LIVING ON THIN ICE

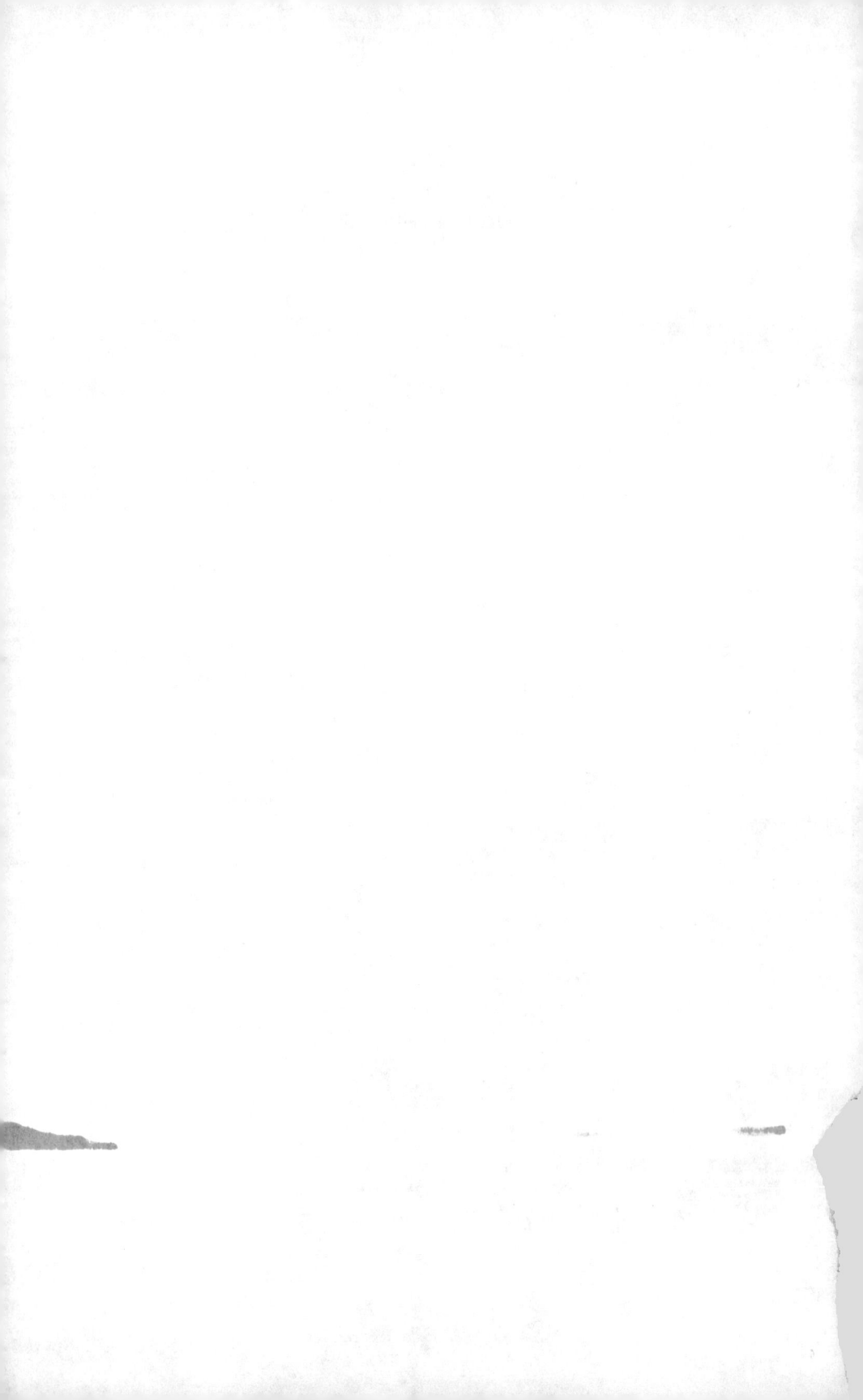

Living on Thin Ice

The Gwich'in Natives of Alaska

Steven C. Dinero

berghahn
NEW YORK · OXFORD
www.berghahnbooks.com

First published in 2016 by

Berghahn Books

www.berghahnbooks.com

Library of Congress Cataloging-in-Publication Data

Names: Dinero, Steven C., author.
Title: Living on thin ice : the Gwich'in natives of Alaska / Steven C. Dinero.
Description: New York : Berghahn Books, [2016] | Includes bibliographical
    references and index.
Identifiers: LCCN 2015047950 | ISBN 9781785331619 (hardback : alk. paper)
    | ISBN 9781785331626 (ebook)
Subjects: LCSH: Gwich'in Indians—Social conditions—Alaska—Arctic
    Village. | Gwich'in Indians—Ethnic identity. | Arctic Village (Alaska)—
    Economic conditions. | Arctic Village (Alaska)—Environmental conditions.
Classification: LCC E99.K84 D56 2016 | DDC 305.897/20798—dc23
LC record available at hmp://lccn.loc.gov/2015047950

British Library Cataloguing in Publication Data

A catalogue record for this book is available from the British Library

ISBN 978-1-78533-161-9 hardback
ISBN 978-1-78920-834-4 paperback
ISBN 978-1-78533-162-6 ebook

For My Father

Who First Sparked My Interest in Alaska,
Its Environment, Wildlife, and Peoples
in 1966

Contents

Illustrations, Maps, and Tables

Illustrations

Maps

Tables

Acknowledgments

I first arrived in Arctic Village, Alaska, on a cool, dreary, cloudy Sunday afternoon in early August 1999. After a quick four-wheeler ride, I rolled into the gravel drive of Timothy Sam's home, disoriented, tired, and entirely uncertain about where I was or what lay ahead. But Timothy, who sadly passed away in 2007, would serve in the coming days as my "teacher-professor." From him I would learn much about Nets'aii Gwich'in history, values, and, especially, subsistence. And yes, about Nets'aii Gwich'in struggles as well.

In the coming weeks, months, and years, I would return to Arctic Village repeatedly. Each time, I would learn more but only if, as one of my key mentors Lincoln Tritt (who also died, sadly, in 2012) told me repeatedly, I would *listen*. As a fast-talking Easterner, this was my greatest challenge. I had to learn that in Arctic Village, the less said, the better. Communication takes many, many forms, and talking—well, let's just say that the Nets'aii Gwich'in aren't known to talk your ear off. But if you are patient and willing to listen, then you can learn more from the Nets'aii Gwich'in than you ever learned from decades of formal education in the classroom.

And learn I did. Not only did I learn from Timothy and Lincoln but also from virtually every other community member I encountered over the years. Therefore, many thanks are now due to my numerous friends in Arctic Village who opened up their homes, hearts, arms, and lives to me during the past fifteen years. Without them, needless to say, this work could never have been possible. In particular, I wish to thank the following people for their generosity during this research:

Trimble and Mary Gilbert, Evon Peter and family, Bobby and Annette Gilbert and family, Jim and Julie Hollandsworth and family, Albert Gilbert and family, Brenda Gilbert and family, Virginia Gilbert, Edward Sam, Audrey Tritt and family, Dena Tritt and family, Debbie Tritt, Raymond Tritt, Naomi Tritt, Isaac Tritt, Kenneth Frank and Caroline Tritt-Frank and family, George and Tiffany Yatlin and family, Mabeleen Christian and Joe Chilcote and family, Darryl "Scott" Clow, Brewster Johnson, Marty Russell and Mitchell Ned and family, Marjorie and Danny Gemmill and family, Faith Gemmill, Fanny Gemmill and family, Lisa Frank and Lynnea, Fabian Frank, Jeannie Frank, Sarah James and family, Gideon James and family, Lillian and Gerry Garnett, Tonya Garnett, Steven and Gayle Tritt and family, Lorraine Tritt and family, Donald Tritt, Franklin Tritt, Allen Tritt, Joel Tritt, Mildred Allan and family, Ernie Peter and family, Kias Peter Jr., Joanne Bryant, Margie Martinez, Shawn Martinez, Cissy Wiehl and family, Bertha Ross and family, Jonathan John and family, Abraham John and family, Joyce John and family, Marie John and Harvey, Marion and Charlie Swaney and family, and Jimmie John. Unfortunately, these thanks come too late for some. These include Bob Allan, Callahan Tritt, Moses Sam Sr., David Panigeo, Ruth Nikolai, Albert James, and Kias Peter Sr.

I want to offer special thanks to Calvin Tritt and Louie John. Calvin and I have spent many hours over the years talking about the Nets'aii Gwich'in village, history, religion, memories of the past, and hopes for the future. From my very first research trip to the village when he, Timothy, and I worked on rebuilding the wooden floor of the "new" village chapel to our work on the old chapel years later (see chapter 2) to our long evenings spent discussing world politics, Calvin has always shown me patience, kindness, and respect. He has helped me to understand the Nets'aii Gwich'in in unique and compelling ways. I cherish our friendship.

As for Louie, he is my Gwich'in brother. He and I have spent many days, weeks, and months together talking, laughing, and yes, at times, disagreeing. Louie is a unique man, with a unique mission in life. I am indebted to him in ways large and small, for he has taught me so much about his people, his family, and himself as well. I *listened* to Louie, and as a result, I learned. Thank you, *Jah*, for everything.

Over the years, I have also received assistance from a variety of agencies to facilitate my travel and research. Though the following views are mine alone, this volume could not have been completed without generous support from the following:

National Geographic Society/Waitt Foundation
National Science Foundation—Award No. EEC-0332608

Alaska Humanities Forum
National Endowment for the Humanities
Philadelphia University

Thanks must also go to Editorial Associate Duncan Ranslem, Production Editor Jessica Murphy, my peer reviewers, and everyone at Berghahn for their assistance once again in helping me to put years of material into good order. I am quite indebted to all for their detailed attention, comments, and constructive criticisms in bringing this volume to fruition.

In addition, I wish to thank my children, Ari Dinero and Maya Dinero. They spent much of their childhood in Arctic Village because of me. Often, they helped me to see the place through the youth's perspective. Truly, I am thankful that they were with me, creating memories that will last a lifetime.

Lastly, I wish to thank Lore for being there to take on the enormous task of encouraging me throughout the writing of this volume. The following is a labor of love, but at times, like any author, I have hit moments of question and uncertainty. Nevertheless, through it all she was there, offering moral support and more. In short, Lor, I couldn't have done it without you.

Philadelphia, Pennsylvania, USA
21 June 2015

A Note on Methodology

My objectives when I first envisioned this study sometime in 1997 or 1998 and the outcomes are similar, though certainly not identical. At the outset, my interest in studying Arctic Village's development and growth was primarily from a planning perspective. Given my training and interests in developing world settlement systems, I came to this particular indigenous community viewing it as a case study, providing a microcosm of the manifest issues and concerns that virtually all hunter-gatherer communities have experienced to some degree since European contact and colonization.

While these interests remained ongoing, in time other issues and opportunities developed that also attracted my attention. Chief among these was my involvement in two major development projects, one concerning the local church, the other on e-commerce, coordinated through the local high school. More to the point, my academic interests also evolved. As I spent time in the village, a cluster of interrelated issues undergoing change in the community repeatedly came to the fore during numerous discussions with the villagers: the climate, subsistence practices (namely, their decline), and behaviors among the village youth. Over the years, it became clear to me that from the Nets'aii Gwich'in perspective, these issues, while not initially my primary areas of emphasis, were the key indicators of the future strength and direction of the community's social and economic development.

Thus, given the longitudinal and interdisciplinary nature of the study, various complementary methodological approaches were used that reflect the complexity of this work. For chapter 2, for example, considerable archival research was conducted primarily at the Alaska and Polar Regions Collections and Archives of the Elmer E. Rasmuson Library at the University of Alaska, Fairbanks. Other archives consulted included those of the Episcopal Diocese of Alaska (Fairbanks) and the Archives of the Episcopal Church (Austin, Texas).

I carried out structured interviews with my interlocutors through-out the research period primarily in face-to-face meetings. Given the nature of the community in question, these meetings often took on an informal but serious tone. Many if not most took place in homes, schools, or even outdoors; very few took place in formal settings such as offices. In all cases, informants were aware that my interest and questions were not for me alone and that anything said might later be written down for public consumption. In this regard, the protec-tion of my interlocutors' identities is crucial; even in cases where some said it was "no big deal," I have anonymized some names when the material under discussion is in any way controversial or potentially embarrassing.

Much of this project emphasizes if and how the villagers are ad-justing to new technologies and lifestyles, brought on by interactions with outside influences (especially White/European contact), and in turn, how they are now fairing in an age of changing climactic condi-tions, country food availability, and distractions being experienced by the younger generations in particular. In order to address these larger questions, I sought to gather some quantitative data via a series of household surveys in Arctic Village from 1999 to 2013. Indeed, an anal-ysis of both the quantitative and qualitative data I collected from these surveys provides the bulk of the empirical material on issues such as educational development in the village (chapter 3), among other con-cerns that appear in the chapters to follow.

I acquired permission of the tribe before entering the village the first time (following Norton and Manson, 1996: 857) by submitting a preliminary proposal to both the Arctic Village Council and the Tribal Council at Venetie. In this proposal, I explained to the community why I wished to conduct research in the village and how this research might potentially benefit them in the future (859). Upon receiving per-mission to visit the village, I initiated preliminary work on the first household survey research instrument before I started the research in 1999. After much discussion with community members, I then be-gan my first study and adjusted the instrument subsequently in order to achieve better results. In so doing, the research became richer and more robust with each household survey that followed. I also changed the questionnaire based on my own experiences. Early on, for exam-ple, I did not fully appreciate the crucial role played by the motorboat when hunting on the Chandalar River. After taking some hunting and fishing trips with villagers, I began to gather data about this critical form of transportation. Through informal conversations during each stay in the village, I got a better sense of what questions I should be asking and which were largely irrelevant to the community. On each questionnaire, for example, I posed a variety of questions on educational achievement and other personal characteristics, as well as wage employment status, subsistence activity, attitudes toward community living conditions, living experiences and travels outside of the region, and so on. With each iteration of the survey, I also asked increasingly more open-ended questions in order to allow respondents to address issues they felt were especially important, and in greater depth.

I was not the first to use a structured household survey in the indigenous North; John A. Kruse, among others, used such tools since the late 1970s in his work among the Inupiat (Kruse 1982: 5), as had Jack C. Stabler in the Northwest Territories. Like Stabler, I also used structured interviews with residents and other "informed" individuals (Stabler 1990: 64–65) in addition to implementing the planning survey. I discussed the instrument with a variety of Nets'aii Gwich'in and non-Gwich'in community members prior to implementation in order to avoid asking sensitive or otherwise problematic questions that could jeopardize the data-gathering process. Following Richard A. Caulfield (1983: 8–10), the last to conduct a survey in the town (in the early 1980s), I defined a "household" as an occupied dwelling unit. I surveyed both men and women; as was the case with Caulfield, men in the first survey and in subsequent surveys were overrepresented due to several social and economic explanations. As Caulfield notes, men tend to play the role of household head in the Nets'aii Gwich'in community.

I also used "information recall" (following Caulfield 1983), allowing respondents to remember or estimate such information as their percentage of annual consumption of food harvested from the local land (what I refer to here as "subsistence rate," see chapter 5). I interviewed Nets'aii Gwich'in, non-Gwich'in Native, and non-Native village residents (although there are very few non-Gwich'in villagers) in order to gain as clear and complete a picture as possible of present village social and economic conditions. Like Caulfield and Kruse, I paid each respondent a small gratuity ($10) for their time spent answering the first survey questions. By 2013, I had increased this amount to $20 per questionnaire. I implemented the first survey in August 1999. Of the forty dwelling units occupied during the survey period, I was able to gather data from thirty-five households (87.5 percent). In general, the interviews lasted from half an hour to two hours, although the average time spent with each respondent was about thirty-five to forty minutes. It was my observation then—further confirmed in later surveys—that the Gwich'in genuinely wished to share their views and stories with me. As Lincoln Tritt had said, it was my job to *listen*; many were quite forthcoming as a result.

In June and July 2006, July and August 2011, and June 2012, I implemented follow-up surveys that included questions on service provision in the village, including education. I posed virtually the same questions on each survey concerning the role of the school and educational development in the village. However, some questions were modified, added, or improved from survey to survey. In 2006, thirty-nine households were surveyed. In 2011, the village continued to grow and forty-six households were surveyed. In 2012, forty-eight were surveyed. Upon completion of each survey, all quantitative data were coded for analysis using SPSS Statistics for Windows. Given the small size of the data sets, chi-square significance testing was used for all quantitative data, where $p \leq .05$ (Poppel 2015).

The implementation of the March 2013 Youth Survey was similar though not identical to the approach followed above. As one might imagine, institutional review board protocols demanded that I tread lightly when interacting with interlocutors under the age of 18. I did so only with the written permission of a parent or guardian and, even still, spoke to children aged 8 to 12 only with an adult present. The survey was cleared by village adults in advance and consisted of benign questions that merely sought a sense of how the children view their school, village, and futures (i.e., what is your favorite subject in school?). Lastly, although I seek here to quantify issues such as community views on the development of the village by using some standard planning tools, I combine these tools with participant observation methods, recognizing that approaches like the static survey often have limited use in indigenous village environments (see my lengthy discussion of these methodological challenges in Dinero 1996).

Much if not most of what follows stems from my personal role as participant observer in Arctic Village over the period of study. Indeed, I believe that I gathered particularly significant data in the village simply by living there and speaking informally with people each day—most though not all of which confirmed data gathered through the more formal process. Still, a few provisos must be noted in this regard: 1) the villagers always knew that I was there as a researcher, even if I also participated in various local activities; I always made clear my purpose for asking questions and never sought in any way to mislead someone into speaking their mind; 2) all quotes found here, therefore, are true to the villagers' own words. In some instances, I have edited for clarity, but what is written here is what was said to me. As noted, sources are anonymized when necessary. As such, this book combines a variety of methods, including some more recent approaches to the material such as autoethnography. In short, I am drawn to this framework because it "acknowledges and accommodates subjectivity, emotionality, and the researcher's influence on research, rather than hiding from these matters or assuming they don't exist" (Ellis et al. 2011).

Thus, I went from being an Outsider "studying" the community (1999) to one who gained intimate knowledge of events and activities within (2014) simply because I was there, experiencing and being a part of those events. When I was not conducting interviews, I myself was picking berries, fishing or "hunting" (i.e., I was along for the ride, no gun in hand), or hammering or digging or cooking. In other words, I increasingly became more of a participant in village life and less of an observer of it. This text illustrates the nuanced experience of the participant observer: on the one hand, I am of course still an Outsider, an academic studying a community, a culture now in the throes of challenging circumstances. On the other, I also spent time working with and on behalf of villager interests, particularly with regard to the Church (see chapter 2). The chapters that follow reflect this role; using a "layered account" approach (Ellis et al. 2011) allows me to interweave literature, quantitative data, qualitative data, and my own reflections into the presentation of a comprehensive tapestry of compelling material and analysis.

Introduction

Alaska has long provided Americans in the Lower 48 states, as well as peoples around the world, with a multitude of romantic ideas and images. To many, this is a land of wide-open spaces teeming with abundant wildlife. Bears, wolves, caribou, moose, and sheep roam below a midnight sun that never sets or in the shadows of the northern lights perpetually dancing overhead.

In recent years, a spate of reality television programs that have sprung up on cable networks reinforces these views. A "Jack London" lifestyle prevails in such shows; there are few roads (and those that exist are quite treacherous), and survival for both "man and beast" is precarious and hardscrabble. Life in America's "Last Frontier" is one of outdoorsy strength, independence, fortitude, and take-no-prisoners gutsiness not found elsewhere. Reinforced by the media coverage of former Alaskan Governor Sarah "Mama Grizzly" Palin's 2008 vice presidential bid, such fancies about the state, its people, and its culture have become increasingly common throughout the latter twentieth and early twenty-first centuries. In short, Alaska sparks the postmodern imagination; it is one of the few places left on the planet that is seemingly "untouched" and "primitive"—a so-called frontier teeming with possibility and potential.

Moreover, of course, residing throughout this vast land are the "Eskimos," or at least some vestige of Native peoples who, according to popular stereotypes, ride swiftly across the tundra by dogsled, dressed in oversized parkas and skin mukluks. Very few Americans in the Lower 48 have ever interacted with actual Alaska Natives, who remain the stuff of high school English class reading assignments. Even visitors of the state are unlikely to venture out into the Native bush; rather, a more likely scenario includes a chance encounter along Two Street in Fairbanks or Fourth Avenue in Anchorage during a search for souvenir trinkets on a cruise side trip. The romantic image of the benign Native hunting seals in the Arctic with a primitive spear—the winter sun just barely peaking over the horizon—in total peace and harmony with the natural environment and essentially frozen in time alongside the sea ice begins to fade, only to be replaced with other equally destructive images of the Native as lazy, an alcoholic, or, worse, an obsolete anachronism in the modern era.

The Disneyesque visions of Alaska and its Native peoples are all well known. In an age of rapid change spawned by globalization, Orientalist ideas and images about Alaska, especially her Native peoples, often do a disservice rather than make a true contribution to a more accurate perception of what is in fact happening in Alaska today. The purpose of this study is to contribute toward a better understanding of one tribe,[1] the Nets'aii Gwich'in of Arctic Village, and to correct many of the misleading beliefs now perpetuated about this land and her people.

To be sure, I do not claim to offer a complete picture of every aspect of Alaska Native life in the early twenty-first century. Rather, I seek to provide an important window into the rapidly changing world of an Alaska Native community emblematic of such indigenous communities not only in North America but indeed across the globe. I have no interest in romanticizing the past or writing about "noble savages" now passing from "tradition" to "modernity." I strive neither to nostalgize nor to present the Gwich'in as static beings who belong on a museum shelf. Rather, I believe the following pages well reveal that theirs is a culture that continues to grow and evolve; the narrative presented here tells the story of who the Gwich'in once were, who they are now, and, most importantly, who they are becoming.

* * *

I begin the first section by introducing the Nets'aii Gwich'in, who they are and how they came to live in Arctic Village in the early decades of the twentieth century. While their story is similar to other Alaska Native tribes that began to settle throughout the latter nineteenth and early twentieth centuries—to be sure, such a narrative has befallen many indigenous communities through North America and indeed the globe—it is particularly filled with interesting and charismatic individuals who played significant roles in the settlement and development process. Moreover, I seek to show in this and succeeding chapters of this first section that the colonial impact on the Nets'aii Gwich'in, though certainly considerable, was not in and of itself an avenue to "cultural destruction." Rather, only in the latter part of the twentieth century, several decades after initial European contact, did the Nets'aii Gwich'in community of Arctic Village begin to show signs of wear and decline currently viewed as "typical" of postcolonial indigenous environments.

In chapter 2, I delve into this issue, namely the initial impact of contact with the White, non-indigenous world, in greater detail. I show that Episcopalian Christianity was pivotal in facilitating the community's concentration and eventual settlement and that this highly aggressive aspect of colonialism has a complex history in the Arctic. The role it played in erasing indigenous, land-based spirituality and other social values is undeniable. Yet, I argue too that the Episcopal Church served well to bridge Nets'aii Gwich'in and "White" cultures in creative and distinctive ways. Here I rely on materials such as archival sources concerning and written by the Church's Native and non-Native "founding fathers," as well as data I personally gathered via participant observation while working in the village on a church reconstruction and historic preservation initiative (2002–2005). My task in this chapter is to suggest that in truth the introduction of Christianity was a unifying force in the early years of Nets'aii Gwich'in settlement; just as communal cohesion began to unravel in the final third of the twentieth century, so too did religious activities, behaviors, and affiliations.

I then turn in chapter 3 to the role that schools and education also play in facilitating settlement and social change within the Nets'aii Gwich'in community. Using data from the 1960s to the present, including data gathered from several household surveys over the past fifteen years (six in total), I address formal education as a tool of assimilation, acculturation, and, in effect, attempted "de-nativization" of the Nets'aii Gwich'in community. I introduce a theoretical framework at this point that in essence suggests that the narratives of "civilization" and "cleanliness" or "hygiene" may be seen as similar if not identical objectives when pursued within the context of colonization. Yet here again I show that formal education arrived late in the village environment, taking form only midcentury. Again, I seek to argue that such efforts dovetailed well with other social and economic changes then occurring both within the community and indeed through the United States at that time.

In chapter 4, I quantify and qualify how the Nets'aii community has evolved into its present state. The Nets'aii once lived largely independently in geographically dispersed camps. The imposition of the European settlement model in the early twentieth century brought on greater communal organization and with it a new, functional form of community development. And so, as the Nets'aii Gwich'in' settled at Arctic Village over the past century, they should have also embraced the provision and use of publically planned services. These utilities

include such basic infrastructure as water and electrification, as well
as health care services. But is this entirely so? Using village planning
theories as my framework for analysis, I assess the degree to which
the village operates today as a cohesive whole. In other words, I pose
a basic but crucial question as I conclude this section: is Arctic Village
truly a "village" in the Western sense of the word, or is it more like the
traditional Nets'aii Gwich'in hunting camp comprised of a group of
families, residing in homes, who, though drawn together by outside
forces, no longer see themselves as a single unified community?

The second section begins with chapter 5, in which I problematize
the issue of subsistence activity, practice, and behaviors in today's
changing global economy. On the one hand, the Nets'aii Gwich'in still
practice hunting, fishing, and gathering at exceptionally high rates
relative to other twenty-first century indigenous populations. On the
other, these practices are in rapid decline in many though not all quarters. In this chapter, I document these changes and analyze both quan-
titatively and qualitatively what the role of subsistence is among the
Nets'aii Gwich'in at present and what it might be going forward. As
subsistence is the heart and soul of any Native community, this chapter, purposely located in the center of this narrative, is in fact the core
of my argument, for without hunting, fishing, and gathering, many
would argue, the future of the Nets'aii Gwich'in appears to be a bleak
one. The Nets'aii Gwich'in are the "Caribou People," but without the
caribou, who are they and what sort of future lies ahead?

Of course, changing subsistence behaviors are related to several
factors, including a fluctuating climate. I quantify and qualify these
changes among the Nets'aii Gwich'in in chapter 6, showing that the
subarctic boreal forest region provides an ideal environment through
which to analyze the impact of warming upon flora, fauna, and, ultimately, those who interact with this natural setting on a daily basis.
In effect, the case presented here supplies an ideal study of the issues
that the Gwich'in are facing at present, as well as what is likely to come
for those of us who live in the urbanized South. The Nets'aii Gwich'in
community's experiences provide numerous examples of what the
entire global community, indigenous and non-indigenous alike, will
face in an era of globalizing technologies and rising political and environmental threat, as well as ways to overcome and adapt to these
challenges.

Chapter 7 picks up on the theme of "where do we go from here?" By
concentrating on the youth (for the most part, those under 18 years of
age) as central to the future of the Nets'aii Gwich'in—a thread found
throughout all four chapters of the second section—I address the

ways, especially since 1970, younger generations now live in the village community. Indeed, the "vill" may occupy the same geographic location but is sociologically a very different place from only a few short decades ago. Communications and transportation technologies have irreversibly altered the face of Native bush village life. New opportunities, as well as challenges in the form of the "three S's" (substances, sex, suicide), make village life extremely difficult for today's youth. Here I highlight material gathered from the general literature, as well as my own interviews, household surveys, and even a survey of the youth themselves, all of which confirm that the Arctic Village of today is a new entity with issues and concerns the likes of which the early founders could never have anticipated.

This leads me to the concluding chapter, chapter 8. Here I speculate about the future of the Nets'aii Gwich'in community in general and of Arctic Village in particular. Villagers will often repeat the phrase, "We don't know *where* we are anymore!" The feeling of disorientation in the new society and global economy of the twenty-first century is truly overwhelming. There is no doubt that the community is under siege from a multitude of social and economic forces: ongoing oil drilling interests in the neighboring Arctic National Wildlife Refuge (ANWR) that threaten wild food resources, poverty and unemployment, substance abuse, teen pregnancy, outmigration and brain drain, and on and on. Here I turn to an analysis of social media to better understand how today, just as the Nets'aii Gwich'in settlement system is beginning to alter and fray, new virtual networks may sustain and support the expression of Nets'aii Gwich'in identity and unity well into the future.

I conclude this final chapter by suggesting that reports of the death of Native cultures like the Nets'aii Gwich'in of Arctic Village are premature at best. While the Nets'aii Gwich'in people of today differ greatly from their ancestors, likely to spend more hours each day watching television or posting on Facebook than hunting caribou or moose, one thing remains consistent: the Nets'aii Gwich'in remain a proud community, able and willing to adjust to change over time and to overcome adversity.

Every fall, without exception, the call *"Vadzaih!"* (Caribou!) can be heard across Arctic Village; each year, men, women, and children continue to head up mountain on their four-wheelers to camp, hunt, eat, and sleep. Some then head back and forth (a minimum of ten miles round-trip)—sometimes more than once in a day—to get supplies and to visit those villagers down below who no longer go up mountain to hunt but who support and sustain their friends and relatives, as well as anticipate their success. It is the twenty-first century in North America, and still the hunt goes on. Animals are harvested across the Yukon Flats, and the village freezers are slowly but surely filled. The Caribou People of the Chandalar have lived in this region for some ten thousand years and continue to do so today. We have much to learn from their example.

Note

1. Alaska Natives are divided into tribes not only based on heritage (e.g., Athabascans) but also by community. In short, throughout, I will refer to the Arctic Village "tribe" and the Native Village of Venetie Tribal Government (NVVTG), which includes the Village of Venetie and Arctic Village.

SECTION I

At the turn of the new millennium, many felt it was time to stop and take stock of where humanity had been and, more importantly, where it was heading. From theoreticians like David Harvey and Francis Fukuyama to *New York Times* writer Thomas Friedman, from CNN, MSNBC, Fox News, and every source in between—men and women of every political persuasion expressed the belief that the turn of the century and the millennium seemed to coincide with a major social, economic, and political paradigm shift. Such a shift signaled the end of something that could never be recovered and the beginning of something perhaps great, perhaps wonderful, but all the more likely frightening, sinister, and worthy of concern. Thus, in the early twenty-first century, we are repeatedly bombarded with cataclysmic images of melting icecaps, exploding buildings, and seemingly unprecedented levels of conflict, violence, and hatred that threaten every species on the planet, including us, and ultimately the planet itself.

Within this context of major global change, fear, and uncertainly is where the following case study must be situated. In an ever-globalizing world where overpopulation, scarcity, and social and economic injustice are common watchwords, the study of a small indigenous population living at the edge of the subarctic, in what was once total obscurity, can now take center-stage. No community large or small is immune today, if ever, from the powers that swirl around us. Indeed, that is what I hope to show in the following pages. While many politicians, academics and policymakers seem to be preoccupied with global change as if it is some new and distant process that only arrived on North America's shores one sunny September 11th morning, there is nothing new here for the indigenous peoples of this continent. Imposed social and economic change is a given—ongoing, familiar, and to be expected. Moreover, as will be demonstrated in the following narrative, imposed change can be resisted, adapted to, accommodated, and, if need be, rebuffed altogether.

In this context then, it is only fair to begin here by asking some basic questions: who are (were) the Nets'aii Gwich'in of Arctic Village?

Where did they come from? And, above all, why, in an age of globalization—when major social, economic, and political shifts seem to be
overtaking the planet at astronomical speed—should an outsider even
really care about such a small community of Alaska Natives living hundreds of miles from what many would even consider civilization? The
chapters in this section will address these questions and more. These
very forces demand that communities such as that under study now
draw our attention, for they are to a great degree the canaries in the
coal mine. What is happening in—and to—communities like Arctic Village, Alaska, is but a harbinger of things to come in neighborhoods, villages, towns, and communities large and small across the globe today.

This, in fact, is what this book will address: change. Whether that
change is for good, bad, or otherwise is up for debate. But if nothing else is certain about the Nets'aii Gwich'in and Arctic Village, they,
like everyone in the world today, are changing but in directions largely
unpredictable and at such an accelerated rate that the dizzied outcome
is at best an exciting new adventure and at worst a terrifying, out-
of-control, brakeless ride over unknown, treacherous, and potential
deadly terrain.

But is change new per se? The Nets'aii Gwich'in would of course tell
us otherwise. Indeed, the Nets'aii Gwich'in's story that follows should
teach us that the perspective expressed of present events is largely Eu-
rocentric. If globalization in the new millennium is to be viewed as a set
of processes that, when combined, allow for increased socioeconomic
integration as a result of improved communications and transporta-
tions systems that overcome the "friction of space" (Harvey 1996: 422),
then one must reassess the whole conceptual framework as it applies to
the Nets'aii Gwich'in. Truly, there is nothing new here under the midnight sun, as this popular story, told orally for generations, illustrates:

> Many years ago the Kutchin [Gwich'in] Indians fought with their neigh-
> bors. The Kutchin were afraid of other people. When the people were
> fighting they hurt each other. Many people were killed. One Indian be-
> gan to think about how it would be if there were no war. His name was
> Dacheltee.
>
> "People can be happy if they don't fight," Dacheltee thought. "They will
> not be afraid anymore."
>
> Dacheltee thought and thought. At last he decided to talk to the other
> Indian chiefs. Sometimes Dacheltee went down the rivers in a boat made
> of caribou skin. In the winter he went in his sled pulled by dogs. He went
> across the mountains and talked to the Eskimos. He went a long way and
> talked to many people.

"I think we would be happy if we did not fight," he told them.

The chiefs talked with Dacheltee about war. They talked about how people would live if there were no war. They would not be afraid if there were no war.

After Dacheltee talked with the chiefs, they decided there would be no more war. After that the Kutchin Indians did not fight with their neighbors. They traded with their neighbors for the things they needed. Dacheltee and the people were happy now.

Dacheltee helped the people in other ways too. He helped the people build a caribou fence. A caribou fence was made of logs. The logs were tied to trees. Snares made of thin pieces of skin were tied to the logs. The fence was made in a circle. There was a hole in one side of the fence. The men stood on the side that did not have a hole. They had bows and arrows ready. The women and the children drove the caribou through the fence. The men killed the caribou when they got caught in the snares. The people got many caribou this way. They had meat to eat and skins for houses and clothes.

One day Dacheltee and his family and friends were coming home from hunting. They were tired. When they got to the top of a hill they decided to rest. All the children sat down around Dacheltee.

They liked to hear him tell stories. Dacheltee liked to tell them about the sun, moon, and stars.

"Somebody must live on those things," Dacheltee told the children. "Maybe someone made the sun and stars," one little boy said.

The people were rested. They got their things and started on their way home.

"Maybe some day we will find out who made the world and all the things in it," Dacheltee told the children.

The years went by. People began to trade more and more. They began to take dried meat down to Fort Yukon. The Indians traded the dried meat for tea, sugar, and other things they needed ...

— Maggie Gilbert, as told to Marian Nickelson, circa 1969

The story narrated above is one of many that were once handed down from generation to generation but have recently become less familiar to many if not most in the community. Rather, a White, postcolonial version of history overshadows much of what was once common knowledge. Yet such stories clearly reveal insights into not only the past but also some of our present priorities, fears, and conundrums.

It is only logical and of necessity to carry out a study of the Nets'aii Gwich'in of the twenty-first century by first looking back in time. We must seek to understand their history—of who they are and how they came to settle at Arctic Village—not merely via convenient academic constructs but also, whenever possible, by relying on Gwich'in narrative or memory. Like any colonial narrative, the story of the Nets'aii Gwich'in has taken on a life of its own, being shaped to fit a certain set of preconceived ideas, attitudes, and beliefs.

As yet one more in a series of such observations, the story being told here also runs the risk of further reifying the colonial narrative, suggesting that globalization has brought new thoughts and behaviors to the Nets'aii Gwich'in. Yet, as the narration noted above illustrates, internecine conflict, cross-cultural trade, and a sense of intellectual curiosity about the unknown need hardly be ascribed to a twenty-first century mindset. These ideas and more are all present in this brief narrative. Every effort will be made here to acknowledge that the Nets'aii Gwich'in are not passive recipients of the impacts of White-induced "modernity" or of other similar forces acting *upon* them but rather active participants in their own lives and, further, in their own destinies.

CHAPTER I

How Did We Get Here?

An Overview of the First Century

So finally they said "Let's all live in one place and vote to have one leader, and we will see what happens." So from around Arctic Village we went down to where the trail meets from Fort Yukon. That's where we stayed. They say that so they can tell anyone coming along either trail about their plan. So that's what they did.

— Maggie Gilbert, quoted in Craig Mishler (1995)

A Background Geography and History of the Nets'aii Gwich'in of Arctic Village, Alaska

The story of the Nets'aii Gwich'in's settlement at Arctic Village has been told and retold over the years by a variety of interested outside observers (see, for example, Caulfield 1983; Hadleigh-West 1963; Lonner and Beard 1982; Mishler 1995). Still, in order to provide context, it is necessary to repeat some of this information here.

In short, the Nets'aii Gwich'in were a nomadic hunting and gathering tribe living in the region now known as northeast Alaska and northwest Yukon, Canada, for several millennia (see Map 1.1). As elder Moses Cruikshank explains in Mackenzie's biography of Johnny Fredson (1985: 5–6):

The Netsi Kutchin [also "Natsit Gwich'in" as it appears in Osgood 1936 or "Natsitkutchin" in Mason 1924: 12, meaning "strong people"] of the Chandalar region were Athabascan Indians who had hunted the muskeg and scrubby forests of the Yukon Flats northward toward the snow-capped Brooks Range, and traveled northeastward toward the Yukon Territory for trade with the coastal Eskimos [i.e., the Inupiat] for more than a thousand years. They didn't own much, only what they could

carry on the hunt—a knife, some baskets, snowshoes, warm skin clothing, and until white traders came, only bows, arrows and spears to hunt
with ... The skins of caribou and moose provided almost everything else
they needed.

The environment made the Nets'aii Gwich'in people who they were
in ways large and small. In turn, the Gwich'in made and remade their
environment over the millennia, shaping it to conform to their needs
while also responding to its strength that would ultimately, along with
other social forces determine their fates.

The region that the Alaskan Gwich'in call "home" is comprised of
nearly 37,000 square miles of land (Andrews 1977:103) located in the
interior region of northeast Alaska known as the Northern Plateaus
Province (Wahrhaftig 1965: 22). The area has historically experienced
extreme temperatures—90 degrees Fahrenheit is possible in summer
and –50 degrees or lower in winter. Summers are typically more mod-
erate, however, usually in the 60s and brief in duration. Sunlight is
plentiful (Illustrations 1.1 and 1.2), as are a variety of species of vo-
racious mosquitoes. Winter lasts from mid-September, when the first
snows fall, until breakup in mid-June. In reality, it can snow virtually
any day of the year. Much of the winter is also enshrouded in a blue
haze, not so much dark as lacking in actual direct sunlight (see Illustrations 8.1 and 8.2). The region varies from marshy lowland valleys to
flats that stretch for miles beyond the Yukon River's banks to foothills
of the Brooks Range. These hills generally reach summits no higher
than 1,500 to 2,500 feet. Boreal forest covers the land (Slobodin 1981:
514) comprised of permafrost. Flora is limited to lichens, conifers, and
the like; fauna includes bear, moose, caribou, and small furbearers
(Wahrhaftig 1965: 23).

Historically, the Nets'aii Gwich'in (also referred to in the literature as "Chandalar Kutchin"; see Slobodin 1981) were seminomadic
hunters, gatherers, and fishers, structured in small groups and bands
known as "restricted wanderers" (Hosley 1966: 52) whose community
pattern "adapted to scattered or seasonably available food resources"
(VanStone 1974: 38). Thus, the region's severe geography dictated the
lifestyle and behavior of the people. While larger mammals served as
the primary food source, smaller mammals (beaver, ground squirrel,
Arctic hare) were used for clothing and trade (Slobodin 1981: 515).

It is uncertain exactly when the Nets'aii Gwich'in of northeast Alaska
were first contacted by Europeans. While some argue that first contact
occurred in 1847, with the establishment of Hudson's Bay Company at
Fort Yukon (Hadleigh-West 1963: 21; Nelson 1986: 13; Slobodin 1981:

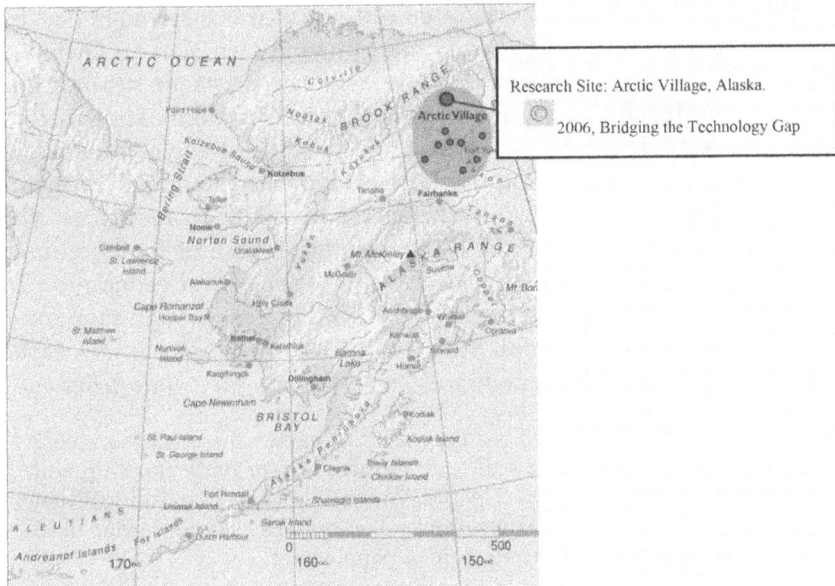

Map 1.1 Arctic Village and neighboring Gwich'in villages in the Yukon Flats.

529), others indicate a later period, the 1860s (Caulfield 1983: 88), when the Roman Catholic Church and the Church of England began sending missionaries to the region (see chapter 2). Either way, interaction occurred with those of both French and English origin beginning in the latter part of the nineteenth century. As will be seen in greater detail (chapters 2 and 3), the colonization process was rapid and thorough, and would ultimately have a long-lasting impact on the Nets'aii Gwich'in with permanent outcomes and ramifications.

The village was founded in 1908 (Caulfield 1983; Hadleigh-West 1963) or 1909 (Lonner and Beard 1982) and named Vashr'aii K'oo, meaning "Creek with Steep Bank" (Mishler 1995: 434). The origins of the name "Arctic Village" are unknown (Hadleigh-West 1963:17). Chief Christian (1878–1947) was, in effect, the founder of the village when he built the first cabin for him and his wife, Rachel (Peter 1966; Nickelson 1969b; I. Tritt 1987a). The building of a cabin was itself an innovation; only with the introduction of the axe was log cabin construction a possibility, and the poor ventilation of the buildings, heated by wood stoves, often led to various health difficulties. Thus, more than a decade later, a few skin houses still existed in the community alongside the small log cabins (Mason 1924: 27).

Although some have reported that settlement was fostered in part by the purported murder of a White man by unknown Nets'aii Gwich'in assailants (see Stern 2005: 34), little evidence exists to substantiate this conspiratorial claim. Rather, as the more commonly known story goes, the Nets'aii Gwich'in people came to settle at the confluence of the Vashr'aii K'oo Creek and the East Fork of the Chandalar River for very rational reasons related to the access of wild food resources. The village is ideally located in the direct migration path of the Porcupine caribou herd, which is central to the tribe's social and economic survival. Similarly, there is a wealth of fish in the area, though numerous creeks similar to the Vashr'aii K'oo that also teem with fish intersect the Chandalar. As one elder related to Mishler (1995: 457) some years ago:

> There was no village [yet] but they used to gather there [at the creek] during spring break-up. So they all gathered there until break-up and also for fish. So that's what they did. We were living there, fishing. Chief Christian was there. We really depended on him. He was not having hard times and had no children. He helped people a lot.

It was at this point that the community determined to settle in one place and to follow a single leader who would run the political and economic affairs of the community:

> So that's what they did. They told everybody what they had planned. They all thought that was a good idea. So everybody got together. In those days there was hardly any money. Our main thing was getting food to eat. So they elected Chief Christian for their leader at Arctic Village. People all helped one another. They helped one another with wood, food, and other things. They all worked hard to do this.

> So that's how Arctic Village became a village. The kids used to pack water for each household. And they did the same with wood. There used to be wood piled up in front of the houses. Those were happy times. (459)

While this version of events is certainly compelling, settlement not only hinged upon food availability, which presumably had always been a concern from time immemorial, but was also further incentivized by two social institutions imposed by the outside, namely the church and the school. The missionaries had come to the area beginning in the 1860s (Caulfield 1983: 88). Formal education was introduced thereafter, designed to teach the Nets'aii Gwich'in Western cultural values (Hosley 1966: 231) and how to follow Christian social mores (VanStone 1974: 87). As I have noted previously, "the creation of schools and the requirement that all children attend them played a direct role in the settlement process of the community" (Dinero 2003b: 143).

Integration into the regional economy via the fur trade also helped in fostering permanent settlement at Arctic Village (Hosley 1966: 153). In the early days, furs were traded at the local store for basic provisions, but in time cash became an increasing part of the village economy as villagers made the 17-to-23-day round-trip journey to Fort Yukon to acquire more specialized commodities such as ammunition and tea (Peter 1966). Since the early 1840s, during the Russian-American era, Gwich'in trappers had traveled regularly to the fort to conduct commerce, especially with coastal Alaska Natives (Inupiat) and other local peoples (Bockstoce 2009: 212–16). The cyclical dynamic of introducing fur trapping to the Nets'aii Gwich'in subsistence culture, selling furs for cash, and subsequently using cash in commercial establishments to purchase non-Native food, clothing, and other fabricated goods including firearms (Bockstoce 2009: 212; Mason 1924: 25) was a major social and economic development that would permanently alter the course of Nets'aii Gwich'in society.

The village was slow to grow to a significant size of permanent settlers. Those who settled at Arctic Village then—or even now—should be recognized as the most committed and determined of Native villagers. It is, in effect, one of Alaska's furthermost outposts, far from other Gwich'in settlements and White communities. As Clara Childs Mackenzie suggests, in its early years especially, Arctic Village was the most distant and remote of Gwich'in villages, making it all the more challenging to get there (1985: 112).

Thus, when researcher and anthropologist Robert McKennan traveled to the village in 1933, for example, only nine people were present upon his arrival, and the village was comprised of about a dozen cabins (Mishler and Simeone 2006: 168–69). Katherine Peter notes that throughout this period into the late 1930s, there was still constant movement between Arctic Village and neighboring Gwich'in settlements including Fort Yukon, Chalkyitsik, and Venetie. For the most part, the Gwich'in remained largely nomadic to this point, having little if any interaction with the outside world short of the ongoing trading activities at Fort Yukon. Increasingly, this began to change, as the men went out to hunt more frequently on their own while the women stayed at the village to care for their children, who began to attend school more consistently (Peter 1992: 91).

Indeed, the population of Arctic Village fluctuated considerably throughout the early years as seminomadism persisted, dropping to negligible numbers around World War I before beginning to climb steadily after World War II and the creation of the Venetie Reservation in which Arctic Village and the Village of Venetie are situated (see

Illustration 1.1 Main Street, Arctic Village, Alaska (July 2011).

Dinero 2003b: 145). The reservation, created in 1943 to promote social and economic development in the Native sector via "a fixed, limited, and protected land base" (Hosley 1966: 206), fostered internal stability and also drew external pressures that encouraged further settlement. Between 1950 and 1960, the permanent village population more than doubled. With settlement, temporary tentlike shelters were replaced by log cabins (Hadleigh-West 1963: 311). Yet, as "traditional" nomadism declined, the community maintained a significant degree of residential mobility.

That said, settlement at the village cannot be viewed as entirely "voluntary" or in any way as a benign or benevolent process. Isaac Tritt Sr. noted that, due to a lack of reliable food supplies, life in Arctic Village was typically much more challenging and the population often smaller than in other communities—Venetie or Fort Yukon, for example—with easier access to these resources (1987a). Therefore, to fully understand the Nets'aii Gwich'in of Arctic Village in the early twenty-first century, it is important to realize that settlement in the early twentieth century occurred largely due to external economic and social forces acting on the community from outside of their control and, to a degree, of their full appreciation or comprehension.

As elder Sarah James put it in one of my earlier interviews with her (8 August 1999):

We were forced to settle here. The White people came with disease and change. They wanted to put Western education here. We were forced to settle in one place so there would be enough kids for a school. If we didn't settle they would take our kids away, adopt them, send them to mission schools.

So we settled here. We have fish here year-round, so we can always have fish. This is a place where caribou are likely to pass, so that's why we settled.

We supported the school getting started, but I still was sent to boarding school [because] half the time the school [in the village] was barely operating.

By being near the timberline, this is also a good trapping area. So they [i.e., the White men] also introduced us to trapping.

The Church was also a big part [of settlement]. They bring in used clothes. We had a bishop, Gordon. He flew a plane, and would bring in oranges. It was the only time we got [things like that] ...

Before the White people, it was a time of plenty ... [Now] there were a lot of people on the land, and it was harder to find food ... Then they brought in the game warden. They put in regulations on game. If they get caught killing out of season, the head of the household, the husband, was arrested. Without a man who will provide for them? The game warden would look at the bones the dogs were chewing on; we had to hide the meat. We used piles of willows to hide it if the airplane came. As I was growing up, it made me feel like—well, what would you feel if you had to sneak around and your parents were a part of it?

To be sure, the coming of White settlers had mixed outcomes. White men brought alcohol and disease, but they also brought doctors and cures. Medicine and religion went hand and hand. The traditional shaman was not powerful enough to fight the new diseases the Nets'aii Gwich'in encountered, which, in time, would further strengthen the power of the Christian church (Mackenzie 1985: 8).

The creation of the Venetie Reservation did not fully resolve all land claims issues and struggles between the Nets'aii Gwich'in and the White settlers, who were slowly but surely coming to Alaska throughout the postwar period. Politicization of Alaskan Gwich'in interests also increased in the 1950s as the community struggled with the United States federal government to protect and maintain its traditional lands. The Nets'aii Gwich'in sought to increase the amount of land beyond that initially allotted to the reservation in 1943.

In 1950 and again in 1957, Arctic Village petitioned the US Department of the Interior to enlarge the Venetie reserve west and north (Lonner and Beard 1982: 101), but to no avail. Rather than surrender-

Illustration 1.2 The village context—the Vashr'aii K'oo Creek as it drains into the East Fork of the Chandalar River (July 2011).

ing land, the US government adopted a different approach to dealing with Indigenous Americans. By the early 1960s, the Johnson Administration had implemented its Great Society initiative, which extended into Native Alaska. On the one hand, the Nets'aii Gwich'in of Arctic Village benefited from the War on Poverty plan, insofar as new housing and buildings were constructed to help improve the communal standard of living (at least, from a Western perspective). At the same time, however, the programs also fostered increased dependence on the government and greater participation in the cash, wage-labor economy (131–32).

Soon thereafter, in 1971, the Alaska Native Claims Settlement Act (ANCSA) was developed and implemented, a major outcome of which was the creation of 13 Native regional corporations and 203 village corporations (Arnold 1976: 146). The regional corporations were to serve as for-profit companies, as holders of traditional Native lands and the resources therein that invested their by-products in order to "promote the economic and social well-being of [their] shareholders and to assist in promoting and preserving the cultural heritage and land base" (Doyon 2015). The village corporations were governed separately from the regional corporations and did not "replace village councils or the governing bodies of municipal governments" (Arnold 1976: 160).

Thirty-seven villages were included in the Doyon Native Regional Corporation, established in Alaska's interior region. Arctic Village and Venetie determined they would take title of their own reserve rather than participate in the land claims settlement. In so doing, the Nets'aii Gwich'in opted to take fee simple title of the 1.8 million acre Venetie Reservation from the federal government, furthering Nets'aii Gwich'in control of natural resources in the region (Stern 2005: 47). Bureau of Land Management studies at the time indicated that the area in and around Arctic Village potentially held gold, iron, zinc, tin, lead, tungsten, silver, chromium, and other minerals, and that oil and natural gas might also be found locally (DCRA 1991).

Thus, the 1.8 million acres were patented to the Venetie and Nets'aii corporations. As "tenants in common," the two villages shared the land, dividing on a percentage basis, with 303 total residents and others with land claims in Venetie and Arctic Village combined. Venetie was given 156 out of 303, or 51.5 percent interest of the land, and Arctic was given 147 out of 303, or 48.5 percent interest of the land, as a temporary first step. The ultimate goal was to control the land and its resources, and to go through the necessary legal processes that would lead to that end. "Subsequent to acquiring the patented lands, the two corporations transferred title of the land in trust to the Native Village of Venetie Tribal Government [NVVTG] for the purpose of managing the land and its resources. Following this transfer the two corporations dissolved" (DCRA 1991).

As a result of working out these various legalisms, the NVVTG (which, as noted, includes both Venetie and Arctic Village) would be independent of the Doyon Native Regional Corporation, and Doyon would have no obligation to the government (Arnold 1976: 200). In the words of Alaskan Gwich'in community leaders (Arctic Village Council 1991):

> Our system of self-regulation and self-determination is based largely upon self-respect and self-esteem, which allows us to then work for the common good of our village ... Our leaders believed ANCSA was a trick to "ripoff" the land from Native people. We feel we were right in our decision to stay with the way we know best, our Indian way (38).

While "rip off" may not necessarily be the right term to describe the ANCSA settlement, it is true that the settlement was not fully resolved at this juncture. Years later, the United States Supreme Court, in a unanimous February 1998 ruling (not 1988, as reported in Stern 2005: 48), determined that while the Nets'aii Gwich'in did hold the land in perpetuity, the reservation lands were not completely under Nets'aii

Gwich'in jurisdiction when it came to certain conditions (i.e., the reserve is not "Indian country"). The tribe cannot, for example, levy taxes on non-Native outside interests such as private contractors operating on tribal lands.

Moreover, throughout the early 1970s and thereafter, following the building of the oil pipeline out of Prudhoe Bay, it also became increasingly common to suggest that the "traditional" Alaska Native was now on the verge of "extinction," about to be replaced by the business-savvy, "oil age," materially oriented capitalist (Jorgenson 1990; for an alternative perspective, see Haycox 2002: 283). This sentiment has been suggested in such popular literature as John McPhee's *Coming into the Country* (1977). The image of the "Brooks Brothers" Native (see Kollin 2001: 168–69) has also been reinforced by academics who suggest that capitalism began taking hold in Alaska Native communities with the creation of ANCSA, if not before, fostering an achievement orientation that supplants an ascriptive culture and facilitating the development of a new class structure that includes the creation of an "Alaska native bourgeoisie" (A. Mason 2002).

By the late 1970s, Arctic Village, if not the Nets'aii Gwich'in in general, *had* changed a great deal when compared to only twenty years earlier, despite efforts to opt out of ANCSA and to maintain control of the land and its resources. New oil-related job opportunities on the North Slope, as well as new "income" provided by the permanent fund annual payments, which had also been created by the oil industry, all served to bring new wealth to the community and with it, new spending behaviors (Nickelson 2013). New buildings, such as a communal laundry (see chapter 4), were added to the existing log housing, church, and school

Caulfield (1983) cites several of these changes, including "the availability of limited wage employment opportunities and government transfer payments, changes in resource distribution, the use of new technology such as high-powered rifles, outboard motors, and snow machines, changing demographic patterns, and resource competition" (101). The preponderance of all-terrain vehicles (ATVs) on village roads occurred during this period as well, lending to greater geographic dispersion of village residences away from the old village center, especially in the direction of the airport (now known as the Airport Road) and the mountain (now known as the Mountain Road). A large peeled-log Community Hall, perhaps the most notable building in the village, would not be added until 1988.

Concurrently, the Nets'aii Gwich'in leadership increased its efforts to exercise greater power, particularly in relation to the federal and state governments. In large part, this was due to an increasing perception among residents that outside interference and control (seen most clearly, perhaps, in the proposal developed at this time to conduct exploratory oil and gas drilling in the ANWR, the traditional calving ground of the Porcupine caribou herd) were directly endangering their subsistence lifestyle and culture. Indeed, the Nets'aii Gwich'in began to see themselves as a "state within a state" in the early 1980s (Lonner and Beard 1982: 107) as they sought control over outsider access to the community, its lands, and its resources.

The Nets'aii Gwich'in leadership sought greater centralized control of village resident behaviors as well during this time. The Arctic Village Council—elected annually and comprised of a First and Second Chief, six members, and an alternate ("Village Focus" 1991)—took on the increasing role of providing moral, as well as legal, guidance. Historically, the chief acted as a representative, chosen by the group for his knowledge and courage in hunting and conflict with neighboring tribes (Osgood 1936: 129). In this regard, the new leadership model was not unlike the Nets'aii Gwich'in's traditional model, in which large groupings of bands (of ten to fifty unrelated families temporarily organized for major functions such as hunting, warfare, or trading) were led by administrator-style leaders, who "directed rather than participated in all major tasks" (Slobodin 1981: 522).

In essence, then, two trends began to emerge during the post-1970 period. First, Western elements of "modernity" arrived in Arctic Village, in the form of new technologies, values, and lifestyles. Second, political activity heightened in the village and broader community, as the Nets'aii Gwich'in struggled to fend off outside political control of their lives, while exercising social control within the community itself. While the Alaskan Gwich'in community underwent great change since European contact and especially since World War II, the Nets'aii Gwich'in of Arctic Village clearly remained just that—strong and proud members of the Gwich'in people. This sense of Gwich'in identity and purpose stemmed from the internal strength of the people and their rich history and culture, as well as from their ability to socially and politically mold newly imposed Western-style values and systems to further their own purposes. Perhaps this is best revealed by the voluntary adoption of a Western innovation—community planning—as a vehicle through which to perpetuate traditional Nets'aii Gwich'in values and ideals.

By the late 1980s, the community had changed in innumerable ways, and the village was, to a great degree, unrecognizable when compared to conditions just two or three decades earlier. Yet, one may still question whether, and to what extent, the village itself was by this point functioning as a single entity with one voice, one identity, one direction. This issue will be taken up in detail in chapter 4, but before doing so, I digress in the pages that follow by addressing how two primary institutions, the Church and the school, played a central role in the ongoing social and economic evolution and development of the Nets'aii Gwich'in community. As will be quite evident, these two institutions together both reflected and formulated the early years of growth and expansion in Arctic Village. Without a doubt, the impact of their role can be felt to the present day.

CHAPTER 2

Episcopalianism Comes
to Nets'aii Country

Gwich'in Christianity has become a way to affirm and embrace the
old ways and the new ways, without losing cultural cohesiveness and
solidarity. The Gwich'in are brilliant theologians. Gwich'in traditional
culture is much closer to Christianity and Jesus than the dominating
culture—Christian or not.
                                    — Rev. Mark MacDonald, Bishop of Alaska (2001)

It is impossible to separate the settlement of the Nets'aii Gwich'in at
Arctic Village from the concomitant arrival of Episcopalian Christianity to the region. What is significant and must be kept in mind here is
that, unlike other aspects of imposed colonial culture, the Christian
Church remains exceptional in the community as an institution that,
despite its White European origins, is still largely loved and embraced
by most, though not all, community members. The reasons, I contend,
for why the Church in specific and Christianity in general are able to
enjoy this exceptional status are rooted in their history and in how
they came into the community from the outset.

In this chapter, I set out to look at the history of Christianity's arrival to the Yukon Flats region, specifically Arctic Village. However,
this religion's appearance cannot be separated from a significant and
charismatic figure in village history, Albert E. Tritt—nor, as one of the
founding fathers of the village, can Tritt's role be overstated. Yet, those
who saw him as a role model—in terms of his position as both a religious and political leader—were at times at odds with other community members. This "rift" of sorts within the community was to play
out throughout the twentieth century (Nickelson 2013); Tritt's family
was often in conflict with other village residents (G. James 2002), creating an uneasy dynamic.

Further still, Tritt's building of the Bishop Rowe Chapel secured his role in the community and, further, finally made permanent the settlement of the Nets'aii Gwich'in at Arctic Village. In turn, the building also further concretized the role of Christianity within the community. The triangular relationship of the institution of Episcopalian Christianity, the leadership of Rev. Albert E. Tritt, and the physical presence of the Bishop Rowe Chapel together served as key anchors in the social development of what would eventually become the permanent community of Arctic Village, Alaska.

Traditional Nets'aii Gwich'in Spirituality

It is rather difficult to acquire information about Nets'aii Gwich'in spirituality prior to the arrival of Christianity that is not filtered through the perspective of outside or White observers. Relatively little is known among the community members themselves. Understanding of the pre-Christian period was limited at best. As one elder put it: "They were good people, but they didn't know the Christian way. You do something wrong and you die. You're stuck. If you fool around, you're not living very long. That's what the old people told the young" (I. Tritt 1987b).

One excellent source of information about the days before European contact is Johnny Frank's testimony, found in *Neerihiinjik*, edited by Craig Mishler. Quoting Frank at length:

> In those days, we didn't know anything about God. Still, something really odd happened. People still say there is no secret about us up in heaven. But besides this they also talked about the Devil … The Russians were the first to help the Indians around here. We also heard that after them the English people landed somewhere down that way. But we didn't get any help from them. Because of them many Alaskan Indians died off from all the diseases they brought over. But before that, our people didn't die from diseases, and people didn't get hurt. And it was really because of lots of people that they lived so well.

> Nobody knows how long there have been men on this earth. Even the small animals that were alive back then were people, they say. The wolverines, the wolves, and the brown bears were all people. Even the foxes were people. The fish in the water were people, they say. But there were no moose in those days. They say all the animals died from the great flood long, long ago … In those days all the fish and all the small animals and big animals were human. And yet they all spoke one language, they say. (1995: 17, 19, 21)

Another noted exception is the Arctic Village minister and traditional chief Rev. Trimble Gilbert, one of the very few village residents
who is familiar with the pre-Christian era and who acknowledges
that this period even existed (Hadleigh-West 1963: 36). Understandably, however, his perspective concerning the early days before contact
tends to emphasize the degree to which the arrival of Christianity was
a positive force (Gilbert 1996). For example, he writes that early on,
before Christianity arrived in the region, life was very difficult for the
Nets'aii Gwich'in, and many struggled and starved:

> And there's a lot of different ways that people have problems during that
> time. And when Jesus was preaching on his sermon on the mount in
> Matthew chapter five and Jesus was talking about the pour people, the
> ones that are really thirsty, people suffering, there are many different
> ways people suffer in there before Jesus come and Jesus talk about peo-
> ple. That's the same way I look at that [period] now [before the] first
> clergy arrive from Canada. People love to hear it, the Word of God, and
> they all believed, have true faith. Once they hear the good news. And they
> really become, they all become very strong Christians in this country.
> (Gilbert 1996)

Gilbert goes on to explain that once the Nets'aii Gwich'in were introduced to Christianity, they embraced it fully, reading from the Bible
and holding prayer services, both on a daily basis. He emphasizes too
that those who prayed hard worked hard and that prayer, work, and
contemplation all were facets of early life in the new village settlement.
He writes:

> And when people travel and they make sure they are going to have service
> in the evening after all the hunting is done during the daytime and the
> people coming home from long hiking with snowshoes break trail all day
> looking for animals. After everybody come home, and they know for sure
> they going to have serve that night. Evening service. Sounds like there is
> a lot of people, a whole camp, I don't know what they've been using for
> bibles maybe the small one … they carry around … everybody goes, once
> everybody ready for the service, then they all put on their snowshoes and
> they all run or walk to that camp and the evening service …

> And I think that during that time in the cold winter when they traveled
> without food that they never stop believing in God, that they still follow,
> and Jesus and all they can, and all they depend on is in our heavenly fa-
> ther … And this is the way that they survive and many, many years they
> having hard time but they never did leave this country …

> And the way I look at [the early village leaders] is that they never stop
> working even when they are eighty years old. They work hard for a liv-

ing and I remember they get up early in the morning all of them early in the morning and they cook for themselves three times a day and they don't stay up very late either in the camp, they all go to sleep and they get up early in the morning, around five. And they do something in the morning. So my thought about later on is that they are very strong and healthy and trained people. So what they teach us is the true life. So many of them said if you take the word which is good for your life and learn more about bibles, what bible says is true if you live by it you're going to have long life. This is one of the good teachings for everyone. So this is the way our Episcopal Church came into this country many years ago in 1847 and some later in the whole Yukon flat people are very strong Christian people. So that Church is still there and we should really think about our Great grandfathers and grandmothers who used to live in this community why did they have a good life. (Gilbert 1996)

Gilbert's thoughts, as well as Johnny Frank's, are instructive. As elders, their observations provide much to the younger generations who may know little about their own history and heritage. In addition, much of our knowledge of precontact Nets'aii Gwich'in spirituality also comes from external sources. By combining the observations of the outsider with those of communal memory, a broader picture of spiritual development may begin to take shape.

For instance, Western sources generally accept that Nets'aii Gwich'in spirituality was similar to other Alaska Native traditions; as an example, Nets'aii Gwich'in tradition traced creation to supernatural spirits in the region. As hunters and gatherers, a connection with the land was understandably strong. The Nets'aii Gwich'in held that there was little if any distinction between the human and animal worlds. This was most especially true when it came to the caribou, an animal believed to share a physical connection with the human race in a literal sense (Dinero 2003a: 9).

Gwich'in spirituality prior to contact also included belief in a variety of supernatural beings. Most prominent among them was the bushman, or the "Na'in" (Hadleigh-West 1963: 37; McKennan 1965: 77; Osgood 1936: 160; Slobodin 1981: 527). Outsiders or others encountered in the bush who were not recognized by community members were at times thought to be such creatures. White authors have written about such topics with romantic fascination, suggesting, for example, that bushmen were humans who at one point were forced by starvation to resort to cannibalism. As a result, they left the community and lived in the bush in caves or underground. In effect, these men were pushed to the periphery of the community through blood feuds or other communal strife, forced to live outside of the village in holes or other unenviable places (Mason 1924: 60).

As Richard Slobodin suggests, bushmen may be viewed as isolated men who became ostracized by the broader community for failing to offer mutual support in times of need. Though stronger than humans, due to their supernatural condition, these beings could be "overmatched" and overpowered under the right circumstances, but their origins stemmed from their dysfunctional or inadequate role in the community:

> If [a] family happened to find game and was unable to bring food to the main party in time, so that the others died, tradition holds that the line family of survivors avoided other people thenceforth. As an informant put it, "They were too sad to be with other people. And besides, they were afraid of the people." The survivors, it is said, would build a pit lodge with a carefully camouflaged dome roof, avoiding the use of fire whenever other humans were in the vicinity. Such people became bush men. Other bush men were individuals, sole survivors of single or paired families whose other members had fallen victims to misfortune. (Slobodin 1960: 127)

In addition to the bushmen, some authors also mention the "brush man" or *Tinjih Rui* (Gwich'in, the "black man"), who was said to be tall and thin with an odd appearance and held miraculous powers, including exceptional abilities of locomotion (Mason 1924: 58–59). Some suggest that this being was similar but not identical to the bushman or Na'in, although Cornelius Osgood believes that the differences between these beings was limited at best and that they are likely various aspects of the same creature (1936: 160). In any case, Mason contends that there are differences and that belief in the "wild bushmen" tended to be more common among the men, while women and children were inclined to fear the brush man (1924: 60–61).

Robert McKennan notes that belief in such supernatural beings was said to exist up until the early decades of the twentieth century (1965: 77). Slobodin notes too (1960: 127) that by the 1930s, elders continued to press forward with this belief while more "modern" sensibilities began to prevail among the younger generations. Yet, when I personally encountered someone (or something) I could not identify while hiking Dachan Lee Mountain in the summer of 2011, no one I told seemed surprised.

In short, the "person" I saw was no more than 50 to 75 meters ahead of me—male, with short straight dark hair and clearly Gwich'in in appearance. He was tall—easily 6 feet—stood ramrod straight with his arms stiffly held at his sides, and wore jeans and a black leather jacket. His feet were never visible to me, but was not difficult to spot; at that point on the mountain, I was above the tree line (the meaning of "Dachan Lee" in English), where one can see for several meters in any given direction. I called out to him several times, although I had never seen him before. No reaction, no response. The village is so small; I had been there several times over the years. How was it possible that there was someone here I had never seen before, and more to the point, how did he get up here? Villagers rarely hike the mountain; they use their ATVs. Moreover, he was alone. Why?

What happened next was even more implausible. As I got closer to him, he literally glided straight up the mountainside, as if he were on an escalator. He just seemed to coast in one smooth motion. Anyone who has climbed this mountain knows that at this point the incline is somewhat steep, covered with boulders that one must bypass with care—but not, apparently, this fellow. I followed in close pursuit. Reaching the top minutes after he did, I looked around. There is nothing on the crest of that mountain but sun-bleached caribou antlers, caribou and bear sign, old rusted cans, and charred lichen where campfires once burned. No trees. No bushes. And on that sunny July morning, no other people for miles around either.

Initially, I was gently ribbed about what I saw or may have seen when I caught up with friends later (perhaps because, as Michael Mason notes [1924: 66], discussion of such beings with outsiders requires caution in the "modern" era for fear of ridicule of one's cultural beliefs). However, I was eventually regaled with several stories of what others had also seen during their numerous trips "up mountain" over the years. By comparison, my story was neither unique nor all that bizarre or extraordinary.

Indeed, the supernatural aspects of traditional Gwich'in spirituality cannot and should not be easily dismissed, as they provide a significant scaffolding and support structure that transcend every aspect of pre-Christian society. Shamans, for example, also played an important role in traditional Gwich'in society and culture. A shaman was said to develop his powers in his mid-teens. In time, once this power was fully developed, shamans would adopt a "companion animal" and carry various animal-related paraphernalia with them, such as the head of that animal.

Shamans served in a variety of functions. Economically, they assisted in bringing success to the hunt. Their ability to intercede between the animal and human worlds was essential in drawing the two together in order to facilitate success in acquiring food in a harsh and unforgiving environment (Osgood 1936: 158). Moses Sam, for example, told the following story in this regard (1987):

One old-timer told me a story that a long time ago people starving and don't know where he's gonna get food. And medicine man, he talked to him. And he make a big fire, people circle around, circle around just singing. And the medicine man just sing. And all the people follow. Circle around to the fire. The medicine man, he sing. The big pile of snow, he just go in there and he grab a caribou horn ... [then] he pull it out.

That's medicine man. Then in the early morning people just go out. Everybody go out there. When the daylight come, they see caribou. He use the bone marrow to find it. The caribou try to run away but he had the bone marrow. So he saved the people's life.

Shamans also acted as medical professionals. They knew the land and its resources well and could use various plants and animal resources to cure sickness, help with childbirth, and aid in other similar needs. Again, the shaman served as intermediary, being most familiar with the natural world and recognizing what is foreign or abnormal. His role was to remove or eliminate that which was harmful or unnatural, using all means at his disposal (Dinero 2003a: 10).

Upon European contact and the arrival of Christianity to the region, the role of the shaman saw immediate decline, but shamanistic behaviors, values, and beliefs would persist for decades to come (Dinero 2003a: 12). The "meshing" of the traditional with the White, Western, Christian, European system of religious thought was revolutionary, with ramifications reverberating to the present day.

The History of the Church and the Role of Albert E. Tritt

The early origins of Episcopalian Christianity in the Alaska Interior follow a trajectory of White imperial intervention and conquest. The Church came to the region, via Anglican Canada, after the Hudson's Bay Company built a trading post at Fort Yukon in 1847 (Mishler 1990: 121). However, it was not until the latter part of the nineteenth century that the Church penetrated the most distant Native communities in the territory, home to the Nets'aii Gwich'in Athabascans of the northeast region. Both White anthropologists and Church officials have documented the events that occurred during this period and their early aftermath (McDonald 1863; Nelson 1986; Slobodin 1981; Stuck 1916, 1920; Wooten 1967).

Archbishop Hudson Stuck, the first archdeacon of the Alaskan diocese, for example, writes of how this region of Alaska was allotted to the Episcopal Church as part of what amounted to a "gentlemen's agreement" (1920: 13):

> A meeting of the secretaries of the principal missionary boards was held at which an informal working agreement as to the allotment of certain regions ... was reached ... It was a wise, statesmanlike thing to do; it has resulted in an almost complete absence in Alaska of the unfortunate, discreditable conflicts between rival religious bodies which have not been unknown elsewhere.

The missionaries of the day were apparently willing to recognize that each church had "limited resources" and it was only "reasonable" that those who had already converted to a particular faith of Christianity were to be left alone (Mishler 1990: 122). Still, Mishler suggests, the Episcopal Church succeeded in winning over the hearts and minds of the Nets'aii Gwich'in by the mid-1860s (1990: 125) only after a lively competition had ensued with the Catholic Church, during which this "agreement" was often ignored.

The missionizing of this region of Alaska used a multipronged approach. On the one hand, missionaries such as Rev. W.W. Kirkby, who arrived in 1861, were sent directly into the field to work with the population and to teach them about Christian beliefs and values. Successful aspects of the appeal to Gwich'in sensibilities included speaking the local language and showing an appreciation for local customs and habits; additionally, Mishler suggests, some locals were "bribed" into conversion through the attractive offer of tobacco (1990: 122). But perhaps to greater effect, these same missionaries located and educated Native community members, who were to prove equally if not even more effective in transmitting Christian views to the people in a more easily understood and accepted way (Dinero 2003a: 7; Mishler 1990: 125). The millennia-old culture, beliefs, and traditions of the Nets'aii Gwich'in were all now under attack from insidious means that were difficult to detect or fend off. Another missionary, Rev. Robert McDonald, made his first visit to the region in 1863 and found that the Gwich'in were a curious people, eager to hear about Christianity and to adopt its practices (McDonald 1863; see Dinero 2003a: 7).

Such unguarded receptivity also appears to have come at a high price, for those carrying the message of Christian teachings and beliefs were firm in their convictions, and non-Christian behaviors were viewed with contempt—or worse. Archbishop Stuck was beloved by many in the Native community; he strove to respect Native culture and traditions and was thus highly regarded. Yet, when it came to the question of traditional spirituality, Stuck was firm in his highly ethno-centric and imperialist views. He writes:

> The "animism" of the Yukon Indians was a *gloomy and degrading super-stition*. It had not anywhere, I think, the *horrible accompaniments* of hu-man sacrifice and cannibalism found elsewhere, but it lived in a constant dread of the *baleful activities* of disembodied spirits, and in constant sub-jection to the shaman or medicine man, who possessed the secret of propitiating these spirits and of subjecting them to his own commands … Many of the thaumaturgic stories told of these conjurors suggest the possession of clairvoyant and hypnotic powers. The people, without ex-ception, cowered under this *sordid tyranny*, a prey to its panic terrors …
>
> [T]hat the Indian race of interior Alaska is threatened with extinction, there is unhappily little room to doubt; and that the threat may be averted is the hope and labour of the missionaries amongst them. (Stuck 1916: 317 as quoted in Dinero 2003a, emphasis added)

The contempt for traditional Nets'aii Gwich'in values and culture that underpinned the views of one of the Natives' most influential and highly regarded longtime friends and supporters is not likely to sur-prise the twenty-first century reader. Given the era, the values of the missionary effort, and the mentality of those who led this movement, imperialistic attitudes were to be expected. Of far greater interest here, however, is the question of how the Gwich'in were socially encapsu-lated into this new mindset—for it is one thing for outsiders to degrade or undervalue one's history, heritage, and cultural traditions. It is an-other thing entirely to foster a sentiment through which a community begins to alter course, slowly but surely accepting foreign set of values and beliefs that vary from, if not contradict entirely, the bedrock ide-ologies of the past.

By the turn of the twentieth century, the conversion of most of the Gwich'in to Episcopalian Christianity was clearly well under way. Yet, as the furthermost northern Gwich'in community, the Nets'aii of the region who were slowly settling at Arctic Village continued to practice more traditional aspects of pre-Christian spirituality. In this regard, the most significant figure in this transition was Rev. Albert E. Tritt. By all accounts, Tritt may be viewed as one of if not the central founding fathers of Arctic Village, though his biography has yet to be written. Lincoln Tritt, one of his grandchildren, was perhaps best suited to this task (L. Tritt 1999), but when he passed suddenly in late October 2012 while still working on Tritt's papers, few were able to quickly step in and fill his shoes. I have previously documented a portion of what exists in written form by Western observers (see Dinero 2003a). In addition to Tritt's own materials, there is some unpublished material about the man and his beliefs that further an understanding of who he was and, more importantly, his contribution to the evolution and development of the Gwich'in community as it has moved into the twenty-first century.

In short, Tritt must be recognized as an exceptional spiritual leader who had numerous charismatic qualities as well as unique talents and abilities in hunting, fishing, and gathering. He was—to quote one of his grandsons, now a village elder—"an amazing man. He was spiritual and traditional and he was a good hunter" (G. James 2002). Rev. Tritt (1875–1955) was the first Nets'aii Gwich'in Episcopalian deacon to come from Arctic Village. From all indications, his conversion to Christianity did not seem to occur by chance. Indeed, his father had studied under Rev. McDonald during his time in the region in the 1860s. Throughout his journals, Tritt discusses the important role his father played in imbuing him and his siblings with reverence for the Bible and its teachings.

In 1895, at the age of 20—not at the age of 15 (see McKennan 1965: 87)—or possibly as early as 1887 according to his son (see I. Tritt 1987a), Tritt saw his first Christian Bible, which made a great impression on him. He was determined to learn more, but only in 1914 did he acquire his own copy after having used others' copies over the years. As Tritt recalls in one of his journal entries: "When I am walking I first think all about the Bible. There [are] not any boys like me [and] that is why I think about it all the time and I am learning it quick[ly]. My father tell[s] me the words that I don't know [and] when Sunday come[s] my father talks [about] the Bible [with me]" (A. Tritt n.d.).

It is, of course, difficult in retrospect to fully analyze Albert Tritt's attitudes or motivations during this key period. He was young, intelligent, and impressionable, seeking new insights that quite clearly resonated for him in the Gospels. However, what is notable here is that Tritt recognized Christianity by its very roots as a means to ever-greater strength and power. He had access to the Christian liturgy in *Takudh* (pronounced "Dago'o"), developed by the Anglican Canadian Archdeacon Robert McDonald in the 1870s. This written version of Gwich'in well served the community for decades, providing a considerable sense of spiritual unity and identity through the written Word.

Still, Tritt's desire to embrace Christian teachings and his eventual movement toward becoming one of if not the most influential missionizing influences in Gwich'in history stemmed, in part or in whole, from his belief that the White man's elevated status came from his ability to read and write. Thus, by embracing Christianity and its primary text, the English-language Bible, Tritt approached Christian teachings with exceptional commitment and fervor. His son Isaac once said of his father: "He believes it pretty bad. He read the Book ... all of it. And they [his friends and followers] read it too ... Then he makes a Sunday school too. And he makes a service *every night,* every day ... [and] they learn pretty quick ... because it's in their own language" (I. Tritt 1987a).

McKennan writes in his 1933 journals that Tritt literally spoke English in the manner of the Bible, something he found "most astonishing" (Mishler and Simeone 2006: 176). Tritt even wrote his own journals in a biblical fashion, following a manner similar to the Book of Genesis. For example, he began his journals by listing the many names of those who lived in the region at the time, before entering a narrative of his thoughts, experiences, and ideas. As Lincoln Tritt (1999) studied these readings, he realized that in many ways, *how* Rev. Tritt wrote down his ideas was as important as *what* he wrote:

> At first, I thought he was copying the format of the Bible, but then I realized that in order to learn about our past, we have to be able to identify with it. As a result, we learn about "who we are" and "where we came from." These two knowledges of identity are what gives us our humanity. As a result, we acquire the ability to learn instead of being programmed. This was the way the people in the past learned and the way my generation learned as children in the woods. This was where we learned how to use all our senses, sight, hearing, smell, taste, and feeling with all our nervous system. These heightened our awareness and it also made us a part of our environment.

In a 1987 interview, Rev. Isaac Tritt Sr., Lincoln's father and Albert's son, confirms Lincoln's beliefs. Speaking to an interviewer from Fairbanks, he repeated, in brief, the genealogical history of the Nets'aii Gwich'in as he had learned it. The story is remarkably biblical in its basic elements but also reflects the challenging conditions that had once existed in the region and how only struggle and perseverance to hunt and gather food saved the people:

> Way before, the people and the Eskimo were not friends together. Jealous I guess. So they make a war. Not Arctic Village area but down by Venetie and Allakaket. Two hundred fifty or two hundred years ago, there is war; they fight together. They killed them all. Only four woman left and one man. They made a life some way. At the same time he's married [to them].

> The first woman he has five children I think, and the second one, I don't know how many, but the third one had a big family. The fourth didn't

have any, no children. These are the ones that come out to Venetie and
Arctic Village.

So they make their living there with water, fish. But it's hard to make a
living there with fish. At that time no fish net, no hook, no fish wheel,
nothing. They don't know how to make a fish wheel, nothing. So people are hungry. So they come here, they hear about the caribou, so they
come up here. So lots of people come up here.

That first woman, a generation in Arctic Village, and the second woman
is in Venetie, their last name is Roberts, and first one is here and the last
name its Tritt, and here I know by this time, the last name is Sam. And
the fourth woman didn't have no kids. And these are the original people
of Venetie and Arctic Village—one Gwich'in, one people. (I. Tritt 1987a,
edited lightly in order to preserve the tone and verbiage used as spoken)

Indeed, Albert Tritt's ability to draw together the teachings of the
Christian Church with a subsistence lifestyle in such a remote Arctic
region (later to be perpetuated by his children and grandchildren) and
to guide the people to a better understanding of their place within the
physical and spiritual worlds is considerably significant. His conversion seemed to follow a model straight out of the scriptures that he had
so strongly embraced.

McKennan (1965: 87) writes that Tritt related an exceptional story
to him about the events that unfolded during this transitional process
of conversion. After returning from a Christmas service in Fort Yukon,
Tritt went home to Arctic Village with his mind filled with questions
about Christianity. "For forty days I wandered crying in the wilderness," he told McKennan, trying to understand the Bible. During this
quest for understanding, in true apocalyptic fashion, he was struck by
a blinding flash of light and fell in a faint. When Tritt recovered con-
sciousness, he was a new man who knew his vocation lay in bringing
the Gospels to his people together with reading and writing. As Mackenzie explains, Tritt's learning continued throughout extended stays in
Fort Yukon. He initially served as a lay reader in Arctic Village, where
he earned a stipend of $10 per month, and was ordained as a deacon
in 1925 (1985: 112, 116). The Episcopalian Church's use of community
members as unordained lay readers in Native regions was not unprecedented; on the contrary, such individuals were extremely helpful to the
Church's evangelizing efforts, given their familiarity with the indigenous cultures and languages of the communities they served.

The level of Tritt's Christian learning during this time is noted by
John Fredson, himself a Native missionary, in his documentation of "A
Trip to Arctic Village" in December 1922 (Fredson and Sapir 1982). As
I discuss in greater depth in one of my earlier works, Tritt's reputation

continued to spread far and wide, though not everyone within Arctic Village was enamored with his directives (Dinero 2003a). Village elders Chief Esaias and especially Chief Christian had been recognized as the first official "chiefs" in the village who acquired their status via wealth and position as "big" men (see also Stern 2005: 33). They oftentimes served as Tritt's primary political rivals in the community, seeking to counter and question his ideas and motives, and to draw the villagers' loyalties in a more pragmatic-leaning direction. Clearly, Tritt was highly intelligent and gifted, but he was a man of the cloth with ideas that struck some as fantastic if not difficult to fully comprehend; White outsiders, in the meantime, only further perpetuated a narrative that suggested his exceptionality was freakish rather than uniquely gifted (McKennan 1965).

Nevertheless, others invited Fredson and Dr. Grafton Burke, a medical missionary from Fort Yukon, to travel to Arctic Village. Notably, Burke would be the first White man to ever visit Arctic Village (Mackenzie 1985: 116), ushering in a new era of exposure to Outside values, attitudes, and beliefs. Fredson tells of his meeting a young man whose name was "Drit" (that is, "Tritt") upon arriving at the village in the winter of 1922. Tritt told Fredson that he wanted to know more about the Bible. As Fredson explains: "Until long past midnight he asked us questions about the Bible. As he always studied it, he knew quite a bit about it" (Fredson and Sapir 1982: 41–43).

By this time, Tritt had been studying the Bible for several years but would seek to further his understanding of its meanings throughout his lifetime. An ordained priest, Burke led the services during the five-day stay at the village, during which a wedding took place and a child was baptized. Overall, Burke and Fredson later noted the high level of participation from adults and children alike, further evidence of Tritt's teaching efforts and talents among the congregation. Indeed, the level of Christian observance in the community attracted the attention of Archdeacon F.B. Drane, who took over Hudson Stuck's duties upon his death in 1920. As a result, Drane also visited Arctic Village in 1923. Drane's reaction was similarly filled with praise, only further confirming the contention that Tritt was a highly motivated, intense figure.

This intensity was reflected in McKennan's journals, written a decade later, in which he describes a man so strongly committed to his quest: "Verily he is half-mad, a mystic and a seer of the type that in another age and another culture would have been a St. Augustine or a St. Francis, or possibly a Cromwell. After my visit with him I think I know why the natives of this village decamped so suddenly after his arrival" (Mishler and Simeone 2006: 177).

Albert Tritt's commitment to the spiritual world was extraordinary; at the same time, he also was a talented hunter who knew the land well, understood animal behavior, and provided well for his wife and family. I have documented many stories of Tritt's exceptional accomplishments and behaviors while out on the land and will not repeat this material here (see Dinero 2003a: 18–21). Still, it must be emphasized that Rev. Tritt's efforts to bridge the White world, embodied by his commitment to the Episcopal Church, while maintaining a strong connection to the Nets'aii Gwich'in tradition and heritage, rooted in the land and its resources, served as an early model of successful coexistence between these two milieus and worldviews. Such an accomplishment was perhaps best exemplified via the construction (and later, reconstruction) of the Bishop Rowe Episcopal Chapel, the very embodiment of this synergistic relationship.

The Building and (Rebuilding) of the Old Bishop Rowe Chapel

No building in Arctic Village holds more significance than the old Bishop Rowe Chapel. This iconic structure embodies the social and cultural history of the Nets'aii Gwich'in in a multitude of ways. The building of the church, and its later reconstruction and historic preservation, say much about who the Nets'aii Gwich'in were, who they are, and who they aspire to be.

From the outset, the building (and rebuilding) of the old Bishop Rowe Chapel was an exceptional accomplishment for such a small and poor Alaska Native congregation. Yet, in many ways, the building of the church well reveals that Rev. Albert Tritt was a visionary who set exceptional goals and exercised the leadership necessary to accomplish them. According to Tritt's son Isaac, this was not the first time efforts had been made to build a church: "Way before they, [Old John, a central figure in Nets'aii history who may be viewed as one of the "founding fathers" of the village, along with his followers] tried to make a church building at Old John Lake. But the foundation is soft. So they moved here [to Arctic Village], they forgot it. They tried to make log houses over there [too], but like the church it was too soft, so they came here" (I. Tritt 1987a). Albert Tritt's journals indicate that "church" services had been held in Nets'aii Gwich'in camps as early as the 1880s but without the benefit of a permanent building (see Stern 2005: 23).

The village was established on the shores of the Chandalar River with the building of Chief Christian's cabin (see chapter 1). Soon thereafter, Rev. Tritt began building the Rowe Chapel as the Nets'aii Gwich'in started to settle along the Vashr'aii K'oo in the mid-1910s. It was completed in 1917. Upon F.B. Drane's visit to the village in the 1920s, Tritt explained that in order to construct the chapel, "he brought the logs, and hired the young men of the village to help him build an ordinary sized cabin ... He managed to pay those who helped him with the work, [and] only [one person] worked without pay" (Drane 1922: 151).

In addition to workers, Tritt also had to acquire adequate materials for the building. As I have previously noted, this was no easy task. As one villager, a child at the time, explains (quoted in Dinero 2003a: 14):

> They went downriver—it was closer and easier than going upriver, even though the logs were smaller. The whole village moved down there, even the kids. They all cut logs, and made them into rafts, eight or ten logs tied together. They had no nails in those days. They pulled the rafts from the banks. In shallow water or when going around a bend, they got into the water in order to pull the raft through. They had no rope in those days, so they pulled the rafts with pieces of braided caribou skin sinews. These proved to be easy to make, and were very strong. To build the church they mostly used an ax and a Simon saw.

The use of local labor and materials was, of course, necessary given the difficult nature of the project. Rev. Tritt approached the building of the chapel as he did many of his works: with an intense commitment and an approach and mentality that had not yet been fully integrated into the communal fabric of the Nets'aii Gwich'in community at large. Tritt's perspective bridged many worlds, including those of the past and the future, of the White outsiders with whom he interacted with increased regularity, and of the Nets'aii Gwich'in who had lived on this land for millennia. However, he recognized too that many yet feared the changes the community faced; not all Nets'aii Gwich'in welcomed innovation in the early twentieth century.

During construction, Tritt did not explain what the building would be, only that there was pressing need to build expeditiously and immediately. Upon its completion, he told only Chief Christian that it belonged to all villagers for their use as a church (at this point the structure still looked like little more than a large cabin). Tritt was to then serve as the church's lay reader. As elder Moses Sam explained at length during a 1987 interview:

> Albert Tritt wanted to build a house for new church. For everybody. Just went down across the river, he went looking for good logs. He went down about four miles to find good logs, and everybody found good logs.

He brought them to the bank, even with dog team. All the logs were piled on the bank.

At that time nothing to eat, just dry meat, dry fish, that's all, nothing else. People hungry, but he want it done, so that's why the people do it. Pile it on the bank.

After they finish they make big raft, all the people pull it, with dogs and a big harness, a bunch of dogs. The people didn't eat good but he wanted to finish that church. So they started to build a big house, which was then going to be the church. Big pile, all the village, they build a log house even though the people were hungry.

People wanted that church, all day long they built it [even though they were hungry] and then Albert Tritt was happy. And then he used it, he used it many years.

Stories about the construction of the chapel, the settling at Arctic Village, or indeed virtually any major event in the history and life of the Gwich'in, such as the life events of Rev. Tritt (Dinero 2003a: 19), are almost always accompanied by hunger and the need to hunt. The very first words of the documentary *Gwich'in Niintsyaa* (1988) concern the story of near starvation and of a family living off one porcupine leg for several days until they could find additional food resources. Indeed, as Slobodin notes, many Gwich'in stories concern physical hardship or even death due to deprivation: "In the past, when starvation threatened a large group of the people or a number of small camps within a restricted area, so that it became impossible to seek further for food, there was a strong tendency for the people to draw together or to remain together, awaiting death as a cohesive group" (1960: 127). Thus, the concept of hunger here signals the degree to which the people were unified in their efforts to unite with a singular goal, drawn together by the charismatic leadership of Albert Tritt.

The completed chapel quickly became the central focus of the village. Though small and slight in stature, the church would in many ways overshadow all structures around it. When McKennan visited in 1933, he noted that the village was comprised of a dozen cabins and the small chapel. Also evident was a large half-finished building—a school—that lay empty, the floorboards having been recently scavenged to construct coffins (Mishler and Simeone 2006: 169–70). Perched above the Vashr'aii K'oo at the confluence with the Chandalar and the Brooks Range beyond, the chapel also increasingly drew villagers together as a focus of settlement, cohesion, and in time, village identity. Yet tensions among and between the village families remained, as not all agreed with Tritt and his "schemes" (likely, a result of jealousy); was this the best use of villager time and resources? Unity would not come quickly and easily to the Nets'aii Gwich'in, but if ever there were one focal that most could agree on, it was the value and significance of the old Bishop Rowe Chapel.

After five years, the chapel had gained recognition even beyond the village, including among officials at the Episcopal Mission in Fort Yukon. In anticipation of the visit that John Fredson and Dr. Grafton Burke were planning to the village in late fall, the villagers voted unanimously in the summer of 1922 to enlarge the building and add a steeple (see Illustration 2.1). As Tritt explained at the time, "the first church was different than now. It was hard for [the congregation] to sing—especially when scattered [in the room], and I thought they would be ashamed of it [when the visitors came]. If they sat near each other I thought it would be better, so I made a long table in the Church and long benches on either side, so they sat facing each other. I did this because when [the] first Church was built they wouldn't sing" (as quoted in Dinero 2003a: 15; no known photos of the original chapter exist).

In order to enlarge the chapel, the decision was made to rebuild it altogether. Tritt's friend and colleague Gilbert Joseph (Rev. Trimble Gilbert's grandfather) led the construction project. The old church was torn down, and a new one, nearly double the size of the first, was erected at the same location, using logs acquired by Joseph. While the original building was 17 feet by 17 feet, this chapel was 17 by 26 feet. The builders—Old Henry, Jimmie Peter, Joseph, and Tritt—also added a belfry. One elder recalls: "They used a two-hand saw to cut the planks for the top. They also used a plane, which they called a 'horse foot,' to smooth out the wood. The belfry top was the only part of the church where they used nails" (Arctic Village Council 2002).

The belfry was topped with one of the most recognizable images now associated with Arctic Village, a wooden piece by Tritt that can best be described as an arrow-shaped carving. Several interpretations of this figure have been put forward over the years. One suggests that it is seen "pointing to the four cardinal points of the compass … to ward off evil spirits" (Poirier 1975). Another interprets the arrow pointing upward as a reference to the story of Jacob's ladder. Arrows then pointed outward, referring to the sending out the four gospels' message in every direction. Even the villagers themselves have differed on the exact meaning of the carving (Dinero 2003a: 15–16). According to Chief Christian, the arrow signified "that the house was God's dwelling, not to be used as a roadside shelter by wayfarers." Chief Esaias, on the other hand, suggested that the arrow was meant "to point straight to heaven."

Illustration 2.1 Rev. Albert E. Tritt and the original Bishop Rowe Chapel, circa 1933.

Perhaps the best interpretation ought to come from Tritt himself. In one of his personal journal entries, he writes: "The furniture [furnishings?] of the church we made it by the way of God's work. [With regard to the carving, the] two round wood [forms] … stand for [the] Sun and moon; 3 round wood forms [are] for the stars. The arrow is God's words that point out in [a] sword and knife. With this, God's words, he confirm[s] these men in victory, Moses, Joshua, Gideon, Barak, Sampson, Jephtha, David, Samuel and all the angels (Heb. Chapter 11, 32–34) ... Then at the point of the arrow the enemy will fall [on] that double blade[d] knife through the earth" (A. Tritt, Box 1, Folder 8: 142–43).

A flagpole was also added, which would not be the last time Tritt showed a patriotic side to his values. As I have noted (Dinero 2003a: 20), he was a staunch opponent of the Nazis during World War II and sought whenever possible to encourage the Gwich'in to remember that they were not only Alaska Natives but Americans as well. As Isaac Tritt Sr. (1987b) explains:

> My father [Albert] tell the people how to get the flagpole. Because he put the toboggan down at Fort Yukon to bring up here and then he got it like same way. So that's why they get the flagpole ... Then a bunch of people go up the river went to the other side to look for a flagpole. And when they find a good flagpole and then the people come together. And they pray, and sing. And then after, Gilbert Joseph, he chop it and then they cut it down. And they clean it, and the people going to use a rope, and then they bring it here. They don't use it there.
>
> And then after fix it good and then make a hole in the ground before Dr. Burke come, to make a flagpole ... and Dr. Burke, he put a flag on.

According to Isaac Tritt Sr., the visitors also brought an altar cloth, a cross, and a "board" with the name of the church written on it.

As the village grew, so too did the congregation. In this way, we see that the physical building well parallels the village as whole, growing and developing alongside the community before experiencing a phase of slow decline, but this was long in the future. Before then, the chapel was rebuilt a third time (see Illustration 2.2) beginning in the summer of 1937. Albert Tritt initially lacked help in completing the job and had to abandon the project until 1940. Understandably, the fatigue of constantly rebuilding and maintaining the structure had taken its toll; the builders who participated in the reconstruction in 1940 largely came from Rev. Tritt's immediate family. As was the case in building the original chapel, additional materials for the reconstruction were again floated upriver tied together as rafts. The church was totally reconstructed in only two weeks, although further repairs took place throughout the following winter. Significantly, the orientation of the church was rotated 180 degrees so that the front door now opened to the south rather than the north.

Like the first reconstruction, the builders used some of the same logs and parts from the previous building. However, the overall appearance

Figure 2.2 The Bishop Rowe Chapel, circa 1960.

changed when they replaced the round belfry and entranceway with a square tower (Illustration 2.2)—7 feet wide and 6 feet deep at the base, tapering into a pyramidal shape at the top some 25 feet from the ground. They also added a vestry behind the altar at the rear of the chapel measuring 12 feet wide by 8 feet deep. Rev. Tritt had always wanted a vestry and welcomed this new addition. This room eventually took on a second purpose: to store bodies prior to burial, particularly in the cold winter months when the grounds of the nearby cemetery are rock solid. The chapel roof was comprised of sod on logs, like its predecessors, and supported internally by a large log "spread laterally midway at the room from eve to eve, with a pair of shorter logs rising from its center to a V to provide support for the two surfaces of the medium gable roof" (Poirier,1975).

For decades, the rebuilt old chapel was used extensively as a religious and cultural center (Illustration 2.3). Only when the villagers had finally outgrown this building was an entirely new chapel built several meters to the east in what would become the new town center in the late 1960s. By that point, the fruits of Rev. Tritt's brave and innovative efforts had become obsolete, forced to give way to a new era of much more rapid change and uncertainty in the village. A journalist summed up the sentiment of the times well when he wrote:

The sagging old Bishop Rowe Chapel is the historic landmark of Arctic Village. But its days are [now] numbered. They are preparing a new church on a hill nearby ... Now crumbling from old age and harsh weather, the antique church still glows inside with warmth. There is delicate Indian beadwork across the altar. On a wall placard is this hand-written prayer of Arctic Village: "Dear God, take care of me and help me find animals. Amen." (Patty 1969)

The new Bishop Rowe Chapel (Illustration 8.1) in the new location was consecrated in 1971 (Dinero 2003a: 17). Some fifty-plus years after its initial construction, the old Bishop Rowe Chapel finally was abandoned for good. During the decades that followed, the old chapel continued to fall into severe disrepair. The roof caved in, and overgrown willows encircled its foundation. At one point in the early 1970s, a truck struck the middle of the northern section. Over time, logs disappeared, presumably to be used for firewood (Arctic Village Council 2002). Later, florescent orange paint graffiti was found on the rear side, likely the work of bored village youth. In short, by the end of the twentieth century, the building—like the village itself—bore little resemblance to the grand structure that had been erected by the village elders sixty years earlier.

Illustration 2.3 Christmas pageant, old Bishop Rowe Chapel (December 1963).

The Final Reconstruction of the OBRC
and Religious Practice Today

On 19 July 2002 at 8 p.m., I convened a meeting in the Arctic Village
Council building. In attendance were First Chief Evon Peter and villagers Naomi Tritt, Isaac Tritt Jr., Sarah James, Kias Peter Sr., and Timothy Sam—all descendants and relatives of Rev. Albert E. Tritt. White
outsiders included Robert Mitchell (an architect from Anchorage), and
me. I had initiated the meeting to discuss the development of a project—envisioned a year earlier at the behest of villager Calvin Tritt, one
of Isaac Tritt Sr.'s sons—to reconstruct the old chapel a final time.

For over an hour, plans were made to reconstruct the chapel, which,
though now on the US National Register of Historic Places, had largely
been neglected since its abandonment in the late 1960s (Illustration
2.4). It was noted that for years, many proposals had been put forward concerning its reconstruction and historic preservation but that
none had come to fruition (Arctic Village Council 2002). It was noted
too that the chapel held great significance for the Nets'aii Gwich'in
community—for those residing in both Arctic Village and throughout
northeast Alaska and northwest Canada. The purpose of the reconstruction was to create a cultural center in the heart of the "old town"
section of the village, a longstanding idea that had first been brought
to my attention years earlier (Kias Peter Jr. 1999). There, the villagers
would house written, graphic, audio, and visual media about Rev. Tritt
and the Nets'aii Gwich'in people as a whole. Some of these materials
were removed decades ago (Arctic Village Council 2002), but at the
new center, they would finally be returned and made available to both
community members and tourists passing through who wish to gain
a greater appreciation of this Alaska Native village and culture. Lastly,
the center would serve as a focus of communal pride, memorializing
Rev. Tritt and other significant leaders in the history of the development of the Gwich'in Nation.

The reconstruction project continued over the next three years, concluding in 2005. The project cost just over $100,000, which I raised
from the State of Alaska Historic Preservation Fund; the Episcopal
Diocese of Alaska; the National Park Service Historic Preservation
Fund Grants to Indian Tribes, Alaska Natives, and Native Hawaiian
Organizations; the National Trust for Historic Preservation; the Alaska
Humanities Forum; and Philadelphia University. Following in the tradition of Rev. Tritt, we relied almost exclusively upon local laborers,
who were paid for their efforts, while Camp Towanga of San Fran-
cisco, California, provided some volunteer labor. Fifty percent of the

Illustration 2.4 The old Bishop Rowe Chapel in disrepair (August 1999).

project budget (2002–2005) was spent on local labor, 25 percent on outside consultants (three total), and 25 percent on building tools and materials ("Bishop Rowe Chapel Budget" 2005).

From the outset, the project closely followed the US Department of the Interior's standards for the reconstruction and preservation of historic properties. Historic photos gathered from archives and villagers' collections played a key role in reconstructing the building, which was placed in the exact location and position as was the 1940 rebuilt version. The goal was to ensure that chapel's final appearance (Illustration 2.5) was similar to the period when the building was still in use (Illustration 2.2). Thus, all visible materials used in the reconstruction are indigenous to the region; artificial materials and processed lumber are not visible. To the degree possible, the lumber from the chapel was reused (about 75 percent of the building shell); only when logs were severely decayed were replacement logs substituted. In addition to the use of indigenous building materials, hand tools were used in the construction of those parts of the building visible to the outside observer.

Throughout the project period, the council repeatedly emphasized that the process as well as the materials ought to reflect the historic meaning and significance of the structure and of the man and community that had initially built it. As one elder put it:

I was a little boy, but I still remember how the church was built. They used wooden pins. The only time they used nails was in the front, by the doors. I think we should go ahead and turn it [into] like it was in the old days. In those days they planed it with a horse plane. (Arctic Village Council 2002)

The interior of the reconstructed building was furnished with accoutrements that were originally housed there (altar railing, altar cloth, wooden cross). However, though holding the appearance of a religious edifice, the building would no longer be used as a church; the deconsecration ceremony carried out by Rev. Mark MacDonald—the Bishop of Alaska—and his colleagues in August 2004 ("Faith Endures" 2004) made this point clear to villagers and outsiders alike.

To this end, materials collected for the cultural center exhibit were initially housed in an adjoining cabin, not in the reconstructed chapel. (In time, however, this cabin would again become a residence, and some materials would be relocated.) In planning the reconstruction, two replacements in the chapel building were determined to be necessary—the bell and the wood stove. Both would be appropriate to the time when the building was abandoned. The building, it was determined, would not be heated by modern electric monitor, despite a recent shift by the villagers toward their use. Upon reconstruction, no stove was returned to the chapel, in the hopes of preserving the building for as long as possible. However, a bell that appeared to be virtually identical to that which had been in the belfry and moved to the new Bishop Rowe Chapel was secured via eBay from an old schoolhouse in Ohio and was eventually hoisted up by a series of pulleys into the newly reconstructed building.

In short, to the degree possible, the final reconstruction of the chapel was carried out in a manner that the villagers hoped would reflect the true appearance and "feel" of the building as it was originally designed and built by Rev. Albert Tritt and his family and friends decades earlier. The overwhelming participation of villagers in the reconstruction, many of whom were Tritt's grandchildren and other relatives, only further reflected that the reconstruction had precedence in earlier rebuilding activities by Tritt and his fellow villagers and family members. This fact speaks then to the authenticity inherent in the reconstructed Bishop Rowe Chapel (Illustration 2.5).

The history of Episcopalian Christianity in northeast Alaska should not be viewed as a parallel force with Nets'aii Gwich'in history. Rather, the story is directly interconnected and intertwined with every aspect of Arctic Village's early settlement and of its ongoing development today. Almost singlehandedly, Rev. Albert Tritt, followed thereafter by

Illustration 2.5 The reconstructed and historically preserved Bishop Rowe Chapel (March 2013).

his son Isaac and other key community members, helped to develop what former Bishop of Alaska Mark MacDonald has called "indigenous Christianity." MacDonald explains, "Though their own practices were outlawed, indigenous peoples used and adapted Christian forms of faith and worship to help carry their traditional worldview and values" (2012: 318). This practice can easily be seen among the Nets'aii Gwich'in who, to this day, have found creative and strategic methods of incorporating Christian belief systems into the everyday while simultaneously maintaining a strong sense of identity that transcends time going back generations. Yet, if one looks at the role of the Church in the early part of the twenty-first century, it, like other aspects of Nets'aii Gwich'in social life, requires new assessment and definition.

Evidence suggests that the youth of Arctic Village (not to mention many adults) are not as engaged in religious life as were their parents or grandparents. With the exceptions of Christmas and Easter, church services often draw few participants. Elders and women tend to populate most of the pews on any given Sunday morning, a trend that was already apparent nearly a century ago (Mason 1924: 58). Much of the motivation behind preserving the old Bishop Rowe Chapel was to remind the village youth of their familial, especially Christian, roots, but few if any hold a strong connection to or involvement with the

Episcopal Church today (see chapter 8). Rev. Trimble Gilbert (1996) summarized this point well when he wrote: "In the past you couldn't say 'no'; you would do as the Church asked. Today, it is hard to find this sort of commitment among the local youth."

As Gilbert moves toward retirement, few if any local candidates are prepared or willing to fill his shoes. This concern for young religious leadership is not new; as early as 1987, Rev. Isaac Tritt Sr. stressed that the young people of Arctic Village were not engaged with the Church and that an outsider would likely succeed Gilbert as village minister (I. Tritt 1987a). On the one hand, the Nets'aii Gwich'in of Arctic Village are undoubtedly a religious, believing Christian people. Religious references, prayers, and other manifestations of spiritual need and belief are commonly seen in Nets'aii Gwich'in Facebook statuses (see chapter 8). Yet, in terms of daily practices, the Episcopal Church appears to be struggling to hold onto an active core of participants. Local clergy and trained laypeople have aged; meanwhile outside interests have been drawn to the village, where Bible camps and similar activities associated with other Christian groups and denominations have been introduced, which, while attractive, pulls the youth in new directions that are not shared by the older generations.

The villagers themselves are cognizant of and concerned about this shift yet express fear and exasperation as to how to change attitudes. A 47-year-old woman villager noted to me in 2011:

> People need to get involved with the church. We need a choir, where we could sing gospel songs. The kids today—when we talk about the Lord Jesus—their faces change. We say, "Merry Christmas," and they say, "Let's gamble!" But we don't gamble on the holidays. I tell them, "Let's go to church." I loved it when I was a kid. I don't see any of this anymore. They're not interested in anything around here anymore.

Two other women echoed these sentiments in 2012. The first, age 41, suggested:

> I think there should be more church activities and socializing about the Bible. There's so much gossip. I hear so much gossip; there's gambling and I wish we had Bible studies so we wouldn't have anyone arguing or fighting. Every day there's someone fighting in front of the council or the post office. If they put God in front of them, it would not happen.

A 48-year-old woman concluded:

> Religion-wise, [the kids] don't even go to church, or if they go, do they know why they're going? In my younger days, we knew about stuff like that. No one is doing anything—I'm not either. What's holding me back?

Her query is profound. The communal ennui that presently grips the village community is forceful, existential, and for many if not all villagers, overwhelming. A renaissance in body, mind, and spirit is long overdue, and if the divinity introduced through the charismatic presence of Rev. Albert Tritt cannot serve as its chief arbiter, then what can? There is no simple answer to this question. However, before delving too deeply into this concern, it is first necessary to better ascertain how the village came to be in its present state. For this, I now turn to the role of education, the Church's "conjoined twin," for together, these two pillars have helped to form the foundational basis of the history and socioeconomic development of the settlement of the Nets'aii Gwich'in at Arctic Village—for good and for bad.

CHAPTER 3

Cleanliness, Hygiene, and Civilization Discourse

The Educational System, Past and Present

The child [of Arctic Village] may have no motivation impelling him to learn to read. He may be bilingual and he probably won't speak standard English. His background of experience will not include electrical appliances, cars, television and numerous other items that influence the daily life of most non-Indians.

— Marian Nickelson (1968)

The Historical Context of Schooling in Native Alaska

The introduction of an organized educational system in Arctic Village must be placed within the broader historic context of Christianization put forward in the previous chapter. Like missionization, the imposition of formalized schooling was a key agent of conquest and colonization long before Alaska achieved statehood. As such, the use of formal, Western, "White" educational structures has been well recognized as a primary vehicle for the forced assimilation of Alaska Native peoples.

Like churches, schools served as the primary "cores" of settlement for Alaska Natives (Berardi 1999: 335). They provided clothing and employment, and they carried out religious functions within the broader context of the Christian missions. The goals of educators and missionaries often overlapped. Becoming a "good Christian" and becoming a "good American" typically went hand in hand (339). From the outset, Native education largely entailed the imposition of White culture, using intelligence tests that would "prove" Natives inferior to Whites (Pewewardy 2002: 27) and in need of "civilizing" through the educational process. "Modern" educational systems, such as the use of specific curricula and pedagogy based on the scientific method, were therefore designed and implemented according to White, Western ideals and attitudes. Indeed, the provision of educational services to Native children was implemented and instituted to enlighten a new generation in order to detach them—and future generations—from their traditional roots and identities. Formal education in a school setting was a central part of the social conquest of territory, undertaken simultaneously with the political and economic conquest of the northern region.

In this context, the logistical aspects of formal education and Christianization went together as well; visiting clergy often served as schoolteachers. Literacy was especially emphasized in an effort to enable Native children to read the Christian scriptures (Kleinfeld 1992: 2). Similar to the teachings found in the traditional church setting, formal secular education was designed as an agent of development, hygiene, health care improvement, and overall "civilization" throughout Native Alaska. During the pre-state period in particular, "schooling for Alaska Native students ... was originally designed to civilize, Christianize, and otherwise assimilate Indigenous children into Western/White culture" (Jester and Fickel 2013: 189), as well as the economy (McDowell Group 2001, Section 2: 5). In short, "Russian schooling of Alaska Native children had three goals: to 'Christianize' them; to 'civilize' or 'westernize' them; and to make them more useful servants of the Russian American Company" (ANC 1994: 127).

Notably, the intersection of these values directly contradicted Native life. While subsistence culture was based on a coherent interaction between the domicile and the outside natural environment (chapter 6), "the ideal Victorian home was a hub of rationality, in contrast to the supposed disorderly, unscientific, dirty habits of 'inferior' groups (Boddy 2007: 31). The creation of an orderly, cleansed, white (if not White) environment was an essential element of this civilization discourse. To this end, the creation of the federal Bureau of Education established a formal educational system in Alaska in 1884. The Bureau lasted until 1931, when the Bureau of Indian Affairs (BIA) took over Native education. Not surprisingly, a major goal of these agencies was to improve sanitation, both literally and figuratively, in Native communities (Berardi 1999: 332). While the missionizing aspect of Native education changed significantly at this time (although it did not decline entirely by any means), the schools' goals were to encourage Native students to learn basic information while simultaneously "unlearning" their own cultures, languages, and traditions in the process of assimilating into patriotic Americans (Barnhardt 2001: 8).

A primary way this process of "deculturation" was pursued was through a systematic effort to remove the people from the land (i.e., a "dirt"-based culture), thereby detaching them from not only their livelihoods but also the history, heritage, and other familiar elements of their cultural identity that served to inform who they were and what they did. Such efforts were being practiced widely across the globe during this time. Anglican values, combined with Victorian sensibilities, when further inscribed into the intricate machinations of the colonialist enterprise, led to an almost universal effort through which "educating," "civilizing," and "cleansing" became largely interchangeable concepts. "Whiteness" in the racial sense and "whiteness" in the sense of cleanliness were, in essence, one and the same. As Boddy explains (2007: 37):

> Ideas about cleanliness now condensed a range of bourgeois values, among them monogamy (clean sex), capitalist enterprise (clean profit), Christianity (being cleansed of sin), class distinction, rationality. More, a close practical connection obtained between Victorian preoccupations with hygiene and evolutionary thought. Washing bodies, clothes, homes ... [would lead to] "maximizing life" ... Soap was both a symbol and an instrument of "civilization," where "civilization" was meant in a nonpluralizable sense.

As will be seen in the chapters that follow, such processes immediately created a dynamic for stress, tension, and conflict within Native communities. At school, children were taught one set of rules, one way of thinking, one set of values, ideals, and norms, while at home, parents began to struggle with these youths, striving to reinforce and reify an indigenous culture with an alternative set of attitudes and traditions.

The major role of education in Native Alaska at this time was clearly "to ignore the history, culture and language of Alaska Native people" (Barnhardt 1999: 103). "Ignore" is not, perhaps, a strong enough word. Indeed, one might contend that the goal was in fact to manipulate and, as will be seen later (chapter 7), permanently alter the course and trajectory of Native social development. In short, "the education system developed around it the mythology that it was a civilizing force. Native schools were seen by administrators and teachers as having a broad mission to improve the Natives' lives ... The Bureau [of Indian Affairs] was to maintain schools but also extend medical relief, provide sanitary living conditions and assistance, foster commercial enterprises ... and 'relieve destitution'" (Berardi 1999: 339).

In some instances, the concentration of the Native population via the use of schools as "cores" led to conflicts among groups, as well as challenges in accessing enough food to feed larger concentrated populations. However, educators felt that the trade-off of centralization was worth these struggles (Berardi 1999: 336). Still, consolidation led to the increased incidence of disease, though it also facilitated the ability to detect sickness and deliver health care (Berardi 1999: 338). That said, education and Christianization were informed by adjunct ideals; good nutrition, sanitation, and hygiene all led to a clean body and, in turn, a clean soul. Together, these ambitions would lead to the overall civilization of Native society.

Native boarding schools in the late 1800s served as a safety valve to help ease the pressure created by village consolidation and were the chosen way to separate children from their traditional environments and cultures. Following a "civilization-savagism paradigm," in which indoctrination of Native children into White society is a central feature such schools were designed to help "erase Indian identity by eliminating external symbols of tribal attachment and replace their tribal identity with the values and behaviors of *civilized* society" (Jester 2002: 3, emphasis added). Essentially, the view was that in order for these children to be properly cleansed of the harm done to them in the village setting, they needed to be removed from such an environment altogether.

In time, local schools became a regular fixture within village life (Dinero 2004: 404). While this structure might be viewed as a step forward insofar as it allowed village youth to stay closer to home and their families, it was also an additional mechanism of domination, purposeful cultural change, and attempted ecocide: the cleansing process was now relocated inside the village itself. The school building, for example, was designed and introduced into Native communities as a central edifice (Madsen 1990: 43–44). Like churches, schools also came to symbolize a recognition that traditions would now have to transition to a new way of life and Western worldview.

The construction, placement, and existence of the local school building in the village setting were hardly harmonious experiences. These schools tended to represent externally generated and controlled political power, social domination, and cultural hegemony. Typically, schools in rural Native Alaska were (and still are) designed by outsiders. Schools are the biggest buildings in town and often have features and amenities that separate them from the surrounding vernacular architecture. The difference in size, scale and materials is neither accidental nor easily ignored; the power differential is apparent, attracting villagers while reminding them that they are visitors and not owners of a part of their own community. "Although village residents utilize and appreciate many of the physical facilities provided in school buildings, it is worth noting the quantitative and qualitative discrepancy between the facilities available in school compounds as compared to facilities available elsewhere in [many] village[s]" (Madsen 1990: 46).

The placement of schools was also strategic, carried out with fore-thought and purpose. For example, schools were often placed in certain areas in order to help grow settlement and to draw populations in a particular direction, frequently away from what were viewed as old, crumbling, dirty town centers. In other words, placement separated and distinguished the new, clean environments in "isolation from harmful contacts" from the existing elements found in the traditional village (Berardi 1999: 343–44). Thus, schools separated not only in a literal geographic sense but also in a social sense, insofar as Native children were viewed to "suffer" from a variety of deficits and failures, weakness that could only be overcome by saving them from their indigenous environments. They, as well as their parents, were viewed as "less than" everyone else ("unteachable," "weak," "poor," and so on) rendering the educational enterprise virtually impossible to achieve to any reasonable degree (Jester and Fickel 2013: 192–93).

In this respect, new school buildings tended to take on certain aspects of outsider-dominated foreignness, capital concentration, and oppressive power dynamics inside the indigenous village setting. The school has often appeared to many as a rigid, hard-sided structure with limited access to the surrounding village (Dinero 2004). This dynamic has begun to subside in the early twenty-first century as the school is viewed as a more accessible structure, but for many, it remains a fortress within the village boundaries. The imposing nature of the school building is only part of the issue of forced cultural assimilation and the social attack on Native Alaska through the formal schooling structure. Clearly, what goes on inside the building matters as much as if not more than how the building is perceived from the outside. Here, two issues come to the fore: the teaching staff that works in Native communities and their curricula.

Elsewhere, I have discussed use of—and resistance to—the Traditional Native Knowledge discourse (Dinero 2013). As I noted, "much of the value of this information stems from the fact that it has been handed down generation to generation, and that it originates in a Native understanding of the Land, and that which lives upon it" (121). Historically, however, the curricula introduced into Native communities expressed what might be seen as an affront to this relatively innovative approach, that is, Western cultural dominance and authority that was difficult for Native Alaskans to counter to any great extent.

The BIA curriculum, as but one example, was specifically designed *not* to reflect anything having to do with being an Alaska Native (Barnhardt 2001: 16).

Moreover, the agents of the ideas brought to Native communities in the form of Western-oriented curricula (e.g., dependent on the "scientific method") were by definition the schoolteachers themselves. The predominance of non-Native schoolteachers further reified the power of the dominant, non-Native society and a relationship of postcolonial dependency. This, as I have also noted previously (Dinero 2004), resulted in a "clash zone" between Native values and attitudes. As the teachers acted as the primary agents of change, the parents were the facilitators of this change (they sought to acquire a "proper education" for their children, after all) while also serving as their children's defenders and protectors against the forces of deculturation. Such was an unenviable position by definition fraught with tension and the potential for misunderstandings. The possibility for school/household conflict was especially likely given that the teachers often were (and still are) viewed in high regard by the village population. Typically young, female, and full of vigor, the "imported" schoolteacher brought new blood, new life, and new excitement to the village community. For many villagers during the 1960s and 1970s, the new teacher was one of the first White people they would ever come to know.

More to the point, such educators were, of course, well intentioned, if not somewhat ignorant of what a job in the Native bush might entail. Non-Native educators were often unaware of how their curricula were culturally biased and could inadvertently foster a discourse of alienation and marginalization. For Western-educated schoolteachers, the material they disseminated was simply based on "fact." However, for those students in their classrooms who held an alternative worldview, the issue was not that simple. When one is taught "facts" that seemingly contradict one's existing reality (Okakok 1989: 410), confusion and self-doubt are inevitable. Once internalized, these sentiments become self-defeating (Marker 2000: 42), as educational goals become jeopardized by the very system intended to achieve them.

Here again, it is necessary to consider the purpose of formal education in general and its designed function in mid-twentieth-century Native America in particular. In brief, the goal of education is to facilitate change, improvement, and social development. Educators begin with a basic assumption: their charges are lacking; they are wanting; they need "help." The goal of the schoolteacher is to facilitate that positive developmental change. Non-Native teachers were often guilty of perpetuating what Jester calls the "unhealthy Native" construct throughout his study (2002). In effect, these non-Native teachers continued to accept the discourse that had been fostered a century earlier; they tended to view their pupils as perpetually or repeatedly "ill," insofar as Native society as a whole is seen as "sick" and in need of "healing." From poor levels of hygiene to alcohol abuse and fetal alcohol syndrome to youth suicides, Native communities are studied, analyzed, and noted for their high rates of dysfunction, with Western modes of treatment—formal education chief among them—being "prescribed" as the solution to a village's woes.

But are such pupils and their communities truly "sick"? Or are they simply victimized by cultural bias and prejudice, merely different from what White America was familiar with? In other words, are the very Victorian ideals of the 1880s not alive and well in the Alaska Native classroom of the twenty-first century? Today, 90 percent of Alaska's teachers are White while nearly a fourth of the students are Native (Jester and Fickel 2013: 189). The teachers in Native communities in particular, where the Native student percentage is of course far higher, remain largely unfamiliar with Alaska Natives' home life, conditions, circumstances, and values, including their close-knit social structures, extended family relationships, and subsistence activities. Among other differences with White society and culture, the use of nonverbal communication is just one factor foreign to the experiences of most new educators.

Arctic Village is just such a community. But have its children since mid-century "suffered" from a variety of deficits, or does the "sick Native" paradigm play a role here? Today, it may be difficult to know for certain what the conditions were in Arctic Village over the past several decades given that the lens used to view them was not of their own making. However, it is known that many Native communities were predisposed to any of a variety of ills and concerns. A lack of cultural knowledge, uneven power dynamics, and Western-oriented bias are at work during the period in question.

The Role of the Non-Native Teacher in Arctic Village

As was the case throughout much of the Territory of Alaska, formal education began to develop in Arctic Village most significantly in the early decades of the twentieth century. For the most part, little is known about the early days of this educational system. As noted above, the permanence of the village remained largely in flux during the interwar era, and so the "formal" nature of education from the 1920s to the

1940s is somewhat questionable. The village had no school building until 1924, when the villagers built their own log schoolhouse (Gagnon 1959: 1). There were no permanent trained teachers; instead, local villagers served as instructors. For that matter, there was no consistent, significant mass of students in school during this time (Hannum 1955).

Schooling did take place and the territorial government provided materials, but the variable nature of the village population and its seasonal permanence proved destabilizing. Due to its isolation in relation to White Alaska, Arctic Village remained largely off the beaten path well into the twentieth century. As such, the experiences villagers underwent in the late 1950s and early 1960s were particularly acute. Only in 1957 was schooling formalized, with the hiring of a teacher from outside of the community and a regular class schedule. From 1958 to 1959, the construction of an elementary school, a 26-by-76-foot building that housed forty students in grades K–8 (Gagnon 1959: 1), organized the educational process. However, this "solution" did not totally solve the educational needs of the local student population, as the schooling was viewed as weak and of poor quality. As I have noted previously, those who studied in the school's early days do not all have fond memories of the experience (Dinero 2004: 407–8).

However, those who taught in the school during this period are quick to note that the facilities and conditions were inherently problematic as well. The classroom was overcrowded, requiring a split or double session with older children studying in the morning and younger in the afternoon. The students lacked individual desks, which allowed and encouraged copying each other's work, as well as poking, punching, and playing rather than working (see Illustrations 3.1 and 3.2). An absence of culturally relevant teaching materials, compounded by the teacher's lack of any training in the area of English as a second language, exacerbated the daily difficulties in the classroom (Nickelson 1969a).

Anyone who has ever taught school at any level knows that one must face a multitude of issues and concerns in the classroom each day, but especially when teaching outside of one's comfort zone, such as when living abroad or teaching cross-culturally. Such was (and is) the case for most teachers working in the Native bush throughout the middle of the twentieth century to the present. These non-Native teachers, who arrived in Arctic Village with little if any preparation for the job at hand, confronted a variety of challenges. From their perspective, the village was still quite "traditional," requiring a significant amount of time and investment in order to bring its youth quickly and effectively into the "modern" world of a newly evolving post–World War II society.

Illustration 3.1 Arctic Village classroom (1970).

To date, little documentation or materials are available concerning this key period in Arctic Village's educational history, a time that preceded a great deal of social change and upheaval in the community before television, the "snowgo" (that is, the snowmobile, sometimes referred to as the "Ski-doo"), and other amenities had arrived. One can, however, speak with schoolteachers now, well after their tenure teaching in Arctic Village, in order to gain some sense via memory recall of what the educational system was like at that time (see Dinero 2004). Indeed, in speaking with Marian Nickelson, then a young teacher from Montana and today an ordained minister in the Episcopal Church, significant insights are revealed concerning her stay there in the late 1960s and early 1970s. As such, I quote her at length (Nickelson 2013):

> The kids came to school not speaking any English. Trimble [Gilbert] was my teacher's aide. We used life experience stories to teach. The kids would tell a story to Trimble. Each kid had a cheese box. They were in grades kindergarten to third. They would write words [from the stories] on cards, and put them in the cheese boxes. By third grade the kids could read the primers [we had]; they could understand. It worked really well …

> People in the village saw me as the "expert." Whatever I said, went. They had had bad experiences with previous teachers. But I had all the cooperation with the parents.

> As for attendance, we didn't have any trouble. The parents knew that the kids would get at least one meal there [at the school]. Getting the kids fed was a problem, so we didn't have any problem with attendance.

The only disciplinary issue I remember was that the kids could be immature. They would start school at age six. Their parents hadn't disciplined
them till then. They were disciplined by aunts, uncles, older siblings. The
parents would always give in. But the school was restrictive, and the children didn't always know how to handle things. Sometimes they might
cry and cry for long periods. At home, their parents would give in, would
give them whatever they wanted. But school is different, of course, and
some had a hard time adjusting.

Still, given that nearly fifty years have passed since Rev. Nickelson
taught in the village, some variation may exist between the details she
recalls and some of the documentation written at that time. For example, school board minutes from the period suggest that concern for
student attendance did exist and that the school particularly sought
parent assistance in encouraging students to return to school after taking their lunch break (*Arctic Village Echoes*, 15 October 1970; 26 March
1971).

However, Rev. Nickelson also provides for this discussion her own
unpublished works, written during the time she taught in the village.
Such papers are invaluable in offering a first-person perspective of
the situation as it was actually occurring. For example, she writes in
the late 1960s: "The report card may state that the child is in Grade

Illustration 3.2 Arctic Village classroom (1970).

Five, but this does not necessarily mean that he is working at that level. There are, in reality, three groups in the primary grades and two groups in the upper grades that function very well for instructional purposes" (Nickelson 1969a). As she explains, the average student is "[one to three] years behind in his academic work." Indeed, the school, she notes, operated like a one-room schoolhouse at the time. To a degree, the school must still do so today given the small student body (Reed 2013).

Rev. Nickelson's discussion of teaching English is also revealing, as she explains: "One of the greatest challenges is developing a better understanding of English, as the language at home is Gwich'in. This is done most especially through reading. Lack of experiences limits comprehension however." The absence of English language skills also limited students' understanding of math: "Children in the upper grades use the available textbooks in mathematics. However, again much explanation and enrichment is needed before total understanding of the concepts involved is achieved" (Nickelson 1969a). The writings also address Nickelson's memories of children "crying a lot" in school. She notes that the school board held a meeting concerning "discipline" in the fall of 1968, among others throughout the school year. As for the topics discussed at these meetings, she writes: "[The Arctic Village student] is immature. Unrestricted method of discipline at home, at school he just cries a lot [*sic*]. Some children adjust, others cry so much it interferes with their schoolwork." As a result, she notes, some children, when frustrated, sulked and refused to work: "On the whole, Arctic Village children's behavior indicates a lack of emotional maturity" (1969a). The idea that the children of Arctic Village are somewhat spoiled by their parents, and that they do what is necessary to get their way, is an old theme long expressed by outside observers (see Mason 1924: 68).

Lastly, Rev. Nickelson discusses the health of the village children, who, in her estimate, tend to be "sickly." She notes that many appear to show signs of hearing loss—that eleven out of her thirty charges have lost their hearing, nine due to a problem related to "draining ears." She suggests that this makes learning English more difficult. Also, repeated colds keep the children out of school, and, she notes, impetigo is a problem as well, as the children play outside without washing (Nickelson 1969a). Her comments on parent–teacher relations at the time, the isolated nature of the school building in relation to the rest of the traditional village, and how formal education might ultimately impact the Nets'aii Gwich'in community are particularly instructive if not prescient:

The feeling among parents about the use of English varies. Some parents feel that the children should speak nothing but English at school, while others feel that when the children come back from boarding school they speak "real good English" so why worry about it now. But by the time they leave for boarding school it's too late to learn to speak it and they have difficulty in the outside world.

The village is isolated. Meantime at school the children are exposed to one world, then they cross the stream to go home [i.e., the Vashr'aii K'oo Creek; the school was literally built across the creek from the village and the children crossed a wooden bridge to reach school each day, as there was no road (*Arctic Village Echoes*, 2 October 1970)] and they live and experience another world.

The problem is that the parents believe that their children should be educated, but they don't have much experience in education. They themselves aren't educated and don't understand how it works. They just entrust their kids to the teacher. The teacher understands the world of education, but does not fully grasp the values of the Gwich'in community. This disconnect is difficult to overcome.

Rev. Nickelson's papers offer significant insights into the perspective of a schoolteacher thrust into a situation fraught with the potential for conflict on all fronts. In discussing the past, it is one thing to ask villagers today in retrospect what they thought then about outsider interference in the lives of their children, and quite another to get a perspective from someone who addresses this issue at the time in question.

The experiences of Rev. Nickelson as she taught for four years in Arctic Village in the late 1960s and early 1970s well exemplify the quandary of formal education, not only in Arctic Village but also throughout the Native bush. Nickelson came to the village, with a population at the time of some ninety to ninety-five Nets'aii Gwich'in villagers, eager to serve the community. Unlike many schoolteachers, who cut themselves off from the community during their stays in bush villages (Jester and Fickel 2013: 192), she actively sought to play a productive role in the town. She was welcomed and well loved during her stay. She participated in village activities, socialized during Christmas and other holidays, and became an active community member well liked by both parents and children.

Yet, her charge was problematic at best, and her perspective was, of course, informed by her own culturally laden attitudes. For example, Nickelson believed that parent buy-in was crucial to student success. Without parent participation and an alteration in the home environment, she considered, students would not succeed, but the world she had entered was a foreign one and she quickly realized that forces outside of her control stymied her expectations for achievement. For example, in her view, her charges had little motivation to learn to read. Limited exposure to technologies and conveniences familiar to similar-aged children in White communities further limited their understanding of what was being taught (Nickelson 1968).

Rev. Nickelson's self-reflection is but one lens through which to observe the multifaceted aspects of formal education provision in the Native bush at that time (and, to a degree, which resonates in the early part of the twenty-first century as well). The questions she faced remain similar today. How, if at all, might one teach the ideals, goals, and values of the "outside" world while simultaneously teaching that another culture and traditions still have value? Was it possible to battle for the hearts and minds of the Native children in one's classroom—seeking to draw them out of the "dysfunctional" spheres of their parents' homes and redirect them into the modern, developed, healthy environment of the twentieth century—and still suggest to these selfsame children that their indigenous backgrounds were equally relevant and valid?

The perspectives of teachers who taught in the village decades later during the 1990s and 2000s suggest that while materials or facilities may have improved, dynamics between students, teachers, and parents remained conflictual in nature (Dinero 2004). As was the case in the past, these tensions appeared to center on a handful of specific issues. In terms of the parents and other villagers, for example, teachers were especially likely to note tense relations with the school board over decision-making powers, as well as the use of funding and resources. Regarding students, teachers also noted that attendance and discipline required greater structure and authority than they felt existed at home but that they were more than able and willing to provide such regimens (Reed 2013; VonThaer 1999).

The teaching and learning of English remained a contested area, recognized as a necessary, albeit controversial, topic of study. In general, teachers in the village in recent years like their predecessors, tended to be in conflict with village parents, as they placed the greatest emphasis and blame for student failure in the classroom squarely upon the students themselves, their families of origin, and their home environments. As I have noted, the views concerning the schoolchildren in Arctic Village during the latter part of the twentieth century could easily be placed within Jester's "unhealthy Native" construct. The teachers I interviewed for my previous studies appeared to view their charges as inherently flawed and in need of some sort of repair. Without exception, they encountered a variety of difficulties teaching in the village environment. Significantly, they attributed many of their frustrations to what they perceived to be an apparently high incidence of mental disabilities among Nets'aii Gwich'in children. Few if any seemed to identify the role of cultural difference in trying to explain student success, failure, or indeed overall behavior in the classroom.

Moreover, many teachers suggested that fetal alcohol syndrome was to blame for their struggles in the classroom. While this issue may have of course been prevalent for some students, the teachers with whom I spoke did not seem to appreciate that their charges lived in another culture, had different experiences, ideals, and values, and thus may have endured the school setting differently from similar children in a "typical" White non-Native setting. Although the demands and expectations of these educators differ greatly from the Native cultural milieu in which they taught in a number of ways, non-Native teachers glossed over or ignored these cultural differences, failing to recognize that difference does not mean "lesser than," "inadequate," or worse, "sick."

In short, many if not all teachers' expectations, demands, and attitudes coming into the village setting were predisposed such that the educational enterprise was jeopardized before a book was even opened or a word was even written on the chalkboard. The teachers who have come to Arctic Village in recent years have, like Rev. Nickelson, had limited preparation as to what they would find when they got there. Moreover, what little they did know was informed and influenced by a narrative of themselves as knowledgeable, well-intentioned, White, Christianizing agents sent into a primitive, if not occasionally hostile, environment. Their task was to take no prisoners in an aggressive, holistic conversion of the ignorant—to a great degree, a spirited and sacred quest. By definition of any worthy cause, non-Native teachers were assumed to face obstacles and opposition to their efforts. The students were rarely seen as the main problem; they were young and innocent, after all, and simply required a steady and guiding hand including "structure," "hierarchy," and respect for "authority" (Dinero 2004: 414–15). Many were viewed as "undisciplined" and out of control, but this was not seen as their fault per se. The fault lay, rather, in the indigenous culture itself, which needed to be overcome, changed, and in effect, "cleansed."

Education in Arctic Village Today: An Empirical Analysis

Throughout the 1950s and 1960s, local control of children's formal education remained a central issue among concerned parents throughout Native Alaska, including Arctic Village. During this time, the village school was under the supervision and control of the BIA; the local village community contributed little in hiring teachers, developing curriculum, or any other aspect of the formal educational process. The school was in effect an island within the village, separated geographically and in terms of its unique and differentiated status in relation to the rest of the community ("Arctic Village: Crossroad" 1968). The school building was the largest structure and, until the 1990s, was its only "modern," facility, accessible by a single handmade log bridge (which has since been dismantled).

One controversial question concerned whether the state should take over the school from the BIA in order to better attain more localized control of the educational agenda (Patty 1969). Eventually, the school was put under Alaska's administration for one year following much discussion by the school board in the fall of 1969. By that point, the school's population had exceeded an enrollment of twenty-five students (and later was predicted to nearly double to forty-five in a few years), so the need for acquiring a second teacher was particularly acute. The village voted on these changes, which passed 19–11 in favor (*Arctic Village Echoes*, 16 January 1970; 26 March 1971). The issue of local control would remain a problematic concern for decades to come as parents felt a sense of alienation and disenfranchisement from the educational enterprise. On the one hand, parents thought that without a formal, Western education, their children's futures would be affected adversely. Formal education, they came to believe, was the key to a successful future, even if they themselves had not graduated from high school (Dinero 2007: 263).

Yet, conversely, the introduction of formal education in the bush village environment provided an opportunistic venue for cultural change. Arctic Village is located within the Yukon Flats School District (YFSD), which includes approximately 250 students in ten villages spread out over a region equal in size to Washington State (Stathis 2014). The village is several air miles from the school district offices. One villager is on the school board. As a basis of its educational philosophy, the YFSD school board lists eleven "Goals for Student Learning." First among these is that a quality education will provide each student with the ability to develop "the importance of physical and mental health in mind, body, and spirit" (YFSD "School Board Policies": BP 0210).

The district curriculum followed by the schoolteachers of the village has been developed within the broader state context. Over the past decade, the overall number of credits required for graduation has dropped—from 22 to 21 (see Table 3.1)—as have requirements for in-

Table 3.1 The YFSD High School Curricular Credit Requirements (2013–2014)

4 credits of English (Yrs 1-4).

2 credits of math (Yrs 1-4).

3 credits of social studies

2 credits of science.

1 credit of health/physical education

9 credits elective

21 credits total required for graduation, where
1 credit = 35 hours of instruction.

dividual fields of study—math, from 4 to 2; science, from 3.5 to 2; physical education/health from 2 to 1; fine arts from 0.5 to 0; and career guidance from 0.5 to 0 (Dinero 2004: 411). The one area that has increased is electives (which has included such courses as vocational education, foreign language/Native language, river navigation, computer applications, driver's education), from 4.5 to 9 credits, or 43 percent of a student's entire high school experience.

For several years, I have sought to measure and quantify the developmental role of educational services in Arctic Village. Within this context, I have reached out to village parents, seeking to identify their attitudes and viewpoints on the formal educational model established throughout the 1950s, '60s, and '70s. My research questions were fairly straightforward: What is the state of education in the village today? What factors are playing a role in the success or failure of the village's educational agenda? Is the inherent conflict between "well-intentioned," White outsider schoolteachers and village parents still holding sway in Arctic Village today, and if so, is this dynamic to blame for present conditions or circumstances related to the state of education in the village? First, some background information is needed in order to address these queries.

There is one primary school and one secondary school in the village, a new facility built in 2009 (Illustration 3.3). Until then, the same facility had been in use with virtually no major additions, renovations, or improvements since the 1960s. Each teacher teaches all subjects in a class that includes multiple grade levels. Student enrollment has ebbed and flowed over the latter part of the twentieth century. The average school enrollment (for the two schools combined) from 1976 to 1982 was thirty-eight. Approximately two-thirds of the students were at the elementary level and one-third at the secondary level. Throughout these six academic years, only five students graduated high school—four boys and one girl (adapted from Lonner and Beard 1982: 171). By 1995, the official enrollment had reached forty-eight students. Of these, five were in a pre-kindergarten program. Of the remaining forty-three, only seven (16 percent) were studying at the secondary level. In 2000, the same number of students was studying in the schools, but now ten (23 percent) were in high school. Yet by 2005, thirty-three students were enrolled in the two schools, eight at the high school level. The high school population now accounted for 24 percent of the total school population (Alaska DOEED, 2014).

These statistics have changed somewhat over the study period under review, particularly the percentage of secondary-level students now studying in the Arctic Village High School. In the academic year

Illustration 3.3 The new Arctic Village School (July 2009).

2011–2012, thirty-one students were enrolled, about half male and half female. Fifty-five percent of students were in grades K–8 and 45 percent in high school. Four teachers were employed in the Arctic Village schools—three with bachelor's degrees and one with a master's (see Table 3.2). The village's graduation rate at the time was 90 percent, with an average of about ten students per teacher, compared to the statewide average graduation rate of 69 percent and 16 students per teacher (*Local School Directory* 2014). While these are the official statistics, school staff members state that in reality, only 60 percent of those enrolled actually attend on any given day (Reed 2013). The grade 7–12 dropout rate was nearly 28 percent during the 2012–2013 school year (Alaska DOEED 2014).

Perhaps more telling are the results found in the Standard Based Assessments (SBA) in such areas as reading, writing, and science (Table 3.2). Some recent statistics from the academic year 2011–2012, reveal that the school is truly in a mode of crisis. In reading, 15 percent—three students out of twenty—tested as proficient according to the SBA. Eighty-five percent were not proficient, 40 percent of whom were far below proficient. In writing, the results were the same. Fifteen percent tested as proficient in their ability to write in the English language while 85 percent were not proficient. Math presents an even greater concern. Ninety-five percent tested as non-proficient in their math abilities, meaning one student out of twenty was proficient (Alaska DOEED 2014).

Table 3.2 Percentages (Rounded) of Arctic Village Students Testing as "Proficient" According to Standard Based Assessments and Number of Teachers with Terminal Degree Qualifications

	2009-2010 31 students	2010-2011 23 students	2011-2012 31 students	2012-2013 28 students
Proficient (%)				
M.A./B.A. Teacher Ratio	2/3	1/4	1/3	N/A
Reading	18	20	15	0
Writing	12	20	15	18
Math	12	7	5	0
Science	13	17	N/A	11

This trend has existed for several years. The number of schoolteachers (and thus, the teacher-to-student ratio) and their terminal degrees
appear, in part, to help explain these outcomes. However, such a complex issue requires additional data for any broader conclusions to be
drawn. According to the 1999 survey, 100 percent of the fifty village
children were enrolled in school (see Table 3.3). Of these, forty were
studying in the primary school and ten in the secondary school. Of
those household heads interviewed, only 14 percent did not graduate
high school, compared to the previous generation (that is, the parents
of the interviewees) of which approximately 69 percent of the men and
77 percent of the women did not earn a high school degree. The closing
of the local school throughout the 1950s played a major role in these
rates.

I have reported the findings of the 1999 survey in previous studies
(Dinero 2004, 2007). The results of the 2006 and 2011 surveys only
further confirm that the adults in Arctic Village are well aware of the
schools' problems and blame the situation entirely on the school district—specifically, the teachers, who they believe are providing a poor
service to the village children. A culturally relevant curriculum, for example, has long been a decades-long subject of debate. In an internal
planning document (Arctic Village Council 1991), village leaders noted
even then that outsider control had fostered feelings of disempower-
ment in the community. Further, the Village Council charged that the
teachers tended to be "culturally insensitive" (23). Table 3.4 highlights
both of these issues with an asterisk, in recognition that they are longstanding village concerns that have been discussed now for over two
decades. Indeed, a generation later, such concerns continued to be
the subject of discussion among village parents who may have once
been students themselves back in 1991. "The teachers' attitudes are
against the kids. They call them names. They're rude and don't give
them chances," suggested one 38-year-old village mother. "The school
employees don't follow the village rules," added another, a 57-year-old
male resident in 2011. "They drink in town. The principal says they
can do what they want when they are off the clock, on their own time."

Table 3.3 Percentage of Survey Respondents Having Graduated High School

%	1999	2006	2009	2011	2012
HS grad	84	69	70	71	85
Non grad	16	31	30	29	15

Table 3.4 Identified Needs and Criticisms of Arctic Village Educational Services (%)

	1999	2006	2011
Better Curriculum/higher standards*	29	20	24
More/better teachers/Too much turnover*	17	15	44
New/better materials/equipment	17	7	--
Outdoor/Survival curriculum/camping	11	9	6
Better parent involvement/ relations with teachers	--	9	35
More strictness in school	--	9	--
Vocational curriculum	7	--	--
Control/stop truancy	7	--	--
Need Special Ed/Aides	--	--	8

The village leaders have repeatedly stated the desire to incorporate indigenous learning, especially outdoor education, camping, and survival skills, into the children's educational experiences. Significantly, although indigenous education is an ongoing concern, only a small number of village parents have expressed interest in this issue. The incorporation of more culturally relevant, outdoor-related topics into the school curriculum has been raised for some years, but the two most notable issues are 1) the quality of the teachers, as well as their level of commitment and professionalism; and 2) the overall curriculum itself and the degree to which it provides today's students with the material and tools they will need to succeed. A 57-year-old man's attitudes, expressed in 2011, are typical of how many view Arctic Village schoolteachers: "They use teachers who don't even have a GED as substitutes. So the kids see this and think, 'Why should I even graduate? They work here and never got a degree.' There's changeover of principals every year." Terry Reed, principal teacher of the school as of August 2012, does not dispute this claim. He suggested in a 2013 interview that turnover has taken a major toll on the students, and that, unlike his predecessors, he intends to remain in the village (Reed 2013). Keeping this promise, he returned to his post the following year, 2013–2014.

The concern about teacher turnover has been repeated and discussed throughout the literature over the past two decades (see Dinero 2004: 405–6). This phenomenon causes a variety of disruptions to the educational process in the village environment, even though the very nature of outsider involvement almost certainly necessitates that teachers will not commit to more than a handful of years of service in a Native bush village. Adds another 53-year-old man, who grew up during the 1960s, when teacher turnover was less volatile: "The teachers are there and then gone, and the kids have to get used to a new one. They have new ones all the time and this affects their studies. Each one has a new attitude, and a different personality."

While students in the Lower 48 typically expect to have a different teacher each year, the issue in Arctic Village is that these teachers are not simply gaining a new class each year but rather are new to teaching in the bush setting altogether. To a great degree, the teachers of Arctic Village practice on-the-job training nearly every year. By the time newcomers have actually spent a year or two acclimating to their new environment and student charges—finally having a sense of the place—they depart, only to usher in a new teacher who must endure the cycle of adjustment and adaptation all over again. Concluded a 59-year-old mother: "They need to hire people who are serious about the job. They don't hire experienced teachers, who cost more. [Instead they hire] young teachers [who] don't understand the culture and how people live around here."

While teacher turnover is the primary concern expressed in the most recent Arctic Village Service Provision Survey (2011), the most prevalent issue over the decade and a half since I began surveying village households about educational provision is the curriculum itself. On average, approximately a quarter of respondents have identified this issue as the most important of all educational concerns, more consistently than any other. In short, regardless of the teachers and how new or good the building is, respondents believe the material being taught matters most, and that remains the most weak and lacking year after year. Stated one village elder in 2011: "The curriculum needs to be at a higher level. It needs to be more challenging. Graduates need better preparation for college. Right now a lot of them need to be re-evaluated for college. That's true all over the school district." Adds another, a 31-year-old man: "They need to improve the curriculum, to get it up to national and state standards. They [also] need activities for the kids—sports, science, more stuff for the kids to do." Some have suggested additional, more "relevant" topics, such as Native American studies.

Perhaps no other curriculum subject is more controversial than the English language. As noted above, village test scores in both reading and writing are notoriously weak. The school's principal reluctantly admits: "For the past seven or eight years, little if anything was being done here in the elementary grades. The middle-school-aged kids can barely read or write" (Reed 2013). Yet, this issue is not new. Since the 1960s, teaching English in the village schools has been a major concern, alongside the degree to which Gwich'in will remain the primary language of the Gwich'in people. In the early days of this transition, an idea began to take shape that retaining the Gwich'in language was a handicap that might hinder access to broader aspects of formal education and other avenues to prosperity and success (Patty 1969). This contention strengthened over time and took on generational form; in 2011, when I surveyed village residents, 91 percent of respondents had parents who spoke Gwich'in. Of these respondents, 56 percent spoke Gwich'in themselves, and 38 percent said their children spoke Gwich'in. In order to validate these data, I asked the same questions in 2012, when 92 percent said their parents spoke Gwich'in and 60 percent said that they themselves spoke the language. However, only 28 percent of parents said their children also spoke Gwich'in.

And so indirectly, if not directly, introducing English as a "replacement" for Gwich'in appears to yet again serve as a proxy for so much that is going on in the village today, for good or bad. The old system has been rendered obsolete, an anachronism in an ever-globalizing world. In its place is an alternative set of social and economic systems (speaking English rather than Gwich'in, valuing commodity accumulation over subsistence, favoring authoritarian power structures versus familial ties and cooperation, and so on) that now creates the ideal circumstances for what some see as the "cultural destruction" of Nets'aii Gwich'in life and community. Not only do these new ideals irrevocably alter Nets'aii Gwich'in culture and society, but the privileging of these values over their precursors also in effect render all that proceeded them obsolete, archaic, anachronistic, and so on.

The YFSD has acknowledged in recent years that many in the community value the Gwich'in language, at least among the older generations. In recognition of this concern, the district has slowly introduced "culturally relevant" school curricula, which have been largely connected to Gwich'in language instruction. While this may seem like a significant counter to the trends described here, such instruction has been limited to only a few school days each year. In time, such "Native Language and Culture Days" might be expanded to a monthly or even more regular basis (Stathis 2010, 2011). Nonetheless, the loss of the language as the primary form of social and economic exchange and the movement toward an English-dominant culture are indisputable.

Indeed, in 2011, a generational relationship was found through statistical analysis of the quantitative data collected in the Arctic Village survey results. While it was not surprising to find that children were more likely to speak Gwich'in if their parents spoke the language, evidence also showed that the more educated one's parents were, the less likely it was for one's children to speak Gwich'in. In essence, the retention and speaking of Gwich'in appeared to correlate with slowed development as measured by Western standards. For example, those adults whose children spoke Gwich'in were more likely to receive General Assistance (welfare) and Social Security, though not food stamps and unemployment, than those whose children only spoke English.

The use of English has thus come to be equated with "success" and "development" within the Nets'aii Gwich'in community, perhaps with good reason. Concluded one 53-year-old father in 2012:

> I want my kids to learn the English way. They need it for school. I don't want them to stick around the village. I want them to get a decent job … I want my kids to learn English. They have to go to school, to be able to get money. Otherwise they graduate and then just wander around. They need education so when they go to the city into civilization, the city, they'll know what to do.

However, the village youth have not yet fully mastered reading and writing in English, even while Gwich'in continues to decline. Adult attitudes toward the schools in Arctic Village are similar to those expressed throughout the rest of rural Native Alaska. In both instances, village parents typically criticize schools (see Table 3.4) for being inadequate insofar as parents want their children to succeed and move forward, even though "forward" likely means "outward."

For example, only 34 percent of those Arctic Village adults surveyed in 1999 expressed satisfaction with this public service's provisions. This figure dropped to 23 percent in 2006 but rose to 54 percent after the new school was built. The adult residents of the village reported a variety of concerns for the quality of their children's education and how this led directly to the children's lack of success—that is, they placed the strongest emphasis on the facilities, teachers, and curriculum as evidence that the system itself is in dire need of overhaul. Parents were far less likely to suggest that the children played a role in their own education. As one 32-year-old put it, "People in the village should have control and power rather than the school district."

Moreover, there is a growing recognition that the school can do only so much and that parents are losing control not only over their children's education but, to a degree, over their children as well. The latter concern is now being discussed more commonly and openly than ever before. Stated a 56-year-old mother: "The kids don't listen. The teachers need to be encouraged, educated more. The kids are out of control. They need to listen to the teachers and to the elders." Suggested one 53-year-old man: "The parents need to get the kids to school. The discipline at home isn't there. Support from the village in general, in backing up the school—it isn't there. They spoil the kids, they are against the school. They need to support it."

Such sentiment seems to place blame equally on the parents for allowing their children too much freedom and on the village youth, who, it is intimated, ought to know better how to behave and who seem to be quite spoiled. Two additional comments expressed in 2011 confirm this belief. The first is provided by a 47-year-old female villager:

> The kids are bossy. The kids don't show respect. They need to know how it is in the world. The parents aren't talking to them. I try to push them up. The ones in the high school walk all over the parents. The parents don't push them to go to school, to be on time. It used to be that Arctic Village was up there, but not anymore. I wish I was a kid again. You guys have everything—computers, games. I wanted to go to college, but I didn't have the support. So I tell them, "You guys got to think ahead."

Concludes a 69-year-old man: "The kids aren't going to school on time. They stay up all night. Some don't go at all. They miss school a lot. We try to tell them things and they don't want to listen." The lack of appreciation and respect expressed here is clear. The generational shift, which will be explored further in chapter 7, is now a central feature of twenty-first century Nets'aii Gwich'in life.

Educational "Success": At What Cost?

As seen above, the implementation of a formal educational system modeled on Western modes of learning appears to have achieved marked albeit modest success in Arctic Village over the past century. Yet, such "success" must be placed within the broader context of educational development across Native Alaska during this same period. The building of the school once served as an anchor to draw the Nets'aii Gwich'in into settling, essentially abetting a process that helped to cease their nomadic ways. But what appears to have been happening since the 1960s is quite the opposite; those who are becoming or wish to become more educated must go elsewhere. And once they leave, the chances of their ever returning to the village, short of the occasional visit, are slim at best.

Such trends are consistent with recent research conducted across the state. In one survey of Native students, a majority (61 percent) said they wanted to go to college, and 80 percent said their families encouraged them to attend postsecondary education (Doyle et al. 2009: 28–29). In this same sample, the students were asked how they felt about leaving the village and moving to the town permanently. The students who did not want to move to the city were usually male, and their reason for staying was primarily based on enjoying a rural lifestyle (30).

A similar study conducted in the early 1990s had comparable outcomes. Of the 63 percent of students stating they planned to leave the village upon graduation, high school girls were more likely to wish to leave than high school boys were. Girls were also more likely to plan to attend college. The study found that while boys oriented to shop classes like small engine repair or boat building—that is, areas emphasizing skills helpful in the bush—girls were more likely to gravitate toward such areas as business—that is, courses that will take them out of the village. While not necessarily a huge exodus, a gender imbalance could correlate with other social problems for girls and boys alike, such as substance abuse, sexual abuse, and other family or village dysfunction (Hamilton and Seyfrit 1994: 190–93).

A certain irony is evident in this development. In the 1950s and 1960s, being sent to a boarding school was a sort of banishment. With no high schools in the villages, thousands of Natives were sent away across the territory and even further afield, to the Lower 48 states throughout the twentieth century, never to return quite whole or complete (Dinero 2004). Yet today, studies such as those conducted by Diane Hirshberg and Brit DelMoral (2009) find that boarding school students are now significantly more likely than Arctic Village and town school students to expect they will attend college or spend most of their lives outside of Alaska (5). Boarding schools such as Mt. Edgecumbe High School provide students more academic and extracurricular opportunities than their home village schools; for some, they offer an escape from homes with drug and alcohol abuse (8). Overall, such schools may supply rural students with better opportunities for a higher quality of education than is available to them in their home communities (11).

In conclusion, it is problematic that the success of Arctic Village and the Nets'aii Gwich'in now rests upon an educational model that by definition has approached its children as deficient, flawed, dirty, and in need of cleansing and Whitening. Not only has this imposed system largely failed in its stated goals but it has further only caused greater harm than good to the population it purportedly set out to "en-*lighten*." A Catch-22 has now developed in bush villages across Alaska, including Arctic Village. From about 1975 or so onward, the concepts of opportunity, educational achievement, and success have been increasingly equated with leaving the village environment (Dinero 2004: 414). The consensus among educators, parents, and others is that future village life is a "dead-end road" of sorts—that achievement is only to be found in Fairbanks or elsewhere (VonThaer 1999). As one 58-year-old male villager put it in a 2011 interview:

> We need more community involvement with the school, and more school involvement with the community ... Things [in this village] are the same as in the past. There's more technology but people are the same. We have new technologies but the same people, the same fights. It's not advancing. People aren't educated.

> I went and got more training, and now they have to pay me more, so they won't hire me. So I'm losing out, I'm screwed. And what can [my adult kids] do here? This village is like a retirement home.

The fact that this is a gendered movement only further complicates the issue. The question then is whether a more educated young population is to the village's benefit. On its face, the answer would appear to be a resounding "yes." Yet, as the village youths become more worldly and educated, seeking opportunities in not only Fairbanks or Anchorage but also increasingly in locations throughout the Lower 48, their individual prospects appear to be rising at the cost of the village's long-term strength and viability. I return to this question in detail in chapter 7. But before doing so, it will be helpful to examine the evolving conditions of Arctic Village and its ability to serve its residents—young, old, and everyone in between.

CHAPTER 4

The Village, Service Provision, and Economic Development

~⊶∘ᴏᴅ̥ᴏ∘⊷~

We do it ourselves.
— Sarah James, *Gwich'in Niintsyaa* (1988)

Ongoing Development in Arctic Village

As discussed in the first three chapters of this section, the development of Arctic Village evolved over the first half of the twentieth century due to internal change as well as in response to a series of social and economic forces generated largely from outside, nonindigenous sources. Colonial activity, including the powers of the Episcopal Church and government interests, fostered settlement and with it, new behaviors, attitudes, and expectations within the Nets'aii Gwich'in community. Yet with change came a growing sense of lost control over land, resources, and living conditions. As noted in chapter 1, the Nets'aii Gwich'in, by the 1980s, had become more politicized than ever before as outsider interests began to encroach upon their lives and livelihoods at unprecedented levels.

Within this atmosphere of growing tensions, a gathering took place in Arctic Village in June 1988 to address Gwich'in identity and outside threats to the future of the community. The gathering, the first of many biannual meetings to occur in the Gwich'in region, was filmed and made into a documentary (*Gwich'in Niintsyaa* 1988). As Rev. Trimble Gilbert explains in the film, such gatherings had once been commonplace, but this was the first since settlement. In theory, the 1988 Gathering was created primarily in response to the ongoing threat of corporate interests wishing to drill for oil in the Arctic National Wildlife Refuge (ANWR) and to discuss the potential impact and damage such drilling would have on the Porcupine caribou herd and, as a result, the

Gwich'in. Yet, the film makes clear that the gathering addressed much more. Alcohol addiction, Gwich'in unity, and the frustrations caused by the United States–Canada border, among other concerns, dominate the initial discussion. Threats to the caribou are saved for the second half, some twenty-five minutes into the film (*Gwich'in Niintsyaa* 1988).

Perhaps the most telling moment in the film—indicative of the times and of changes to come—is when Sarah James appears. She says to filmmaker Ruth Carroll, "This is *our* meeting. We have to do it *ourselves*. It's *our* meeting." Her words are significant, and for a variety of reasons. By this point, the Gwich'in had acted largely in response to outside social and economic forces for roughly a century. For the most part, the response to outsider intervention had been open, honest, and receptive, but by the 1980s, the Gwich'in realized that such willing acceptance had come at a high price. Those outside forces had effectively struck a mighty blow to the Gwich'in community, dividing the people and even pitting them against each other.

A sense was rising that Gwich'in identity and cohesion, as the film discusses, were being undermined. Yet, new communications and transportation technologies would now allow for greater connectivity. While both the Canadian and the American Gwich'in posted flags in the community hall throughout the gathering, they repeated that "we are one people, one big family" (*Gwich'in Niintsyaa* 1988), regardless of living in a village or in "town," in Alaska or in the Canadian Yukon or Northwest Territories. More to the point, the 1988 gathering inaugurated an era of self-directed organization, community planning, and control. Historically, the Gwich'in had been loosely confederated, as their environment necessitated a lifestyle that was socially, economically, politically, and geographically dispersed and decentralized. Colonization settled and centralized the community but under the influence of foreign, outside powers. By the early twentieth century, wholesale change was under way; communal cohesion had been undermined so extensively that the community was unrecognizable from its former nomadic past. As Osgood (1936: 172–73) states:

> There has been a growing tendency away from communal activity towards individualism with an accompanying disintegration of the old feeling toward the band, the house group and the family. The old class system, primarily based on wealth, which might have been expected to continue because of its seeming similarity with the pattern of the new culture, actually fell apart: primarily, it appears, because of the redistribution of status and wealth under the new economic system and then because it has been overshadowed by new classifications based on intermarriage with the whites and the extent of adoption of European culture.

In effect, social bonds of the past had been broken; at the time, it was felt that there was little to effectively replace them, though this would change as new twenty-first century technologies arose and allowed the Gwich'in to overcome the challenges of geographic dispersion. Still, the idea of a centralized village system functioning under a consolidated leadership had yet to gel or fully solidify by the late 1980s. Rather, "Arctic Village" was, in the truest sense, the village, with all of its various components including housing, stores, schools, clinics, and churches, as well as the surrounding region where hunting, gathering, and fishing took place. This region, which extends for several miles in all directions around the village (including the ANWR), was as much "home" to the villagers as was the village itself. The mountains, rivers, and creeks—indeed, all of the geographic and geological features in and around the village—were as much a part of one's residence as was one's four-walled house. More to the point, the village itself must also be viewed in this context; "home" in the villager's sense of the term extended well beyond one's dwelling to the village and then further telescoped out to the surrounding region.

While "home" for tribes in the Lower 48 states might be delimited within one of the 278 federally defined sites demarcated as "reservations" for Natives (Snipp and Summers 1991: 177), the concept of "home" goes past the Venetie Reservation for tribes like the Nets'aii Gwich'in. To a degree, the expanse of "home" embodied by the concept of village life included "town" as well—in the case of Arctic Village, Fairbanks, and, to a far lesser degree, Anchorage. In this regard, the plane that connects village to town was (and remains) a lifeline of sorts, facilitating an ebb and flow of goods, services, and, above all, people as they circulate in constant daily motion between these two nodes, as well as the smaller nodes of Fort Yukon and Venetie. In the past, these trips took weeks or even months via dogsled, but by the late 1980s, when the gathering took place, the film well depicts that these flows occurred within hours.

In short, Sarah James's words at the time were a harbinger of events to come, namely of a shift toward more centralized planning and development in Arctic Village, which, up until this point, had been haphazard at best. Moreover, while one could argue that the Nets'aii Gwich'in had no choice but to accept the new realities brought on by the White colonial enterprise decades earlier, it is only fair to point out that this paradigm shift was externally imposed. As such, imbedded within it were ethnic, religious, and racial elements and prejudices that by definition served from the outset to despatialize, disenfranchise, disorient, and destabilize. Settlement was, by its very nature, an artificially imposed superstructure.

Still, this dynamic was only further exacerbated when, in the late 1970s and 1980s, the Nets'aii Gwich'in voluntarily began to embrace use of the snowgo, the ATV, the telephone, the television, and, later, the much-prized VCR. These technologies further catalyzed expansion, separation, and distancing of the village members away from each other, alongside increased connections with non-Gwich'in cultures, ideas, and attitudes. This movement was not huge in geographic terms, but socially, a more household-centered culture oriented toward the television, for example, divided rather than unified a community that had typically spent working and leisure time in close-knit proximity of one another.

Thus, the new shift toward the Nets'aii Gwich'in working together to "do it ourselves" while simultaneously decentralizing away from one another would be both revolutionary yet at times contradictory. As noted, the Gwich'in had functioned on their own for millennia; now, they would need to operate independently together. That the Nets'aii Gwich'in at Arctic Village would find such an oxymoronic circumstance challenging as they strove to adapt to the new constraints brought on by such a confluence of formidable socioeconomic changes is, therefore, unsurprising and, more to the point, understandable.

The Development of Planning in the Village: Living Independently, Together

Soon after the 1988 gathering, the Arctic Village Council, led by then–First Chief and Episcopalian Village Priest Trimble Gilbert, published "*Nakai' t'iu'in*, ('Do It Yourself!'): A Plan for Preserving the Cultural Identity of the Neets'aii Gwich'in Indians of Arctic Village" (1991). Members of the Village Council co-wrote the typewritten, spiral-bound report over several months and divided it into two major parts. The first section, sixty-seven pages long, presents a plan for the future development and growth of Arctic Village and includes council resolution topics—some already passed, some only suggested—for future community development. The second part, nearly a hundred pages, is comprised of various letters, interviews, tribal memoranda, and photo essays, which serve to trace and document the village community's history, as well as its values, attitudes, and concerns since European contact and settlement during the previous century. The target audience of the document was the villagers themselves, for without their inclusion and participation, the council believed, any planning in the village in the coming years was destined to fail.

The document's purpose was twofold. First, the council laid out elements that it saw as central in defining Gwich'in identity, as well as what the Nets'aii Gwich'in stood for and believed in. Second, the council attempted to codify areas of need in order to establish a future social planning agenda for the village. The document opens with the declaration that "your own self-esteem comes from your past, our past" (Arctic Village Council 1991: 3). Emphasis is placed on self-sufficiency and independence, but at the communal, not individual, level. The document notes that in the past, cooperation and respect were paramount, but by 1991, internal conflict and schism were damaging the village. Central to this concern is the issue of ongoing family conflict: "Our culture and spiritual well-being is negatively effected [*sic*] when families are a part [*sic*], the younger men are not as involved in learning from the older men when they are separated, and important values are not handed down because of this separatism" (14).

That said, the Community Development Plan (CDP) also reflects the need for a balance between living in community and living independently, as village members have done for millennia, free from outside influences, expectations, or demands, including from one another: "Our system of self-regulation and self-determination is based largely upon self-respect and self-esteem, which allows us to then work for the common good of our village" (38). In this regard, the document notes that the villagers did not (and would not) recognize any outside authority besides their own, as "we are a sovereign nation recognizing only tribal laws" (36). The writers of the CDP sought to emphasize the importance of unity, admitted to current conflict, and urged renewed efforts toward cooperation as the only means to ward off external economic and political powers. They further defined this ideology through "Cultural Policy and Community Value Statements" (33–35), summarized and paraphrased as follows:

The Gwich'in community of Arctic Village must:
- Speak our own minds, and be honest;
- Oppose any efforts by outsiders that threaten our land, animals, or way of life;
- Teach our children the values of our people;
- Preserve our culture through the teaching of our native language;
- Respect and cherish our elders;
- Support Western-style education of the children but with a culturally sensitive curriculum.

Moreover, the CDP refers to several other concerns, especially on the village's economy, educational system, governance, and infrastructure. In addressing economy and education, the document notes the need for a stable cash economy in the village, which was lacking in large part due to inadequate wage labor positions (see Dinero 2003b). The CDP proposed vocational education as one way of solving the employment issue but contends that such curricula would not likely be implemented without more centralized local school control. Ultimately, the plan calls for economic growth but to be undertaken slowly and cautiously (14–20). As for infrastructural changes, the document (28) recommends a new wash building (i.e., a washateria, completed in 2014), a new playground (completed in 2009), airport improvements (completed in 2003), a better health clinic (rebuilt in 2012), restoring the old village church (completed in 2005), road improvements (ongoing), and a youth recreation center (completed in 1998; relocated and improved in the early 2000s). These were seen as important improvements that could, in part, help to further promote the village as a tourist destination (31)—a possible source of outside income (see chapter 8).

Perhaps most significant of all, the document acknowledges the need for better village governance in order to accomplish such goals. Lack of legal knowledge, business administration skills, political savvy, and public relations expertise are all cited as problem areas. In addition, the plan calls for restructuring the council to delegate more authority and states that personal conflicts between villagers further inhibited council decision-making (20–21). The problems highlighted in the document reflect problems found in many small rural communities in the United States and Canada, regardless of their ethnic makeup. In the case of Arctic Village, these concerns were only further exacerbated by the difficulties inherent in the transition from a seminomadic, relatively independent livelihood to a settled lifestyle situated within a global economy and society.

Overall, the council apparently intended the CDP to be not merely a blueprint for the future development of Arctic Village per se but rather a plan for the entire Nets'aii Gwich'in people and nation. This is no small point. In the nomadic past, the social community was in some ways separable from its temporary physical, geographic place, but such a distinction was far less clear by the 1990s. Chief Gilbert and the council realized that social, economic, and communal development for the village and for the people as a whole were intertwined and that planning combined the two. Put differently, the temporary tents did not define Gwich'inness in the past, but by the 1990s, Gwich'inness without the benefit of the physical village was becoming less easily defined. The document provides insights that, in the spirit of Rev. Albert Tritt, combine the newly evolving modern era with the historic identity and heritage that had sustained and supported the Nets'aii Gwich'in people for millennia. In essence, the document sought both to recognize the Gwich'in people's historic past alongside the new realities of the coming millennium and to provide direction for moving forward in a time of uncertainty (Arctic Village Council 1991: 32):

> To us, money is not an end, but a means to make life easier in a harsh environment. Money is used for basic survival needs, not luxury ... We wonder about people who think we are poor, for how can we be considered poor when food, clothing, shelter, laughter and compassion surround us daily?

The issue of monetary worth in juxtaposition with Gwich'in ideals and values was at the crux of many Arctic Village families' struggles at the time and, to a considerable degree, still today. The imposition of the capitalist global economy fostered an inherently foreign mentality yet one that has taken root among some quarters, with devastating results. The CDP offers a cogent response to this, the most difficult and dominant issue confronting the community then—and now (32):

> We value our children, our land, our animals, our lakes, rivers, trees, air, and mountains. We value each other and ourselves as Gwich'in people, not for how many material goods we have or want. We do not separate these things; we are made of these things.

The plan's ideals reveal the concerns and priorities of the village leadership, many of which were consistent with other Native tribes of this era. An emphasis on self-determination, self-regulation, and tribal control of local education, natural resources, employment, and other aspects of socioeconomic development well reflected a village-centered orientation, especially in an era of federal government cutbacks (Snipp and Summers 1991: 170–71). Dependency on federal and state support is an inherent aspect of Native America despite the turbulent Native rights efforts of the 1960s; by opting out of the Alaska National Interest Lands Conservation Act (ANILCA), Arctic Village was able to preserve some degree of self-determination, but such efforts had limited effect given the power of government interests in the region.

Moreover, several issues arise from closely examining the development-planning document. First, the CDP contains no implementation mechanism to actualize most of the priorities discussed. Goals are noted, but a path to accomplishing them is not made clear. More to the point, while the document well reflects the concerns and values of the village leadership and, to a considerable extent, many in Arctic Village itself, planning for development and growth is not the same as policing. That is, the planning document encourages and facilitates both economic change—which is formidable but, with considerable effort, feasible—and social change. The latter was rife with controversy and, despite good intentions, far more complicated to implement. These social changes included Council Resolutions (Arctic Village Council 1991: 42), stating that the Gwich'in language would be spoken a minimum of two days a week, Arctic Village would be alcohol and drug free, parents would "train their kids" to be more mindful and respectful, and, perhaps the most provocative, the village would "deal with" the problem of marriage to nontribal members (a veiled reference to non-Natives, that is, Whites). While each goal is understandable and perhaps laudable given the perceived threats facing the village at the time (and since), such resolutions were difficult to pursue. Furthermore, though well intended, they could potentially prove to be as divisive as they were unifying.

Within this evolving context, community planning may be measured over the past twenty-five years. By looking at the development of Arctic Village from both a qualitative and quantitative perspective, the CDP was successful on a number of levels in moving the village forward, fostering growth, and creating a stronger, more economically robust village environment. At the social level, however, those very concerns that haunted village leaders in the early 1990s are still evident today. If anything, they have progressively become worse.

An Analysis of Planning Outcomes: 1990–2015

As noted above, the Arctic Village leadership set an ambitious agenda for development in the early 1990s, largely in response to the sense that the village had functioned to this point based on what one outsider referred to as a "knee-jerk" approach (Jones 1999). Rather than implementing careful and slow planning, the village tended to react quickly and without forethought, often against what it perceived to be outsider interference, only later to realize the losses such responses would entail.

Interestingly, the concerns of the 1990s eventually found purchase some years later as a result of this new approach, though a dependency on outside assistance rather than total "self-reliance" was apparent from the outset. For example, in addition to reconstructing the old Bishop Rowe Chapel, priorities at the time included protecting Red Sheep Creek in the ANWR from sport hunting, moving the trash landfill farther away from the village, and building and relocating a new school due to environmental contamination detected on the school grounds (Kias Peter Jr. 1999). As discussed in chapter 3, a new school was in fact built in 2009 with federal support, and all asbestos was removed and incinerated. The landfill, a major environmental hazard, was moved farther away from the village at that time as well. Meanwhile, hearings concerning the protection of the Red Sheep Creek area were held in 2010 (USDOI 2012). Despite the region's considerable distance from the village and the logistical challenges that prevent continuous hunting for sheep there, the Nets'aii have longed claimed the region as a significant part of Gwich'in Country that should be protected from outsider hunting and related recreational uses. With concerted effort, including my own brief testimony, the US Fish and Wildlife Service closed the area to sheep hunting by in 2012 (USFWS 2012).

After these environmental concerns had been raised in the early 1990s, Arctic Village expanded considerably throughout the decade and, by the turn of the millennium, stretched well beyond its original core. Centered within a few steps of the old Bishop Rowe Chapel, the village now increasingly oriented toward Main Street—that is, due south (see Illustration 4.1)—off which the Gilbert, John, and Sam families in particular had settled in clustered "neighborhoods" (see Map 4.1). Around

Illustration 4.1 Main Street, Arctic Village, and neighborhood expansion (August 1999).

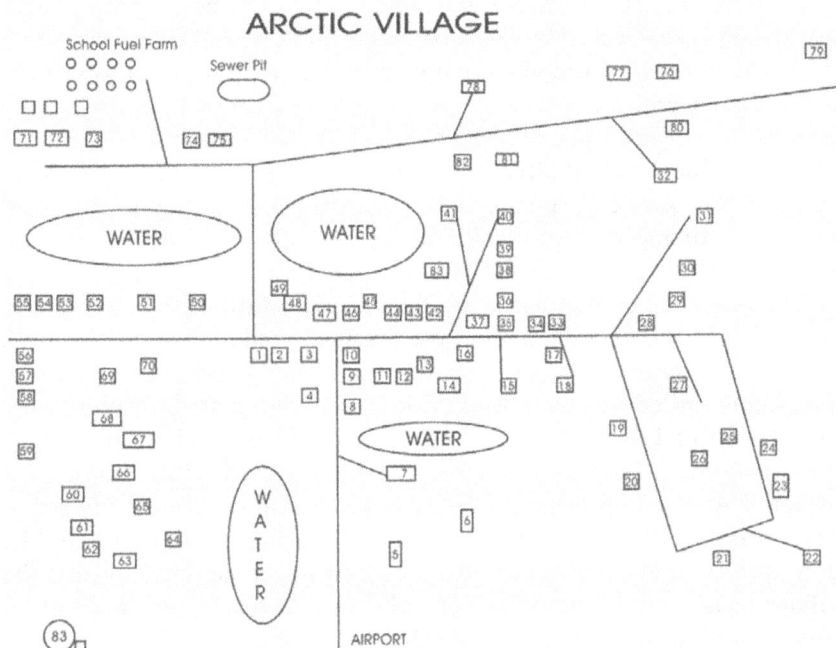

Map 4.1 Arctic Village in 1999.

this time, the US Department of Housing and Urban Development (HUD) initiated a free housing program in the community in order to provide for everyone's needs. Housing stock had aged considerably at this point; little if anything had been built in the village since the 1960s (Jones 1999). Though slow to begin, the program facilitated the building of the first two houses in 1997 and four houses in 1998 (Martinez 1999). Thereafter, one or two houses have been built every year. Much of this new housing dominates Airport Road and, due to the exterior pastel colors chosen by the owners, now composes a micro-neighborhood known locally as Skittleville.

Along with the HUD program, other similar federally funded initiatives at this time began bringing millions of dollars in materials, supplies, and wages into the village. As but one example, a weatherization program to better insulate the village's older housing stock and thus conserve local fuel resources was implemented in the late spring and summer of 1999 and cost nearly $1 million alone (Jones 1999). While a quarter of the funds remained in Fairbanks for administrative purposes, three quarters were funneled into Arctic Village for materials and salaries to local laborers.

In short, while the local council aimed to function as a representative governing body elected by the local villagers to plan the future growth and development of the village, it soon morphed into a grant-writing, fund-raising entity dependent on external resources to carry out its objectives. For example, in order to subsidize skyrocketing fuel costs— the village fuel bill had already reached $8,000 a month by 1999 (Martinez 1999)—Arctic Village turned to a variety of externally generated programs, including State of Alaska energy subsidies and Venezuelan President Hugo Chávez's CITGO-Venezuela Heating Oil Program.

The outcome of this evolving dynamic is multifaceted. As numerous changes and developments were implemented in the late twentieth and early twenty-first centuries, the social fabric of the community was being pulled in several directions. Although a small but growing population of less than two hundred, the residents of Arctic Village were becoming increasingly divided and stratified within these new systems. Access to power and resources increasingly resulted in social and economic dynamics that have only divided rather than unified the community. Intercommunity disputes and anger directed toward the village leadership became two central concerns tearing at the community's foundations (Stern 2005: 75–76).

This contention is evident in a variety of ways, shown here through data gathered from my household surveys. The statistical data, along with qualitative material presented to me at the time, well reveal that over the 2000s and 2010s in particular, the village has witnessed greater dispersion rather than unity of residents in both a geographic and, more importantly, socioeconomic sense. To better analyze these developments, it is easiest to first examine some of the economic data I collected during this period (see Table 4.1).

Each of these indices—employment, households collecting transfers, and reported household income—offers little when viewed individually. When combined, however, the three reveal that village employment rates are very slowly rising. As they rise, transfer payments drop slightly but not in any statistically significant manner; they are still high. Minimally, two out of three households report receiving welfare or a similar form of government support. Household income also reflects a slow but steady improvement in economic well-being. Yet, while the number of households making less than $10,000 per year declines, the percentage of wealthier households (making more than $20,000 per year) also appears to drop. Thus, though Arctic Village appears to be wealthier overall than it was in the late 1990s, that minimal increase is limited at best.

Table 4.1 Arctic Village Economic Indices

Are you employed?	1999	2006	2011	Average
Yes	46	44	50	47
No	54	56	50	53

A: Employment status.

	1999	2006	2011	Average
Yes	51	80	63	65
No	49	20	37	35

B: Households receiving transfer payments. Sources: Arctic Village household surveys.

	1999	2006	2011	Average
Under $10,000	57	59	53	56
$10,000–20,000	29	36	38	34
Over $20,000	14	5	9	10

C: Household income.

However, economic growth may also be examined through material consumption. The 1991 CDP identifies several consumer goods that the village leadership contended were requirements for a reasonable quality of life. Among these, the top three "essential" items that all households ought to own were the four-wheel ATV, the snowgo, and the motorboat (Arctic Village Council 1991: 20). Table 4.2 reveals, however, that such is not the case for Arctic Village households. While what might be viewed as "nonessentials," including the television, the DVD player or VCR, the refrigerator, and the oven range, are relatively

Table 4.2 Household Ownership of Consumer Goods

	1999	2006	2011	Average
Telephone*	67*	52	70	63
TV+	100	100	96	99
DISH-TV*	17*	49	30*	32
DVD/VCR+	97	92	91	93
Oven/range/microwave+	91	85	100	92
Fridge/freezer+	83	82	87	84
Snowgo*	69	54*	67	63
ATV/4 wheeler*	49	44*	35*	43
Motor boat*	n/a	n/a	20*	20
Gaming System+	77	54	39	57
Personal computer*	11*	23*	30	21
------ On Facebook	n/a	n/a	46	46

ubiquitous, ownership of the essential items identified by the CDP and several others, tend to correlate significantly with household income in many if not all of the surveys conducted during the study period.

Throughout this study, all correlations were determined using chi-square analysis (where $p <$ or $= .05$). I used this methodological tool because the size and nature of the data samples collected throughout the longitudinal period of research in an indigenous environment defy European definitions of standard housing units (see Poppel 2015 throughout). During the 2011 Arctic Village Survey, as but one example, $N = 46$. Not surprisingly, ownership of one consumer good tends to correlate with ownership of other goods. For example, those with a telephone also have satellite television, as do those who own a boat. Perhaps of greatest interest is ownership of an ATV. Households with higher incomes are more likely to own such vehicles than those with lower incomes. ATV owners are also more likely to have a telephone—as well as a snowgo, a motorboat, and satellite TV—and less likely to receive transfer payments (i.e., welfare, food stamps). Evidently, the ATV requires a certain level of wealth that not all villagers enjoy. This correlation is seen for boat owners as well, emphasizing the relationship among wealth, access to resources, and quality of life differentials in the evolving village economy.

It is not surprising that ownership of goods correlates with income. However, the consumption of certain goods, regardless of income or owning other goods, suggests that some priorities and concerns in Nets'aii Gwich'in society supersede economics alone. This contention is confirmed when ownership is considered in relation to other criteria, including social indices such as age, gender, and education. For example, ownership of a personal computer grew more consistently and rapidly than any other product measured in the study. While computer ownership correlates with owning computer gaming systems and using Facebook—clearly expected outcomes—it also correlates with having a more educated father and an inability to speak the Gwich'in language.

At first glance, such correlations with social indices might be mistaken as false or meaningless outcomes. What might computer ownership have in common with such issues? Yet, further analyses suggest that a connection is evident. For example, those who own a gaming system are also less likely to speak Gwich'in. In turn, the employed are less likely to speak Gwich'in, along with their children. Those who do speak Gwich'in tend to have less educated parents and are more likely to receive General Assistance, unemployment, and Social Security benefits. Furthermore, those whose children speak Gwich'in are more likely to receive welfare and Social Security, though not food stamps or unemployment benefits.

Significantly, when asked how they identified themselves (i.e., Nets'aii Gwich'in or more generic Athabascan or Alaska Native identities), those who choose the Nets'aii label are also more likely to receive General Assistance, food stamps, and Social Security. This trend was further confirmed by the correlation between choosing the Gwich'in identity and reporting lower household incomes. Thus, a picture begins to emerge in which "Gwich'inness" may be connected with a poorer socioeconomic position. But this alone does not explain the stratified economic circumstances of today's Arctic Villager. In addition, marital status is also strongly associated with economic success and prosperity. For example, single adults are less likely than married or cohabitating couples to own a refrigerator, freezer, or telephone. Furthermore, couples are more likely to have a boat, a four-wheeler, or satellite TV and less likely to rely on Social Security, General Assistance, or other forms of government support.

Such analyses well reveal the stratification of the Arctic Village community over the past several years. While these data provide significant evidence of social and economic change, publically provided services offer further opportunity for growth and development. However, resident use and satisfaction with these services is not assured; the provision of a service and its enjoyment by a majority of users are essential if planning is to be considered a "success." The percentage of respondents expressing satisfaction with the provision of services in Arctic Village presents a mixed outcome at best (see Table 4.3) from which several issues may be highlighted.

First, none of the provisions—be they supplied by the local council, the federal or state government, or other means—are viewed very positively. The service that consistently attained the highest score was water provision, yet there is no running water system or indoor plumbing in the village (with the exception of the schools and, as of 2012, the health clinic). Rather, individual households access water either at the washateria's single tap or—the old-fashioned way—by using large plastic cans at Tritt Creek (known locally as Glacier). The washateria was first built in 1976 and its "water was obtained from an infiltration gallery/well in a nearby lake and carried by elevated utilidor and chlorinated prior to storage in a 10,000 gallon wood-stave tank" (Alaska DCRA 1991). This method worked relatively well but was repaired and improved in 1983. At that time, seventeen homes also were provided

Table 4.3 Percentage of Respondents Expressing Satisfaction with Service Provisions in Arctic Village

Utility/Service	1999	2006	2011	Average
Electricity	51	49	57	52
Sanitation/ solid waste	37	56	54	49
Health/Clinic	49	49	39	46
Education/School	34	23	54	37
Water (Self-service)	69	51	59	60
Air transportation (Private vendor)	63	56	57	59
All Outside Government (State, Federal) Services	26	44	61	44

with a basic indoor plumbing system, which was an almost immediate failure.

Since then, villagers have relied on the self-service system of packing water, as well as the use of outhouses and honey buckets. Some households have developed an informal system of using walkie-talkies in the village to call for a runner who uses a four-wheeler in summer and a snowgo in winter to pack water for a small fee. Interestingly, when analyzed statistically, women expressed less satisfaction than men did with personally having to haul water, perhaps a reflection of the present system's exceptionally demanding nature and inconvenience. That said, those residents with more educated parents were also critical of water provision, confirming that the desire for running water in the village is not merely an issue of gender or physical strength but also a quality of life concern.

Other notable statistics concern air travel, the health clinic, schools, and trash removal. Air travel consistently receives high rates of satisfaction yet is provided by a private airline. Wright Air Service is known to be reliable and safe, but most villagers constantly complain it is "too expensive." The schools received poor ratings up until a new school was built in 2009; similarly, ratings rose when the solid waste system was improved and the dump moved. While ratings for the school have shown particular improvement, women, who predominate in the village as single mothers, expressed less satisfaction with the school in the 2011 survey than did men. Conversely, those who rate the school more highly tend to have fathers with lower levels of education.

As for the health clinic, its history complicated. Once managed by the Tanana Chiefs Conference (TCC) out of Fairbanks, the Council of Athabascan Tribal Governments (CATG) centered at Fort Yukon has recently taken over many of the village's health-care-related responsibilities. The council provides personnel training, visits from aides and clinicians, pharmacological assistance, and the like but has long experienced a great deal of criticism from local villagers (see Dinero 2005: 150; 2007: 264). Although some view CATG as an improvement over TCC (Stern 2005: 63), many feel the arrangement is still not ideal, as the clinic continues to suffer from a lack of equipment and well-trained staff (see Tables 4.3 and 4.4). The clinic was rebuilt in 2012, so residents might now rate it more highly than they did in 2011. Still, at the time of the 2011 survey, statistical analysis determined that more educated residents were more likely to criticize the clinic and less likely than other villagers to use its services. Those with more educated parents were also less likely to use the Arctic Village clinic for their health care needs.

The quantitative outcomes presented above are compelling but present only one aspect of the evolving development of planning in Arctic Village over the past two decades. In addition to the numeric data presented here, I also interviewed dozens of residents in order to gain a direct understanding of how villagers themselves view village development planning. I present empirical evidence of this perspective in their own words with little if any editing. Rather, I seek here to allow the residents of Arctic Village to speak for themselves, responding in a straightforward manner to the following queries:

> How do you feel the village is developing and progressing today? Is the local council effective in planning for your needs and the needs of your family? If so, how so? And if not, why not?

Table 4.4 Arctic Villager Planning and Development Concerns and Opinions

Villager 1: We've built the new school, new housing; we're getting a new Washeteria, a new clinic. The airport is new. We're building the road up to Old John Lake. So what else will sustain us economically? And can we keep these things up? CITGO helps us. We don't have a long-term economic sustainability plan. Tourism has petered out. We have a lot of young people just hanging around. There are so many, so we have to rotate them every two weeks. They have nothing to do, there's too many of them, and we have to hire them whether they are trained or not. So out of high school they are making $25/hour. This is Council policy, the family expects this. So I want to cut this policy just when *your* kid turns 18? It ruins their minds. They make their money, go to town, buy games; they don't save for a snowgo.

We have more carpenters than in the past, but not enough electricians or heavy equipment drivers. When we get CITGO aid, is this really a help? We have a lot of new infrastructure, it's safer, people are adapting to it. But we're losing our language. It's why we're Gwich'in. I can't be Gwich'in unless I speak it.

You got a freezer, before everything [i.e. food] was dry. In the summer everything we eat was dried. A long time ago we'd be out a long time. These kids only go out on a picnic. You have to live out there. These kids are in town, they don't know anything out there. You should catch them when they are young.

--57 year old male

Villager 2: It all depends on the chief. If they're educated [things go well], but some are lazy. Ten years ago we were really in debt. Now it's paid up. So it's better now. We've had chiefs that embezzle. Things are moving in the right direction now.

We could be drilling for oil, gold, uranium, or tourism – using the Reserve. But the majority of the people want to keep it *pristine*. I want to develop it beyond the village. Sixteen hundred of us own 8 million acres [actually 1.8 million]. If we really developed it, we'd be millionaires. But people around here don't want to tear up "Mother Earth" [said with a sneer]. So we are poor, depending on General Assistance. Everything is so expensive without a road. These kids will be good leaders, the ones who go to university. Ten years ago we didn't have them going to college.

-- 53 year old male

Villager 3: The Village is starting to move in the right direction. Things like the Washeteria isn't being run right. We need a communal freezer. The Council Office needs a new building. It leaks; the foundation is messed up. It's workable, but it needs major work. We need an emergency fund for elders, for their maintenance for housing.

The Village should take over, should do something. Single people are getting large houses. We only build two houses a year. People don't have patience. You have to wait to be called to work too. It's how it works, people need to be patient.

It used to be that we used dog teams. You feed the dogs with fish. How are you going to afford gas for your snowgo or 4-wheeler? We'll go back to the dog team maybe?

The biggest part of income here is building houses. Energy assistance is good for the economy too. We'll get a new Washeteria, but we need to pay a little for water. People don't want to pay. The landfill has to be maintained. The old ways are long gone! We have 160 people living here! Things have to change.

The Village is broke doing other people's work. The store is in the best shape it's ever been. There's lots of stuff in the dump that should be recycled. We need incentives for recycling. The old days are long gone and we need to wake up and smell the coffee!

-- 53 year old male

Villager 4: The government has no clue what's happening up here. There are a lot more houses, more jobs are available. The jobs are there, the grants are there. Our people are losing out to alcoholism and drugs. Economically we're doing better. So in our time, we're better off than in the past, but not socially, like in our grandparents' day. I have everything here. I have my land, [but] if I go to Fairbanks, I'll have nothing. My parents' generation thinks collectively, but we think individually. But then, they can't trust each other. How will life be for my daughter? I am already an alcoholic as young as I am. We're slowly losing our culture.

These kids have no respect. When I was growing up we were thankful. Teaching respect is depleting. In the past the community raised the children, not just the parents. Now they worry about getting money to spend it on alcohol and drugs. They don't care for the kids—the kids are doing drugs WITH their parents. Alcoholism, drug abuse, violence, sex abuse – they're all connected.

--32 year old female

(continued)

Table 4.4 *continued*

Villager 5: I have a personal concern. Drugs are an issue. They cost too much. A lot of money is being spent here on drugs. The young generation has nothing to do but kick back, smoke a joint and play video games. We need a bowling alley or an archery range. Something besides drugs. To get kids off of drugs, they need something to do. Snowboards maybe. The kids say it's boring here. They need to get into shape, and make their brains better too. As close as we live to each other, we don't act like we're close. We walk by like we don't even see each other.

> *-- 29 year old male (who during the interview, quite ironically, excused himself for a few minutes, went into an area behind some bushes where we were meeting, and lit up a marijuana joint. He then returned to complete the interview)*

Villager 6: We have problems here with Copenhagen [chew], drugs, alcohol. We brought someone in to teach about condoms and AIDS. There is bootlegging here, and a lot of problems with alcohol. We know who's doing it. Women come to my house—it's like a "battered women's shelter." They feel safe there. We even have our own "Peeping Tom," someone taking women's underwear. And men doing things to kids. But people are in denial here. When things happen, the families back them up.

We're in the Third World yet.

> *-- 56 year old female*

Villager 7: Things are fair here. There are hardly any jobs. There's too much favoritism among certain people. There's poor communication with each other. We don't work together. There's too much gossip. Also, the hiring practices are unfair.

> *-- 43 year old female*

Villager 8: Things have changed a lot. There's favoritism for one family. One family is favored to get a job. There's nothing to do here, nothing in the store, nothing for the kids. It used to be fun for the kids. A lot of people have hatred against each other. They talk about each other. They say things that aren't even true.

> *-- 21 year old female*

Villager 9: There's work only in the summer. There's no work in the winter, and that's what we need. If we don't make money, the Federal government gives us welfare and food stamps. We need welfare because we don't have jobs. It's not like the city. Here, there aren't many jobs: the post office, school teacher, store.

Twenty years ago, we didn't have so many houses, and we now have the new school too. It's good now. It's improved, we have good people working in the store and Washeteria. A lot is still the same though—no economic development or investment in the future. We have a lot of land but we don't know what's on it.

We don't have water and sewer. It would be great if we could keep ourselves clean. I feel dirty all the time. It's hard to go over there [to the Washeteria]. It's not comfortable over there. But we need to stay clean from MRSA and other disease. And we don't have any money to take a shower.

-- 52 year old male

Villager 10: We now tell the BIA [Bureau of Indian Affairs] what we want and they do it. The Government makes sure that our kids eat. In the past, they were trying to brainwash us and take away our values, to break our spirit.

Things suck. Material-wise, it's fair. But morally, value-wise, it's not the way our grandfathers and grandmothers and mothers and fathers wanted us to be. We don't share, we don't love each other we are greedy and trying to get that back is like pulling a nail.

If things don't change we're not going to last. If there's a war we'll be the first to go. I try to live simple. I don't want running water, satellite dish, Facebook. Those are toys. I am a country village girl. I try to think of those values, how to get back to my people's values. We were happier in the '70s. Coming back here after being away was like paradise. Everyone was good to each other then. When our grandmas and grandpas disappeared in the 1980s, then we started to lose our Native ways. When I first came back I thought my people were the best – as the years go by I see they are like everyone I know down in the States.

In my grandma's and parents' time, they took care of each other. It's not just us, it's happening all over the world. Our grandmas and grandpas warned us not to join them, but they didn't listen; there was too much opposition.

-- 65 year old female

(continued)

Table 4.4 *continued*

<u>Villager 11</u>: People don't raise their kids. They don't tell them how to be a kid. They grow up too fast. Kids know about sex, crack. Some kids know all about drugs and alcohol. I talk with my kids all the time. Kids see things here because the parents aren't around; they watch X-rated movies.

I hate it around here – and I don't like using that word "hate." The drugs, the alcohol. Girls around 14 and 15 are drinking, then falling asleep with guys all around. The mothers blame the boys instead of themselves. There's no supervision.

Things are changing for the worse. Money is coming in from the housing, which is good. My family doesn't say we have to hire each other—we're different from some of these families. We're normal. We just stay out of everyone's business.
-- *40 year old female*

<u>Villager 12</u>: I love this village. I wouldn't want to move. I support it. But it's changed here for the worse. People don't follow our tradition no more. It's better if we use our culture rather than the White way, the outside way. Other than that I think it's good.

There's bootlegging and a lot of drinking. We need to prevent it. It's been happening for a long time but it's getting worse and there's not enough effort to stop it.

Family favors family. They protect their family; they say their family isn't doing it. It's stressful. We need more support to stop it. It's mostly the kids, and the parents don't make an effort to stop them. Some of these parents know their kids drink at 16 and don't try to stop them. The parents just let the kids do what they want.

The Council tries to get involved but some of them drink too. It's crazy. Even some of the elders bootleg. Everyone's involved.

People come here to my house because I live outside of the village, and they're hurt. I can't turn them away. They come here to be safe. I've had a lot come here. It's a family situation, family against family, and when alcohol is added, it all comes out. To tell you the truth, I've given up. I can't do it anymore. They're my people, but I just can't do that much.

-- *23 year old female*

Villager 13: In 1960s the community and the teachers worked together. It was better that way. We don't work together now. The kids aren't learning like we did. We send them over there and then they come home and watch TV, and there's no good training at home… [so] I'm pretty low and unhappy. I'm an elder. When I was growing up, a community had unity, we worked together. We donated time; for thousands of years, we shared. This was before the pipeline. After the pipeline, there were more free handouts and that really spoiled the people. It doesn't help them.

People my age, we based our kids' education on fishing and hunting and crafts, and we worked part time. That worked for us—no free hand-outs. We don't want to get spoiled. We try to show this to the young people—you know, role model…

…We've been here—our great-grandfathers and grandmothers did training, boys outside and girls inside planning how to survive. Like your high school and college. This was important, people depended on them. Now it's different. People depend on machines. I still use an axe. But the kids aren't training. It's all over now. It's harder and harder for kids to live in a place like this.

We go to the schools, we talk to the kids about who they are, how to survive, about arts and crafts. It's better than nothing. Language too. They are so used to the telephone and the TV. We had a sled and dogs. They wouldn't know how to do it! We had the dogs and the kids too, working hard in the cold winter. Now the kids complain that it's cold and they need a 4-wheeler to go to the post office!

I pack water, use a sweep saw, it's good for your health. We used to be strong. Now they can't walk – they're overweight – not healthy. That really worries me, anyway…

One of the biggest problems is alcohol, drugs and gambling. You should see our people in Fairbanks. Their minds are all connected to that BINGO. And no jobs – people say this year after year. I try to show the kids, teaching sewing, but kids aren't always interested. But they are happy sometimes to see it. They need to know their culture too. There aren't many people like me—they've all passed on.

More and more people are angry. The alcohol, the drugs makes things worse. Everyone is blaming one another. There's always jobs around here. Stop blaming other people! My mom and dad told me, don't blame nobody, just keep working! We need to help each other.

-- 76 year old male

(continued)

Table 4.4 *continued*

> **Villager 14**: We're in this same boat without a paddle – and we need to paddle real bad! We need professional help.
>
> *We can't do it ourselves.*
>
>   *-- 60 year old male*

Village Planning and the Future of a Functional "Community"

The fourteen men and women quoted above span from 21 to 76 years of age, born between 1935 and 1990. As such, I contend that their attitudes and concerns may be viewed as a reasonably representative sample of most if not all of the villagers who have grown up in Arctic Village during the twentieth and early twenty-first centuries. In general, several conclusions may be drawn from these comments. First, regardless of age or gender, most villagers are fearful for their families and community. Let it be perfectly clear: each and every interviewee loves the village, the Nets'aii community, their families, and their neighbors. Yet every person interviewed voiced concern for their communal future.

This fear may in part stem from a great deal of uncertainty. Many quoted above feel that the past was familiar, known, and understood. The present, however, feels far less so, and the future appears to be even more forbidding and intimidating. One gets the sense that residents believe things in the village are spiraling out of control and want someone—ideally the council or some other government agency—to bring them back to a safer, more secure, predictable state.

Older generations of every culture commonly look back on their lives with nostalgic, sometimes overly sentimental, romanticized thoughts that do not always resemble reality. However, the sentiments expressed above clearly indicate that regardless of generation, every Nets'aii Gwich'in interviewee has identified social and economic problems in Arctic Village that they contend did not exist in the past. More to the point, possible solutions or responses to these issues all fall within the realm of local community planning. Yet to date, the local council has not only proved ineffective in responding to the needs of the community but has also, some suggest, exacerbated divisions, causing further stresses from within.

Historically, the Gwich'in were known to come together in both a literal and figurative sense in times of trouble (Slobodin 1960: 129). This was a population that experienced anxiety largely because of separation and isolation from one another; in a time of emergency or disaster, unity became key. As anthropologist Slobodin suggests (130):

> [S]ecurity is sought in the reinforcement of social ties, signalized by physical proximity. This equation between social and physical nearness is a converse of the expression of social distance by physical distance, as between "rich" and "poor," ... The drawing together of most of the community into a large encampment in a time of alarm, the crowding and pressing of relatives up against a sick person, are manifestations under unusual circumstances of a customary type of Kutchin [Gwich'in] behavior, found most commonly among status-equivalents, i.e., age-mates of the same sex.

But Slobodin also suggests that socioeconomic status among the Gwich'in was historically a "relative matter" and that the society experienced very little stratification, with very little spread between richest and poorest members of the community (131). Yet, by the second decade of the new millennium, such differentiation, individualization, and divisions were manifest, suggesting new social and economic realities for the Gwich'in that were heretofore unprecedented.

The concerns of Arctic Village Nets'aii Gwich'in are significant. However, these issues did not occur overnight, nor did the community exclusively bring them on due to negligence, laziness, or any other simplistic explanations or rationalizations. As the preceding chapters have revealed, the state of the Nets'aii Gwich'in today evolved over a period of roughly a hundred years and stems from the systematic processes meted out by colonial and postcolonial powers that actively sought to alter the course of the community's social, economic, and political trajectory. These forces were largely successful. While the community has held fast to its central identity through the decades, it has done so in new and ever-evolving manifestations. Central to its identity and lifeblood was the fact that the Nets'aii Gwich'in continued to subsist off the land. The land gave the Nets'aii Gwich'in life and in turn, the Nets'aii Gwich'in gave the land an identity; space was converted into "place," into the heart and soul of the people.

However, this lifestyle is changing with increased rapidity. Since 1970, new technologies (especially in transportation and communications), easy access to store-bought food, and a changing climate now foster additional impacts on subsistence behaviors. Meanwhile, the village youth have new priorities drawing them away from what was once a traditional Nets'aii Gwich'in subsistence lifestyle. These issues compose the following chapters of the study's second section.

SECTION II

Nets'aii Country is much more than the settlement of Arctic Village as discussed in the first section. While the village is to a large degree the permanent "camp" where the Nets'aii Gwich'in now reside year-round, the surrounding region similarly informs and supports who the Nets'aii Gwich'in are, what they do, and where their future is headed. The climactic and geographical elements that hold particular significance in Nets'aii Gwich'in heritage, history, and culture are debatable, yet certain spaces and places surrounding the village are iconographic. While it is impossible to note every significant point of reference, there are certain spaces that inform Nets'aii Gwich'in identity as much as, or perhaps even more than, the village itself.

The most notable of these is Dachan Lee, the mountain just south of the village, where a majority of Nets'aii Gwich'in caribou hunting takes place, as the Porcupine herd migrates through here virtually without exception every fall. Experiencing this space year-round, often simply referred to as "going up mountain," is wholly fulfilling for the Nets'aii Gwich'in. This space offers historic, cultural, and mnemonic signifiers found nowhere else in Nets'aii Country. Just as the Arctic National Wildlife Refuge coastal plain holds biblical, Edenic significance to the Nets'aii Gwich'in (Dinero 2003a: 23), the mountain is the Nets'aii Gwich'in Mount Sinai, providing spiritual, emotional, and physical nurturance. It is no wonder that when Rev. Albert Tritt passed away, he did so on Dachan Lee (21).

Old John Lake, some twenty-five miles beyond Dachan Lee, is renowned for its huge stock of lake trout. First Bend, a small outcropping at the first bend of the Chandalar River about half a mile east of the Arctic Village School, is often used for picnics and other gatherings. Fishing by net also is common here. In the area known as Glacier, named after a now-melted field of ice, snow may still be found in the shadows through late June. Located by Tritt Creek, this is also a good area to catch a grayling or two. Second, Third, and Fourth towers, each erected along the Chandalar in the ANWR, serve as watchtowers to scout out wildlife. Fishing by net is common at these sites as well, as creeks empty into the Chandalar, providing pike, lush, whitefish, and grayling in abundance. (First Tower, located within the village itself on a hill at the foot of the Main Street, provides a platform from which the entire village can be viewed.)

The Junjik River meets the Chandalar twenty-five miles or so up-river, a region known as prime moose hunting grounds. There, where the water is sweeter than from an urban tap, several berries, willow, and other grasses grow thick along the river's edge. American wigeons, a species of duck in abundance in the southern Brooks Range, fly low here before the Nets'aii Gwich'in's motorboats, feigning broken wings to draw attention away from nests buried in the rushes.

To demarcate Nets'aii Country—like demarcating Nets'aii Gwich'in identity or, worse, prognosticating about a Nets'aii Gwich'in future—is a fool's errand. Still, were one to suggest a boundary beyond which "Gwich'inness" begins to fade, that would likely be Red Sheep Creek (see USDOI 2012; USFWS 2012). However, this definition is presumptuous and assumes that "Gwich'inness" and subsistence hunting, fishing, and gathering correlate or, further, are the same. But is this contention still true, if indeed it ever was? Must one hunt and fish and speak the Native language to be considered Nets'aii Gwich'in? If so, what is to be said for the growing majority who no longer fit these criteria? The following four chapters address these very questions, for in an age of globalizing flows of capital and finance, innovative communications and transportation technologies, and cultural homogenization, such contentions no longer seem valid.

CHAPTER 5

The Evolving Role of Subsistence in Nets'aii Gwich'in Life

~•••o✦o•••~

[You need to know] how to make a living, cut a caribou, make a fire, make a snowhouse. The kids aren't learning. They aren't listening. You tell them but they don't "take it" [i.e., don't pay attention, don't learn].
— Moses Sam, 11 August 1987

Hunting, Fishing, and Gathering

It is impossible to overstate the importance of hunting, fishing, and gathering in Alaska Native communal life as it evolved over the millennia. Numerous authors over the years have sought to measure the value of this system even today, which has largely been viewed in quantitative, economic terms, by comparing the amount of food gathered off the land with that purchased commercially. A considerable literature has developed around such efforts (see, e.g., Callaway 1999; Kofinas et al. 2010; Lonner 1986; Nuttall et al. 2004).

While I also have previously documented this system's economic functions and values (see Dinero 2003b for an extensive discussion), in truth, the social and cultural aspects of a subsistence *lifestyle* inform the present chapter. Seasonal weather patterns are, without a doubt, central to the lives and life patterns of all Native peoples historically. Such patterns are now undergoing massive alterations, furthering the contention that subsistence behaviors are the key to Native life and that new technological and meteorological developments are now changing realities for Alaska Natives statewide—including, of course, the world of the Nets'aii Gwich'in.

When asked to define or translate the term "subsistence" into their own language, Alaska Natives invariably offer assorted definitions, such as "our way of living," "our way of being," "our culture" (Thornton 2001: 87). So, while outsiders may see subsistence as separate from other aspects of Native culture, Native peoples do not. It is just who they are and, perhaps, what they do—or at least, what they *did*. As is well known, these behaviors and activities were clearly part and parcel of Native education, health care, spirituality, and identity, (93–94). What is also clear is that no Native people live solely upon subsistence to-day, despite contrary romantic allusions. A substantial literature on the "mixed" nature of today's typical bush economy developed in the 1980s and early 1990s (see, e.g., Langdon 1991; Wolfe 1991; Wolfe and Ellanna 1983; Wolfe and Walker 1987). Inputs from transfer payments and cash income from labor are crucial to the persistence of subsistence activities in the twenty-first-century Alaska Native and Canadian First Nation village (Chabot 2003: 30; Dinero 2003b: 151–53).

However, given that all of this and more is the "stuff" of culture and given that Native culture is no longer what it once was, it seems unfair to bemoan the inevitable decline of subsistence behavior as if it is an independent entity. All aspects of Native culture—and for that matter, of global cultures in general—are undergoing change. Alterations in subsistence behaviors, as the previous chapters suggest, as well as the development of new patterns and activities, are not the causes of these changes; they are merely symptoms.

In other words, while subsistence behaviors may be an ideal barometer of social, economic, and cultural change in Alaska Native village life, the first section illustrates that by equating subsistence activity with "Nativeness," outsiders (and increasingly, indigenous peoples themselves) are already writing the epitaphs of Native Alaska. Rather than recognizing the strength and vitality in Alaska Native life that goes beyond hunting, fishing, and gathering, concerned observers seem all too willing to accept that the end of subsistence means the end of the Alaska Native community. I, for one, have not accepted this equation and offer that the following statistics and data suggest that subsistence activities and behaviors—like the state of Native Alaska itself—form a complex picture, requiring careful deconstruction in order to fully grasp the nuanced nature of its present condition and development.

More to the point, Western observers throughout Native North America—and as the Nets'aii Gwich'in case well exemplifies—exercise cultural bias by challenging or questioning the "rationality" of ongoing subsistence behaviors and patterns in the "modern" twenty-first century. Historically, hunting, fishing, and gathering were aspects of an economic enterprise that involves several inputs, demands, upfront resource investment. Today, these activities show signs of vulnerability in the face of various challenges and risks that by definition makes a return on the investment uncertain at best. As Marcelle Chabot suggests: "the lack of time appear[s] to be a major constraint to harvesting activities. Frequent trips between the Village and hunting grounds implied reliable transportation and large purchases of gasoline, increasing, consequently, the expenses for production" (2003: 28).

Yet this system of distribution not only continues to serve economic necessity in the new millennium (although in an altered form and, to a degree, with added economic functions), but more significantly, also facilitates social bonds, solidarity, and communal interactions that, despite contrary fears, are maintained, albeit tenuously, in the village setting. As Chabot explains with regard to the Nunavik Inuit (2003: 30):

> Economic rationality is not the only motivational force involved in behaviour, and other rationalities justify seemingly irrational behaviours. In fact, economic practices are motivated by a large array of social and cultural rationalities. For instance, despite substantial sums of money that hunters and households must invest, gift-giving remains the dominant form of distribution of country food. Producers seek neither profit maximization nor compensation of expenses. It can be suggested that if household production shows a financial deficit, the loss is socially rational.

While it may be increasingly difficult to pursue hunting, fishing, and gathering for economic reasons alone, these activities have indisputable social, cultural, and other values. From an economic standpoint at least, one is fortunate to break even when going out on the land—if not, to lose money in the process. Rather, it may indeed be cheaper to simply purchase meat from the city grocery, even including exorbitant shipping costs (Gemmill 2012).

Subsistence behaviors have long held Native communities together despite increasing economic costs, for the social benefits well outweigh them. Rather, food security has been correlated with cultural cohesion, even in an age of increasing dependency on vehicles fueled with gasoline, imported firearms and tools, and the rising prices of such commodities. In the case of the Gwich'in (including the Nets'aii), fears that skills have been lost or that subsistence behaviors are in sharp decline, have plagued the community for decades. Stated one elder nearly a century ago (as quoted in M. Mason 1924: 24):

> In the old days we used to hunt with the bow and spear. Our young men were strong in those days. We hunted the moose by running him down on snowshoes, and we could run all day, like wolves. Now our young men are become lazy and feeble. They prefer to hunt the moose in the

fall, when he is easy to kill. They ride on their dog-sleds and are afraid
to run all day.

Outside observers have taken up this theme of feared decline of subsistence and the embracing of "White man's food" for decades, and many
contend that the end of the Gwich'in subsistence lifestyle was certain
and imminent. Suggested Michael H. Mason in 1924 (45):

> Imported foods have, on the whole, had a bad effect on the [Gwich'in]
> Indians. They have become particularly fond of tea, tobacco, and flour.
> This does not hurt the older people, but seeing children of five, con-
> firmed drinkers of tea boiled for an hour and stewed all night, and chew-
> ing black plug-tobacco, makes one realize that they carry these habits
> beyond moderation.

Roughly a decade later, Mason's words were echoed by yet another
observer, anthropologist Cornelius Osgood, who suggested that the acceptance of nonindigenous imports was leading to the Gwich'in's un-
doing (1936: 170):

> Matches and iron implements have simplified the cooking methods and
> there is an increasing demand for store foods, the use of which is not
> only a matter of taste but an indication of wealth effecting prestige [sic].
> The smoking of tobacco is almost universal among the Kutchin, and the
> drinking of intoxicants widespread. Perhaps there is less actual starva-
> tion than in the prehistoric period, but that there is any increase of secu-
> rity in the Indian's outlook toward his food supply is dubious.

While the decline of subsistence activities may overall seem to be a
logical outgrowth from new technologies, improved formal education,
increased wage labor opportunities, and the like, the picture is far more
complex than a simple "tradition to modernity" evolutionary trajectory
found within the modernization theoretical framework. Rather, as numerous bits of data reveal, subsistence behaviors continue unabated
but in new forms and with new patterns that call into question how
such simplistic evolutionary arcs have been perceived historically.

Changes in Subsistence in Arctic Village: 1999–2012

Since 1999, I have documented the self-reported subsistence activity in
Arctic Village, as well as the relationships between several subsistence
behaviors and how these tend to correlate significantly with specific
social and economic factors in the community, including age, gender,

employment status, and education (see Dinero 2003b, 2005, 2007, 2013). In general, a variety of patterns may be discerned in terms of which subsistence behaviors are persisting and thriving in the twenty-first century, which sectors of the village population are continually carrying out these subsistence activities, which are not, and why.

A summary of this activity over time may be found in Table 5.1. As the statistics so graphically reveal, hunting, fishing, and gathering have all been in slow but consistent decline since I began gathering data for this study in August 1999. Still, some activities show greater resolve—others less so. Berry picking, for example, has declined but only minimally. This is, perhaps, the easiest task—requiring the least effort, resources, or equipment and carried out by young and old, men and women alike—though it too can be taxing after long periods. Still, berry picking is a low-impact activity when compared, for example, with sheep hunting, which, conversely, requires huge inputs, both financial and logistical. It is no wonder that such hunting has seen one of the greatest levels of decline over time. Sheep meat has never been a major Nets'aii Gwich'in staple because of these limitations (Mason 1924: 25).

Three other activities also deserve some attention here. Trapping for furs is particularly notable given that it has experienced the greatest decline of all activities in the study. Such a profound and rapid

Table 5.1 Arctic Village Household Annual Harvesting Activity (%)

	1999	2006	2009	2012	1999-2012 Degree of Change Only Activity Participants	1999-2012 Degree of Change All Village Households
	N = 35	N = 39	N = 35	N=48		
Caribou	89	67	74	71	-20	-18
Moose	66	49	51	15	-77	-51
Sheep	14	5	0	8	-43	-6
Ducks	74	36*	66	60	-19	-14
Fur Trapping	31	15	23	15	-52	-16
Fish (pole/net)	94	69	80	77	-18	-17
Berries	80	56	71	75	-6	-5
Wood/fuel	89	85	89	77	-13	-12
AVERAGE (All activities combined)	67.125	47.75	56.75	49.75	-31.00	-17.375

Illustration 5.1 Cutting firewood at –30 degrees Fahrenheit (Christmas Day 2011).

change requires further discussion and inquiry, as this development comes with a variety of possible explanations. Lastly, perhaps most notable of all is the decline in moose and caribou hunting. These two animals, but caribou in particular (see Dinero 2003b), are the primary staples of the Nets'aii Gwich'in diet. A decline their harvest suggests a major change in the societal structure and culture of the entire Nets'aii Gwich'in.

However, such statistics do not present the full picture of subsistence behaviors and country food consumption in Arctic Village today. While household harvesting provides one facet of country food use and reliance, sharing continues to supply another to the Alaska Native diet, including that of the Nets'aii Gwich'in of Arctic Village. Meat, fish, and fruit harvested by neighbors and relatives—in both the village itself and neighboring Gwich'in communities such as Venetie, Beaver, Fort Yukon, Stevens Village, and Chalkyitsik—offer additional contributions to the Arctic Village economy and diet (see Table 5.2). Yet, as Table 5.2 suggests, a decline is evident in gifts and sharing as well. While some "super-hunters" (Chabot 2003: 23) have actively continued the tradition of hunting Dall sheep in the Red Sheep Creek area, the only region where such game is accessible, and have thereupon shared these precious resources with the community at large, the consensus is that wild foods have become, albeit by a very small margin, less widely

Illustration 5.2 Gathering fish from a fishnet (Third Tower, July 2012).

Table 5.2 Arctic Village Households Receiving Country Food Gifts from Family/ Friends (%)

	2006 N = 39	2009 N = 35	2012 N=48	A. 2006-2012 Degree of Change All Village Households	B. 2006-2012 Degree of Change Active Subsistence Households Only
Caribou meat	90	83	75	-15	-17
Moose meat	77	89	67	-10	-13
Sheep meat	10	14	42	+32	+320
Duck meat	72	83	69	-3	-4
Fur/s	15	6	10	-5	-33
Fish	80	89	77	-3	-4
Berries	49	60	46	-3	-6
Wood fuel	64	63	44	-20	-31
Average Self-Estimated "Subsistence Rate" (i.e. % of all food consumed off the land annually)	53	52	48	-5	-9

distributed. This pattern is also evident in the distribution of firewood, a highly prized commodity that is now sold regularly throughout the village and rarely given away, except to elders and others who struggle to access fuel on their own.

Although the decline and ultimate "demise" in subsistence activity appears to be self-evident by examining these statistics alone, it is possible, I believe, to further parse out how and why this decline is now occurring and to determine if, indeed, the end of this lifestyle is as imminent as some observers suggest. To this end, I was able to interview nearly all adult residents of Arctic Village during three visits in 2011 and 2012. In addition, I conducted household surveys similar to those conducted in previous years; in 2012 I surveyed forty-eight households (out of approximately fifty-five total), gathering over five thousand pieces of raw data. Numerous associations and statistically significant correlations can be discerned that, when viewed together, help to further explain what appears to be a rather disconcerting trend in Arctic Village subsistence activities and behaviors.

The results, many of which confirm findings presented from data gathered in previous studies in the village (see Dinero 2003b, 2005, 2007, 2013) provide a patchwork of fascinating—and, at times, seemingly convoluted—evidence of the state of subsistence today and a possible foreshadowing of things yet to come. While some findings may

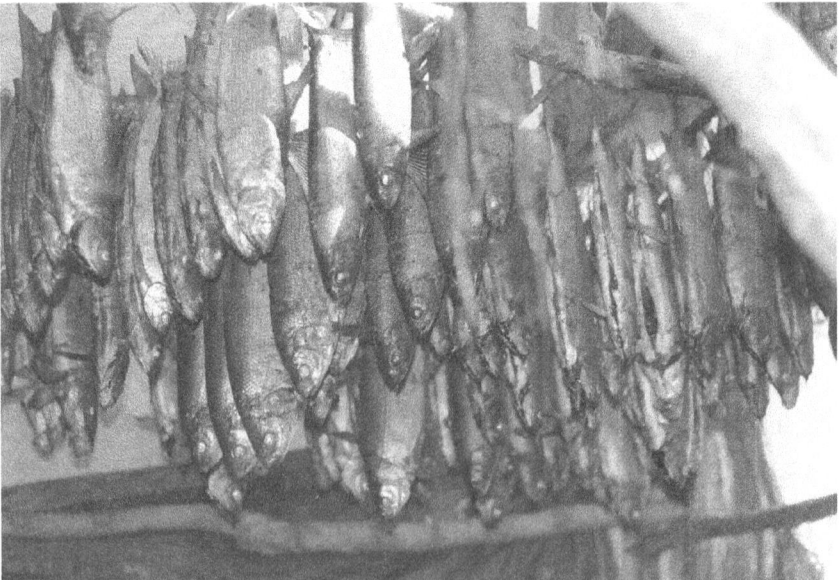

Illustration 5.3 Smokehouse on the Chandalar River (July 2012).

initially appear problematic or perhaps even meaningless, it is my contention upon closer scrutiny that these data help to present an image of a people functioning—and, at least for the moment, succeeding, albeit tenuously—within and across several interlinked economic and social spheres.

Using data from the 2012 survey, age and gender quite apparently continue to play significant roles in subsistence activity. For example, duck hunting tends to be a gendered activity, where men are more likely than women to hunt fowl. Furthermore, these hunters are also more likely to be unmarried; those in married or cohabitating relationships are less likely to go out for duck. Similar social factors predicate the harvesting of two other foods. Berry picking is also gendered, but here, women are more likely to go out than men (though this of course does not mean men do not also gather). Moose hunting, however, is age specific; older villagers (40-plus) are more likely to hunt for moose than younger respondents are.

As in previous studies, education, employment, and related aspects of wealth also play significant roles in the persistence of subsistence activities. For example, villagers with high school educations are more likely to have fished, with either a net or a pole, than those with less education. Curiously, those who are employed are also more likely to re-

Illustration 5.4 Picking blueberries is tedious yet fulfilling and provides hours of socializing (August 2011).

ceive fish as a gift; employed men are also more likely to receive berries as a gift (i.e., those villagers least likely get them on their own). Lastly, again as was the case previously (Dinero 2003a: 156; 2007: 259–60), owning various equipment helps to facilitate certain aspects of a subsistence culture (the ownership of which, in turn, depends heavily on a certain level of wealth). As in previous studies, the most significant ease the transportation process of accessing country food and other resources.

Notably, ownership of several material goods correlates with certain social and economic factors. Data I collected in a 2011 survey, for example, found significant correlations suggesting that those villagers in married or cohabitating households are better off financially. In turn, these households are more likely to own expensive items such as refrigerators and freezers. Higher incomes also correlate with ATV and boat ownership. Similarly, data from 2012 saw a significant correlation between marital status and ATV ownership, where married couples were more likely to own ATVs. The ownership of all such costly items, in turn, plays key roles in the ability to carry out subsistence activities and to store foods taken from the land.

Thus, a constellation of factors helps to explain the continuation of subsistence behaviors that include, in part, both social status and economic criteria. For example, those who still trap for furs are more likely to own a motorboat than those who do not trap. This pattern is especially true of women and older villagers, sectors of the Gwich'in population that have historically been less actively involved in the fur trade (itself an imported economic activity), which required regular travel to Fort Yukon (Mason 1924: 25). In my previous surveys, trapping did indeed correlate with gender (i.e., it was predominantly a male activity) and, again, with income, where wealthier villagers were more likely to trap than those with lower incomes (Dinero 2003b: 153).

As noted, ownership of these vehicles and goods relates directly to the ongoing ability to maintain a subsistence lifestyle—without them, villagers are far less likely to participate. The 2012 data set revealed that the most significant correlations concern the ATV and the snowgo. For example, those women who claim higher rates of food consumption off the land are also more likely to own an ATV. Similarly, villagers who own a snowgo, especially women, are more likely to cut their own wood for heating fuel. Lastly, and perhaps of greatest significance, those villagers who go out for caribou, the primary staple of the Nets'aii Gwich'in diet, are also more likely to own a snowgo. This case is especially true of older villagers and women.

Illustration 5.5 Caribou hunting camp (Dachan Lee, August 1999).

While technology, wealth, social status, and similar criteria all make contributions toward helping to explain how and why subsistence persists in the Nets'aii Gwich'in community, most correlations are found within and between subsistence activities themselves. That is to say, a dynamic exists in the community whereby certain households (i.e., super-hunters) are largely responsible for harvesting a considerable percentage of the country foods distributed throughout the community. Thus, increasingly fewer hunters now get the bulk of the food, utilizing major inputs from transfer payments, adult children's income, and other support in order to hunt. Much of the harvest is for the hunters' own use, but a good deal is distributed to other households that do not carry out a high level of subsistence activity (Chabot 2003: 23–25).

The dynamic between hunting and nonhunting households may be shown in two primary ways. First, those who participate in one activity tend to participate in others, and second, gifts and sharing tend to supplement in a relatively equalizing manner the distribution of the harvest, allowing each household to maximize consumption at the level most appropriate to its individual needs. Beginning with the most pertinent activity, households in which a male had hunted for caribou in the previous twelve months have the highest rates of self-reported consumption of food off the land. Caribou hunters are also more likely to hunt for waterfowl and to cut their own wood for fuel. Hunting for

Illustration 5.6 After the hunt: caribou meat, skin, and antlers being dried (August 2011).

moose, another key element in the Nets'aii Gwich'in diet, correlates with the likelihood of also hunting for Dall sheep. Those who had hunted for moose are also more likely to have hunted for waterfowl. Duck hunters are also more likely to cut their own firewood.

However, distribution of shared food proved the greatest explicator of ongoing subsistence, presenting the highest number of associations. Put simply, the system is self-perpetuating—at least for the moment—and highly rational, which can be illustrated by numerous significant correlations. Households that own a motorboat, for example (by far those that are the most well off financially with the greatest access to country foods found up and down the Chandalar River) are less likely to receive fish as a gift than those that do not own a boat. Boat owners are also less likely to receive caribou meat as a gift. In turn, however, those households that do not hunt caribou are more likely to receive caribou meat as a gift. Like caribou-hunting households, those that hunt moose maintain more self-sufficiency. Moose-hunting households are also less likely to receive gifts of caribou meat. Older moose-hunting families are less likely than nonhunters to receive moose meat, duck meat, or fish as a gift. The exception here is the tendency to receive sheep meat as a gift, but this is true of only younger moose hunters.

So what might one make of all of this information? In short, there appears to be a dynamic relationship within the Gwich'in community in general and Arctic Village in particular between givers and receivers. This collaboration is determined in part by gender and age but also by recognizing who carries out the activities and who "deserves" the gifts based not only on age but also on their willingness and desire to participate in a system of exchange and sharing. So, for example, berry pickers, who tend to be young and female, are more likely to

Illustration 5.7 Tanning a caribou hide (August 1999).

receive caribou meat, duck meat, and fish as gifts. Similarly, those who cut wood, a predominantly male activity, are more likely to receive caribou meat and fish as a gift; younger cutters were also more likely to receive moose meat as well.

Still, for the most part, those who receive one form of country food tend to be recipients of other forms as well, confirming that just as there are super-hunters, there are "super-recipients" of the shared wealth. Recipients of caribou meat are more likely than nonrecipients to also receive moose meat, sheep meat, duck meat, fish, and berries. Moose meat recipients are also likely to receive sheep meat, duck meat, fish, berries, and trapped animal furs. Women and elders who receive moose meat are more likely to also receive wood fuel as a gift. Gifts of fish, sheep meat, and duck meat are also significant correlates but to a lesser degree than caribou and moose. Recipients of sheep meat tend to also receive duck meat. Those who receive duck meat also receive fish and berries. Finally, those who receive fish as a gift also tend to be the recipients of berries. These three animal resources interact with one another in an internal association, where recipients of one tend to receive one or both of the other products as well.

An analysis of the numerous pieces of data presented to this point suggests that while subsistence is in decline in terms of numbers of participants, a great deal of sharing is helping the community to continue the consumption of country foods at a relatively high rate. But is such a model sustainable over the long term? The 2009 data set (Dinero 2013: 123) revealed a strong correlation between age and subsistence activity. Such a correlation was not found in the 2012 data. What was seen, however, was a perception among villagers that the future of going out and hunting on the land is now in jeopardy. Over 81 percent of those interviewed confirmed the belief that the younger generation no longer hunts or carries out subsistence activities. While 33 percent of respondents attributed this to parents failing to take the youth out on the land, 56 percent blamed games, computers, and other technologies. Indeed, a significant correlation was found between those who believe that the next generation is no longer spending time on the land and the belief that new electronic technologies are the underlying problem and the primary distraction.

I will return to the issue of subsistence activity among the next generation in chapter 7, but first, I conclude this chapter by turning to villager attitudes regarding subsistence in the community today. The bits of data above tell only one part of the story. The views expressed provide further evidence of the ways subsistence continues to develop and change in the early part of the twenty-first century.

Subsistence in Arctic Village Today: The Voice of the People

The evidence presented above suggests that participation in subsistence activity is in some decline among the Nets'aii Gwich'in of Arctic Village, with rates dropping from approximately two-thirds of all households to about one-half in just the short period I have been conducting my study (see Table 5.1). While aspects of this change appear to be numerous and multifaceted, the decline can nonetheless be explained in part (though certainly not fully) by some of the factors enumerated above.

Many villagers believe that part of the decline is generational, and the data collected support such conjecture (Dinero 2013). While the quantitative data presented thus far provide one part of the subsistence picture, the Nets'aii Gwich'in have their own perspectives on the issue and on the future of hunting, fishing, and gathering in the community. These issues cannot be divorced—at least in the minds of the villagers—from other social and economic issues that presently shape and form Nets'aii Gwich'in society. Formal education, work opportunities, substance abuse—all of these and more are intertwined in the eyes of the villagers with the ways declines in subsistence are manifested.

Further, such concerns reflect a generational pattern in the qualitative data just as they do in the statistical data. While the older generation tends to bemoan the lost past—the description of which at times borders on the nostalgic—the younger generation complains that the present is moving in a direction that makes subsistence activity and village life difficult for them as well, albeit for different reasons. Stated one 65-year-old woman in August of 2011:

> I remember when there were many creeks all over Dachan Lee [mountain]. Now there's only one. And we never saw this kind of wind before. We get frustrated when we can't get the animals like in the past. There are fewer caribou now and they are scrawny.

> We take care of the land; we do what we are supposed to do. But we give rest to a certain area—people used to do that anyway. As a Gwich'in Nation we used to do that. But we don't do it anymore. Now the kids live on junk food. They grow up on hamburgers and hot dogs and crap. There are a few who go hunting; you can't say all of them are like this. Maybe half. It's sad that not all of them are [hunting, gathering, or fishing]. We don't teach them; the parents are too busy making money to teach their kids.

Her son, a 29-year-old male, offered a different albeit complimentary perspective soon after she stopped speaking:

I'm worried about the caribou. Their meat doesn't look right. Sometimes the meat is green or shiny; it's "colorful." Maybe they are drinking something that's contaminated, I really don't know.

And there was that recent landslide [in the nearby mountains]. Things are changing dramatically here. There are severe storms around here like I've never seen before—wind, lightning strikes. The weather is really severe. We have warm spells in the winter, the permafrost is melting. The sun feels hotter.

Indeed, virtually every interview I conducted throughout the research period seemed to connect changing (i.e., declining) subsistence activity with other meta-changes taking place throughout village life. This general worldview reflects the intersection and conflation of virtually every aspect of Nets'aii Gwich'in cultural values (strength, independence, hard work, self-respect, pride) and of every issue now plaguing Arctic Village and the Nets'aii Gwich'in community (weakness, dependency, insecurity, internal conflict, loss). The subsistence culture and lifestyle historically must be equated with self-worth and physical and mental health (Callaway 1999: 59). Thus, a drop in subsistence activity is not just a decline in a way of life or a lessening of an economic activity. Rather, it signals a further weakening of the very fabric of the Nets'aii Gwich'in community as a whole.

Elder Moses Sam recognized this concern decades ago. Speaking of his fear that the younger generations were not heeding their elders and that life on the land was on the decline, he said (Sam 1987):

[The kids] don't learn nothing! I never teach no more. A lot of time I tell them, I teach them about the bone marrow, everything, cooking, the campfire ... A lot of parents, they don't know nothing.

I try to tell them there is something to learn. They don't learn nothing ... I tell them how to cut it, but they don't do it right. They don't waste it, but they gotta do it right!

Got to be cut right, caribou, moose, fish, there's one way to cut it right. If you don't it will spoil, you can't use it ... Even right now, every spring, I just go fishing on the lake. Every morning, I check the fishnet to see what I've got. I take the fish out, make a smoke, I smoke it.

I fish under the ice, one at a time. Last spring I make a smoke fish; he's still in my box, save it for a long time. A hard time coming, so everything I save it.

The hard times are coming now! You have a grandchild too. When the grandchild is hungry how are you gonna feed him? I'm ready for the hard time. I have a bunch of grocery, a bunch of dry fish, ammunition, matches, everything! I've got enough now. When I get my pension check, I'll get more. I can't give to everyone, just my family, that's all. I'll use ice chisel and go fishing and my family is going to eat fish. Maybe flour, rice, oats. That's the way I figure.

Long time ago when you get a moose or caribou, everybody—whole village—just divide it. Divide all the meat. Each house.

Matches, tea, flour, rice, sugar they would get in Fort Yukon; ammunition too. Now we don't have to worry, we can run out to the store. It's easy living now.

Were people healthier when they ate just meat? Yes!

Decades later, his words are more cogent than ever. Sam could never have foreseen the changes described above, having passed away in 2001 soon after this research was launched. Nor could he have imagined the role a changing climate has now begun to play as it impacts several aspects of the daily lives of the Nets'aii Gwich'in, but most especially in their ability to carry out subsistence activity.

Indeed, villagers commonly watch the 5 o'clock news intently (NBC Channel 2 KTUU out of Anchorage being a choice of many) and conclude from reports of melting glaciers, hurricanes, earthquakes, racially rooted riots, and mass killings that the world is in chaos. Thus follows the belief that in the near future, returning to a culture of total reliance on subsistence from the land will be essential. Such catastrophic if not apocalyptic thinking of course contains some rationality, given both the Christian nature of Gwich'in intellect and the vulnerability inherent in the psyche of a people who now experience increasing fear and uncertainty for their futures, and more so, for their posterity.

CHAPTER 6

The Environment and
a Changing Climate

The elders are saying that time are going faster now, nowadays ... Things are just, I think, as they see it, I think that the way how I see it, I think they're talking about time, it's go by, going by so fast, like summer come, then fall time come, and it just, it's going through quicker than it used to.
— Kenneth Frank, 2 February 2002

The Changing Climate of Nets'aii Gwich'in Country

The changes in hunting, fishing, and gathering activity in Arctic Village have, as discussed in the previous chapter, a variety of explanations. Given the exogenous social, economic, and political forces acting on the community, as well as internal changes that occur as the village develops and evolves, it is no wonder that subsistence behaviors of the early twenty-first century are in flux and, to a considerable degree, under threat.

In recent years, these changes have been exacerbated by a rapidly changing climate, typified by new and uncertain temperature fluctuations, unexpected precipitation, and, in general, unfamiliar variability in wind, storm, and atmospheric activity. To suggest that a changing climate is the primary cause of a decline in subsistence activity would be an overstatement, but these environmental impacts have created a high degree of unpredictability and vulnerability throughout life in the Native bush. Most especially affected are those aspects of accessing game, including its availability and nature, which in turn threaten the long-term viability of traditional subsistence behaviors.

While the scientific community has recently addressed changes in the subarctic region of the lower Brooks Range, where Arctic Village is situated from a quantitative approach, the Nets'aii Gwich'in themselves have observed changing weather patterns, new behaviors among local flora and fauna and, as a direct result, challenges they now face in hunting, fishing, and gathering. Both the "scientific" approach and the incorporation of traditional ecological knowledge (TEK) are used here and in previous studies of Arctic Village climate change in order to better understand how climate, environment, subsistence, and economy all conflate at this critical time in the village's short history (Dinero 2013: 121).

For example, the most evident change documented by the scientific community over the past half century is a general warming trend throughout the North American Arctic, annually measured with an average of 1 to 3 degrees Celsius (about 2 to 5 degrees Fahrenheit) above normal (Fox 2004: 14; Furgal and Seguin 2006: 1965; McBeath and Shepro 2007: 57; Post et al. 2009: 1355). This rise in the average annual temperature has produced or is accompanied by several related outcomes for Canadian and Alaskan indigenous populations. First, warmer, drier summers are increasingly evident (Berman et al. 2004: 407). The permafrost in many areas is now melting as well. Additionally, the freeze-up date is coming later in the fall than ever before while spring breakup is now earlier (Fox 2004: 20; Post et al. 2009: 1355; Rattenbury et al. 2009: 81–82). Winters also appear to be warmer, as reductions in

Illustration 6.1 Flooding on the Chandalar River (August 2011).

the thickness of snow and ice packs in are frequent (Ford et al. 2008: 55–56; Fox 2004: 21). Such changes, along with varying wind patterns, have caused alterations in the physical landscape, particularly land erosion, especially near rivers (McBeath and Shepro 2007: 47).

However, to be noted again, much of this change is ongoing and not in any way consistent or predictable. For example, in the case under discussion, Arctic Village experienced a small snowfall in late June 2011, only days before the annual Fourth of July celebrations. Less than two weeks later, torrential downpours caused the side of a mountain to give way just north of the village; the Chandalar River flowed red in color from the runoff, worrying villagers who had never in their lives seen such a phenomenon (Chomicz 2011). Such unpredictable fluctuations are ongoing. On the Sunday before Memorial Day, 24 May 2015, the temperature reached 75 degrees Fahrenheit, (24 Celsius) when the average temperature for that day is 56 degrees (13 Celsius). Yet, one week later, it snowed all day, albeit with minimal accumulation of 2 to 3 inches (7 cm). Throughout the first week of June, the snow continued, at times mixed with sleet, only to abate by week's end.

Alterations in the flora and fauna of the Arctic also are evident (Gitay et al. 2002: 14). For example, certain types of vegetation with altered appearances (larger, smaller, or a different color) are now found in some Arctic and subarctic regions (McBeath and Shepro 2007: 48). Range expansions of various trees and shrubs are also a direct result of a warming climate (Post et al. 2009: 1355–56). In the case of the region in question, some bird species have begun to display signs of illness while others seem to have disappeared from the region altogether (S. James 1999). The quality (size, health) and quantity of fish is affected as well.

Matthew Berman et al. have documented the projected decline of one species that has particular relevance and importance to the Nets'aii Gwich'in—the caribou. According to the findings at the time, the Porcupine herd population was declining at an annual rate of 3.2 percent (2004: 407). In 2004, the researchers projected that global warming would impact future caribou migratory movements, ultimately resulting in considerably reduced animal availability for harvesting purposes (409). Forty years into the future, they suggested, the herd size would decline by roughly 18 percent. They noted, however, that alterations in the ability to hunt the animals may be a more significant issue than the herd's declining size: "A warmer climate is likely to be associated with more years during which complete freeze-up is delayed, preventing safe overland travel to more distant hunting areas until late December" (407).

Illustration 6.2 Riverbank erosion and willow overgrowth along the Chandalar River (July 2011).

Perhaps the most comprehensive study to assess the manifest ways climate change now appears to be impacting wildlife behaviors, migrations, reproductive activity, and similar challenges across the Arctic was published by *Science* in September 2009. Penn State biologist and lead author Eric Post notes that virtually everything in the Arctic is changing "across the spectrum" in terms of the region's physical geography and ecology. In an interview about the article, he says, "Whether you're talking about mammals or birds, invertebrates or vertebrates, migratory species, nonmigratory species, things that live on land, things that live in freshwater, saltwater, it all seems to ... have been affected pretty dramatically over the last twenty to thirty years" (Post 2009). According to Post, several other concerns in the Arctic are now equally compelling. For example, the study reveals that the animals most directly impacted by warming live in marine or freshwater environments. Animals that directly rely on ice for their survival and livelihoods are some of the most vulnerable to climate variability and rising temperatures (Post et al. 2009: 1355).

Global warming and climate change have multifaceted impacts with extensive possible ramifications (Gitay et al. 2002: 23), but of greatest concern to North American Arctic Natives today is the issue of food security—that is, the relationship between fluctuating atmospheric con-

ditions, country food quality and quantity, and the ability to access
these resources from a shifting physical geography. Local observations
do not always confirm those made by the scientific community. For
example, while the aforementioned studies all seem to suggest that
game resources are on a slow but steady decline, villager perceptions
are mixed. Some offer that warming and longer growing seasons have
increased amounts of vegetation, leading to greater food availability
for game and thus more, not fewer, animal resources overall (Kofinas
et al. 2010: 1350).

More to the point, the idea of food security in Alaska Native communities such as Arctic Village does not, as discussed in chapter 5, merely
suggest the physical support of the community, which is now supple-
mented by food from the local grocery and foodstuffs shipped by plane
from Fairbanks). In addition, this concept applies to the cultural security of the community (Sakakibara 2010: 1009). As Mark Nuttall et al.
cogently affirm: "The living resources of the Arctic do not just sustain
indigenous peoples in an economic and nutritional sense, but provide
a fundamental basis for social identity, cultural survival, and spiritual
life. As such they are as much important cultural resources as they are
economic ones" (2004: 654).

The Nets'aii Gwich'in view the caribou in strong cultural terms
with spiritual roots (see Dinero 2003b). Therefore, the potential threat
this animal faces from climate change is a danger not only to a food
resource but also to Nets'aii Gwich'in identity. Variations in the local climate are thus relevant to how, when, and if caribou may be
harvested but, more importantly, have broader ramifications on how
the people currently view themselves, their culture, their heritage—indeed, their present place in the world—and how they see themselves
in the future. While verifying any direct causal relationships between
the measureable decline in country food consumption by the Nets'aii
Gwich'in and the observable effects of climate change may be difficult, the following data certainly reveal that these rapid changes dele-
teriously impact not only the natural environment but also the human
culture so inextricably interlinked and intermeshed within it (Dinero
2013: 117–19).

Using Local Knowledge and Traditions
to Understand the Climate

Local Native knowledge, traditions, values, and analysis are used to
supplement (though not replace or contradict) scientific observation in

the field. As Chris Cuomo et al. (2008) note, indigenous knowledge is helpful in understanding climate change for the simple reason that local observers can speak from a position of personal experience and memory impossible for those who approach research from the outside. Indeed, they suggest, elders and others ought to be viewed as the "best authorities" on their natural surroundings, as they know the land and its resources better than any outside observer.

As I have noted previously (Dinero 2013: 121), there are both positive and negative aspects to using information gathered from within the community in analyzing the impacts of climate change. Though Native people may be able to offer observations about changes seen in their communities, "they may not, however, be the best authorities on how to solve problems or difficulties that they are encountering along the way" (Cuomo et al. 2008). As the data also suggest, it is necessary to keep the interlocutors' views in perspective. One should respect the informants' memories and knowledge but also acknowledge that such information is not identical to data gathered through random sampling (Kofinas 2002: 66). Furthermore, not all informants' information is of equal value. One must distinguish those who regularly spend time on the land, for example, from those who do not.

Similarly, indigenous knowledge—due to its anecdotal nature—may be contradictory, confused, or incomplete. Jerry McBeath and Carl E. Shepro suggest that not all of their informants made the same observations, but all showed the "sensitive ability to measure highly complex processes" (2007: 62). While such "sensitivity" may not be equivalent with "scientific" processes and systems that analyze testable, measurable changes in the natural environment, I again contend that local knowledge is, in the final analysis, about perception, and for those who experience it and make decisions accordingly, that perception is truth.

In short, the information presented here, while only as reliable as its providers, offers an additional glimpse into the evolving world of the Nets'aii Gwich'in today. While the responses and attitudes expressed are influenced by personal experiences, the climate change debate is an additional window through which to discuss, analyze, and evaluate the ongoing development and evolution of this Native community. Not only is climate change prevalent in this study but so is the manner through which the Nets'aii Gwich'in people discuss, consider, respond to, react to, and adapt to it (see Kofinas et al. 2010: 1355; McNeely 2009). These issues and more are as relevant to the future of the Nets'aii Gwich'in of Arctic Village as is the actual phenomenon of climate change. Evidence drawn from Arctic Villager observations is both qualitative and quantitative. These pieces of data often take anecdotal form, which may appear to be problematic. Individually, the information may seem inconsequential, but when combined, the story being told in the village today, while still somewhat blurry, contains several consistent aspects that provide an ever-evolving picture of the new landscape developing in the subarctic.

Before turning to the data I have collected, it is helpful to consider the perspective of one active subsistence hunter, Kenneth Frank, who was interviewed about his views on climate change in 2002. He retains an acute knowledge of his family history, as well as of the land and its resources, so Frank's comments are especially noteworthy. Over the past several years, he has actively shared his knowledge and experience at academic conferences and other events throughout the United States and Canada. Among the likes of Sarah James, Faith Gemmill, and Evon Peter, Frank is gaining a strong reputation for abetting Gwich'in interests well beyond the Yukon Flats. His perspective is comprehensive in scope and may, for the purposes here, provide a baseline from which to analyze villager attitudes as they apply to how much the subarctic climate is changing and how, if at all, these changes affect Nets'aii Gwich'in culture and society.

Frank does not doubt that the climate has changed in numerous ways over the past several decades and has noted difference in the local flora and fauna of the region. Moose, for example, are now grazing in areas of the Brooks Range where they had not been seen before, a sign of changing availability of vegetation. Trees, most notably spruce and willow (a primary food of the moose) are now growing thicker and taller than ever in memory, indicating a longer, more intense and sustained growing season. Frank notes too that new insects, birds, and other species are now evident, and the Nets'aii Gwich'in lack words for several of these creatures they have never seen. As for the primary rationale that explains these various phenomena, Frank's observations are not unexpected. Confirmed by other villagers, an overall warming throughout the region in the past several decades has fostered these changes and more. As he puts it: "The temperature in the early days were really extreme cold weather in the wintertime, a long period of time too. But nowadays we don't see that anymore. Just every once in a while we see cold weather, you know?" (Frank 2002).

Frank's discussion of a changing climate in and around Arctic Village is not unlike many of the findings I present below. Most intriguing, though, is the way his explanation of recent events helps to reveal how Nets'aii Gwich'in culture, seasonal weather patterns, and animal behaviors can all be seen to mesh into one. With changes in the climate, therefore, must come changes in every other aspect of the Nets'aii Gwich'in lifestyle and worldview. As Frank explains at length (2002):

> In some part of the country, like Arctic Village, in our culture we name those month by the certain things that's happening in the calendar year. Actually, we have thirteen month in our culture, but the Western they only have twelve. Because we do it by the full moon, every full moon is certain part of the month we have for that season.
>
> And February is supposed to be, they call *Veegwaadhat,* it pass over, but another thing too they call it *ahtr'aii zhrii,* wind month, in the early days the wind always come long time ago I remember. But today it don't really do that. That wind is good for animal too like moose. When moose sometimes they be in one area for long time and then like other wolf or something like that, they know it. They know the moose is in that area. And then by losing their ground when the wind come and then they take off and make a big loop, you know like five mile loop. They just run around like that and they get back in different area away from the place where they're at so they lose their spot. The moose are very smart animal, so that's why when the wind, that's why in February it does that, the wind come and moose usually relocate themself. But today we don't see no wind even in February.
>
> So the wind, even in that wind change, and the cold weather too, it start to get, it got really warm. Even in '60 we had lotta cold weather in '60, but very recently up in around '70 it start, weather just kinda like all of a sudden it'd be warm one winter next year it'll be cold next winter and then just go like flip flop. But very recently these last couple years, about three or four years it's just … since about '88 is the only time we had cold weather. [In] 1988 we went up to like 75 below one winter. That was in '88. And then after that it just kinda have little wave like, that's just about all. We don't even see cold weather, we don't even wear parka anymore in the winter.

He notes too that winter snows have become less predictable. Sometimes it snows more than usual, sometimes less, and sometimes it even rains in the winter, all of which in turn affect animals that rely on water-fed plants. Glacial ice that once existed in the area, attracting caribou while fending off mosquitoes in the summer heat, has long ago melted away. Frank says the permafrost also appears to be melting and as a result, some of the lakes are "caving in." Others have simply dried up, affecting many historic fishing areas. In short, villager Kenneth Frank's interview provides a helpful background to better understand a changing climate at Arctic Village. Although he suggests in 2002 that local villagers are not very worried about climate change, my quantitative and qualitative data suggest rising concern.

Local Arctic Villager Observations
Concerning a Changing Climate

Perceptions of a changing climate are just that—perceptions. While most scientific circles now accept climate change and global warming as facts, many still dispute such findings as anecdotal, politically motivated, or worse. My goal in gathering the following material is to use local Native knowledge as a barometer to further measure cultural change. While the details of a changing climate can be argued in Congress and elaborate academic conferences, my interest here is to measure, to the degree possible, local sentiment on the subject. If, as Frank contends above, the public feels the local climate is undergoing transition and if, in response, subsistence behaviors are altering substantially, then this cultural change is very real and worthy of attention and even concern. Put simply, perception *is* reality.

As seen in Table 6.1, locals clearly perceive that the climate in and around Arctic Village is presently changing. As for how, to what ex-

Table 6.1 Observed Areas of Changes in Weather

2009 (*N*=35) 2012 (*N*=48)	Percentage Affirming this Observation		Percentage *Not* Affirming this Observation/ "No change observed"		No Answer	
	2009	2012	2009	2012	2009	2012
Warmer winters	51	54	43	46	6	0
Colder Winters	26	27	69	73	5	0
Warmer Summers	54	54	46	46	0	0
Colder Summers	23	19	77	81	0	0
Dryer Summers	37	45	63	55	0	0
Wetter Summers	34	23	66	77	0	0
More Winter Snow	49	36	49	62	2	2
Less Winter Snow	21	41	79	57	0	2
Thinner Icepack	49	54	46	44	5	2
Thicker Icepack	11	8	83	90	6	2
More Summer Storms	43	38	57	62	0	0

tent, and in what direction, the data is muddled at best and, to be expected, has little consensus, as the use of local knowledge is notoriously challenging and ungainly (Dinero 2013; Kofinas 2002; McBeath and Shepro 2007). Not all observations are informed equally, so some opinions may in truth be more valuable than others. Further inquiry below will illustrate greater consensus here than may initially appear, but at first glance, one conclusion is indisputable: the Gwich'in at Arctic Village sense the weather is "abnormal" but disagree on what that word means.

That said, I have highlighted what I believe can be discerned with some degree of certainty. First, it can be stated with confidence that most villagers believe that winters are in general warmer than in the past, confirming Kenneth Frank's observation above. Second, most villagers believe that summers are also warmer. Of all questions asked, this one received the highest affirmation rate, which, I contend, is significant. Third, there is a fairly strong belief that the ice pack is thinning. This sentiment aligns well with the idea of warmer winters and, more to the point, has considerable ramifications in terms of travel, access, and subsistence-related activities. As for the remaining observations, it is impossible here to draw any certain conclusions. Only through lengthy longitudinal analysis might some possible patterns emerge. That said, these sentiments alone have clearly already begun to impact Nets'aii Gwich'in experiences on the land. Examples are documented in Table 6.2. Here, it is apparent that perceptions have begun to affect some aspects of Nets'aii Gwich'in activities, most especially as they relate to subsistence practices. Though responses in the two study years noted are again somewhat fluid and at times contradictory, many Arctic Villagers generally feel that a changing climate is proving deleterious to their historic hunting, fishing, and gathering behaviors, as well as to the quality and quantity of the resources now available on the land.

The fluidity is easily explained after addressing how well informed the opinions are in the overall context of a changing climate. In other words, not every villager experiences the natural environment the same way. Quantitative analysis reveals that the primary indicators for determining a perspective on climate change often relate to involvement in subsistence activities—though not always, as these intersect with additional factors such as age, gender, education, employment in wage labor, and, in some instances, owning various technologies like the ATV or snowgo that enable travel beyond the village boundaries. For example, through data from the 2012 Arctic Village Household Survey (where $N = 48$), age, gender, use of technology, and subsistence

Table 6.2 Perceived Impacts of Climate Change on Subsistence Activity
(of Those Practicing Subsistence)

2009; N=35 2012; N=48 Does a changing climate...	Percentage of Household Representatives Responding Affirmatively (Yes)		Percentage of Household Representatives Responding *Not* Affirming This Belief (No)	
	2009	2012	2009	2012
Affect *how* you hunt/fish?	65	56	35	44
Affect *how often* you hunt/fish?	45	54	55	46
Affect the *quantity* of the meat/fish that you harvest?	67	73	33	27
Affect the *quality* of the meat/fish that you harvest?	55	40	45	60

practices all influence one's perspective on the observable trend of
rising winter and summer temperatures (Table 6.1). Those who fish
are more likely to note a warming trend and to suggest that winters
are not getting colder. Similarly, those who own snowgos and believe
that the environment is endangered do not believe that winters are
getting colder. Men who regularly use snowgos to travel and hunt in
and around the village are especially likely to suggest that winters are
warming. Women with higher estimated rates of country food consumption (i.e., subsistence) also tend to believe winters are warming
overall, while those with lower rates believe otherwise.

Age plays a key role in comparing the present with the past, of course,
and differences are apparent in perceptions of warming temperatures.
Many members of the younger generation who now cut their own firewood, for example, believe that winters are colder than usual. Even
those younger villagers who receive wood as a gift tend to refute that
winters are warming. Those who have received shared game they did
not have to hunt, such as gifts of moose meat, similarly contend that
winters are colder, not warmer, than usual. Older villagers, including
recipients of caribou, sheep, and moose meat, still are more likely to
express the view that winters are warming.

More telling are the data on those who receive gifts of wood fuel to heat their homes—often the elderly who can no longer go out in the bitter chill to cut the wood needed to get through months of winter. While both older and younger recipients' responses to whether winters were warming are in correlation, older villagers suggest that the winters are definitely warming, while younger respondents suggest that they are not. Furthermore, when asked whether winters were, alternatively, cooling, older wood fuel recipients reiterate the belief that winters are not getting colder. However, members of the older generation who do not speak Gwich'in are less likely to express that winters are warming. To be sure, anyone who is older (i.e., 36 and above) and does not speak Gwich'in must have, by definition, grown up outside of Arctic Village (i.e., they did not grow up locally). Significantly distinguishing is that this group is also less likely than others of their generation to receive wood fuel as a gift during the winter months.

Statistical analysis found that members of the older generation are overall more likely to believe that winters are getting colder, contrary to the general village sentiment. This perspective seems counterintuitive, until additional investigation determined which members of this older generation held such beliefs. Further analysis concluded that what distinguishes this core group of older villagers from the younger generation is that for the most part they are male high school (but not secondary education) graduates who do not speak Gwich'in and are not active hunters or trappers, although they are more likely to fish and to cut their own firewood. These older male villagers are less likely to receive gifts of moose meat, sheep meat, furs, or firewood, and are less likely to own a snowgo or boat. They are more likely than younger villagers, however, to own a refrigerator.

In short, this group—caught between the changes brought on by a fluctuating climate, a new economy, and a society in transition—in many ways embodies much of what is going right (and wrong) in Arctic Village today. On the one hand, this generation represents those who are, or soon will be, the village's elders. Educated outside the village in many instances, these villagers have a great deal of knowledge and employable skills but are presently underemployed. Yet, statistics suggest they tend to be less active hunters, in part a probable sign of age, as older men do still hunt but in time are more likely to rely on their sons, nephews, and grandsons to do so. Financial limitations probably also restrict their hunting activity, as the unemployed and underemployed in the village are less likely to be able to afford the accoutrements required to hunt (see Dinero 2003b: 152–54; 2007: 258–59). Yet, they are still able bodied, and few see them as in need of outside support. Thus, they receive few food gifts and must continue to fend for themselves at a time when fewer hunters provide for a larger pool of consumers as resources off the land dry up literally before their very eyes. Many rely on government assistance as a result (see Dinero 2003b).

Age and gender again proved significant in terms of views toward an increase in winter snow in and around the village. Male duck hunters (i.e., those who predominate the activity) believe there is more snow in recent winters than usual. Those older villagers who own snowgos also hold this belief, suggesting that overall the snow has increased over the past several years. Yet, villagers who own other vehicles such as boats and ATVs contend that winters are no more snowy than usual. In fact, villagers who owned boats expressed the opposite view, believing that nowadays there is less snow than usual. Similarly, those who are less likely to go out on the land in the winter, such as women who receive gifts of wild game, believe there is less snow nowadays. This group also included recipients of fish and caribou meat but not women who received firewood as a gift.

As is the case with the winter months, villagers also note changes in weather during the brief Arctic summer (part of June, July, and part of August). Virtually every social and economic sector seems to believe that summers in Arctic Village are warmer than in the past. Many "hibernate" a bit in the winter as colder temperatures plunge, restricting time spent outdoors to the essentials: hunting or ice fishing, travel to work or school, shopping, cutting wood, and visiting family and friends. However, in the summer, the village is abuzz with motion, noise, and activity. Time spent outside is lengthy and extensive, and changes in the weather are especially notable during this short period when virtually all local housing construction, road repair, and other warm-weather subsistence activities—not to mention recreation—are scheduled.

Thus, every villager—man, woman, and child—seems to have an opinion about the changing summer heat, the increasing fear of sunburn, the rising dustiness around town throughout the summer months, and so on. Those who participate in subsistence, such as male moose hunters, express this belief in the survey, as do older fishermen and women. Curiously, those employed in wage labor, many of whom work during the summer months in construction and related fields, do not express that the summers in general are warming. Yet when asked about the present summer (i.e., of 2012, when the survey was implemented), the employed are more likely than the unemployed to say it is hotter than usual. Younger men and women are most likely to make note of the heat relative to the past. Overall, hunting activity does not correlate with attitudes toward a warming summer, likely in part because most hunting takes place in the fall and winter. However, an indirect correlation still occurs between being active in subsistence and sensing that the environment is changing. Men who do not receive fish, duck, moose, or caribou meat as a gift are more likely to believe the summer months are now warmer than in the past. The only exceptions to this trend are berry pickers—especially older, unemployed men—none of whom believe the summers are warming.

The statistics cited above are but a sample of the recent opinions expressed by the Nets'aii Gwich'in on the most prevalent weather and climate variability now occurring in Arctic Village. While apparently not all residents agree, some general trends occur, mostly concerning a warming trend in both the winter and summer months. More to the point, one's beliefs are clearly colored by the extent to which weather variability directly affects one's daily life. Imagine, for example, one waits all winter for summer's arrival in order to get a badly needed wage-labor job and, once hired, faces constant interruptions, fewer hours, and lost pay due to rain delays. The perception of wetter summers will, unsurprisingly, be of concern to those employed in wage labor positions while those unaffected at home will find the issue less troublesome or noticeable.

Of course, as the data in Table 6.2 suggests, subsistence activities are especially vulnerable to climatic shifts. In terms of these changes affecting *how* the Nets'aii Gwich'in hunt and fish, only the younger respondents tend to answer that climatic fluctuations alter their behaviors. This is not to say that villagers of any age are not cognizant of these changes, but older respondents are somewhat more sanguine about how to adapt to this new reality. Notes one 45-year-old man: "You see erosion. The rivers are wider; they're more shallow. The banks are caving in. You have to travel farther to find moose; they are moving further in search of food, so we have to go further and use more gas to find them." Adds a 62-year-old man: "The ducks are coming earlier now. The snow is different; it's powdery. It gets warmer sooner now [in the spring]. There's erosion, the lakes are draining, the permafrost is melting. The snowgo gets stuck more easily."

In terms of how often villagers hunt or fish, few statistical correlations are found, but a particular set somewhat reveals the increasingly deterministic nature of a changing climate for some Arctic Villagers. A correlation exists between villagers who are not engaged in wage labor and their willingness to fish regardless of changing weather conditions. When asked, this subgroup said that weather does not dictate how often they pursue fishing with either a pole or a net. Indeed, this subsistence activity (as will be seen in chapter 7) is a relatively non-labor-intensive activity requiring limited equipment (as compared to, say, moose hunting). A coffee can, some line, and a lure are all one needs to bring in several fish rather quickly (as Timothy Sam showed my children and me on several occasions). As such, it is not entirely surprising that pursuit of fishing might remain strong, especially among those of limited means, while other activities may decline (see Table 5.1). However, unemployed villagers who receive fish as a gift say just the opposite, as they are more prone to consider weather conditions. Some of these respondents may also fish, but overall, those who have the time, resources, and motivation to seek out country foods for themselves are clearly more likely to do so regardless of weather constraints. Those aided by others through shared wealth and resources have less need or compunction for subsistence activities.

Another constraint influencing these activities is the availability of game on the land. While villagers generally contend fewer animals are available than in the past, some suggest there are more than usual. What is true is that something is "off," something is different. For example, a few years back, the village seemed to be overrun by Arctic hares, but that is no longer the case. Like the moose, the caribou, and the rest of the local ecosystem, what was once taken for granted, as familiar as one's family or the four walls of one's home, is now infrequently seen, ever changing, and never quite the same. Once again, gender and age seem to be the primary determinates for explaining perspectives on food availability. Women are more likely than men to believe that the amount of food from the land has declined. Berry pickers, especially men and the young, say the quantity of food has changed, and men who fish have also noticed a difference.

I am included in the latter group. During my first visits to Arctic Village (1999 in particular), fish were abundant. On one Sunday morning alone, in perhaps an hour, I caught twelve to fourteen large northern pike in a lake just beyond the airport. Pike were plentiful in neighboring lakes as well, though certainly fewer in number. Occasionally I fished Tritt Creek by Glacier, where I would catch a few grayling, again in about an hour. However, by the second decade of my research, the lakes appeared empty. Catching one grayling was difficult. Farther up the Chandalar, however, over a few days in July 2012, I caught by pole more grayling and pike than I could count, the rest filling the nets of my friends, Charley Swaney and Danny Gemmill (see Illustrations 5.2 and 5.3).

My limited experiences notwithstanding, the data collected in the Arctic Village surveys suggest that those who receive gifts of meat, such as sheep (men) or duck (the young), believe there is less country food available than before. Still, the irregular warming, abnormal rain and snow, and new flora also provide additional vegetation on the land, thus game numbers are in flux compared to "the past." Suggests one 62-year-old elder with a bit of irony, "There are more moose, but now [as the lakes dry] there are fewer fish," but, he adds hastily, "the caribou haven't changed at all."

Finally, the question of food quality must be addressed. Here, too, the results seem counterintuitive. On the one hand, the Nets'aii Gwich'in note several examples of how the quality of the food they are eating off the land is changing for the worse. Yet, on the other, the statistics gathered suggest that this difference does not dissuade villagers from harvesting. For example, a 27-year-old man notes, "A couple of years ago we had problems with cysts on the caribou meat, but we cut it off and ate it anyway." Another villager, a 45-year-old man, adds: "I caught a pike with a strange hump on its back. We cut it open and it looked OK, so we ate it. I took pictures first, but it was strange. We are seeing growths on the caribou too." Others say the caribou meat has "white thingies" on it, as well as "strange-looking," possibly contaminated marrow. In short, something does not look quite right to villagers, who tell stories of animals now appearing oddly—most especially, lacking the rich fat they once had.

Illustration 6.3 One of the many Arctic hares to visit the village—and to harass the local dog population (July 2009).

Despite these oddities, the Nets'aii Gwich'in at Arctic Village (as some of the views above indicate) do not tend to express caution in terms of their willingness to pursue subsistence hunting and fishing. Interestingly, villagers who are more educated (i.e., with a high school degree) are less likely than the less educated to note any concern with food quality. Furthermore, caribou hunters from the younger generation are less likely than older hunters to see a change in meat quality. While these results may seem unexpected, one finding perhaps helps to explain these contradictions: villagers with the lowest subsistence rates were least likely to express concern over country food quality. Once again, the villagers' opinions are clearly rational, based on their personal experiences, concerns, and interests.

Ramifications for the Future

The issues of how, if, and to what degree the Arctic Village climate is changing provide a good barometer for assessing various aspects of social and economic differences now manifest among the Nets'aii. Attitudes vary considerably and are largely influenced by personal or household experiences. As such, these perceptions provide irresolvable conundrums. Many may agree that a certain constellation of problems exists, but when it comes to resolutions, individual interests will likely take precedence over those of the group. Of course, this pattern is not unique to the Gwich'in, but in a village of less than two hundred people living in a region that experiences limited population inflow, such a shift is significant and particularly distinct from the Nets'aii communal society before the 1970s.

Thus, the statistics presented above provide a rich kaleidoscope of ideas on the evolving ways a changing climate has affected the Nets'aii Gwich'in residents of Arctic Village. The evidence—infused with personal experiences and combined with centuries of knowledge compressed into small, discrete data sets—is somewhat difficult to fully digest. Table 6.3 provides one additional set of evidence, namely, the accrued words, wisdom, and perspectives of some of the villagers themselves. Like the quantitative material above, these data are raw and largely unedited, and they provide further narration and clarification to ongoing fluctuation at a time when the target is still moving, still changing, still developing on a seasonal—or even weekly or daily—basis.

No single, general set of agreed-upon outcomes can be made on Nets'aii Gwich'in attitudes toward a changing climate at Arctic Village

Table 6.3 Quotes from Arctic Villagers Concerning a Changing Climate

Villager 1: I remember when there were many creeks all over Dachan Lee. Now there's only one. And we never saw this kind of wind before. Now we get frustrated when we can't get the animals. There are fewer caribou now and they are scrawny. We take care of the Land, we do what we are supposed to do. But we give rest to a certain area people used to do that anyway. As a Gwich'in Nation we used to do that. We don't do it anymore.

--65, female

Villager 2: The caribou seem to be around more now. But before the caribou were fat. They're so skinny nowadays. Maybe it has to do with Prudhoe, I don't know. There are no calves around anymore. We care about the animals. We don't shoot them for nothing.

--54, male

Villager 3: You have to compare the weather with technology. Housing is more efficient now. It keeps us warmer. Clothing too. In the old days we had clothing that kept us warm, it's all in the mind. People spend a lot of money but you get the same thing that we got back then for very little money. People get taken. If your hand gets cold, get busy with it, move it around. The deep water gets warmed all throughout the summer then when the ice is forming over the lake it freezes in the shallow parts but only the top freezes below the warm water doesn't freeze and the snow is warm so the water remains warm and keeps the ice thin so the ice opens up and people have to stay on the edge when they drive. We have to wait till the middle of the winter now before we go out into the middle of the ice when we drive. A hill caved in down by the airport then during the winter ten years later the Land next to it between two lakes collapsed but the water in the one lake was higher so all the water went into the other lake and the lake was filled with white fish so those fish ended up on top of the ice in the smaller lake. They all died

Meantime nowadays there's so much rain I don't go out to set my [fish]nets as often. Forty or fifty years ago the caribou didn't have as much food. Now there is a lot of vegetation and they don't have to migrate directly to feed. The caribou paths used to be really deep they always went the same way these are disappearing now. They aren't following the same roots. Even up on the mountain there's lots to feed on. We can't even see moose because there is so much vegetation because there is all this participation. So sometimes it's better to have forest fires to clean out the area.

(continued)

Table 6.3 *continued*

[Also] the caribou is different. Like with farming they make injections so things grow faster. Maybe in nature too they're eating differently and now they taste differently. Not all of them but some don't taste right. Caribou used to taste great. It's not like that anymore…

-- 73, male

Villager 4: It's too hard now. It's just easier to buy food from the store.

--39, male

or, for that matter on how these changes in turn impact subsistence activities. Recent scientific studies reveal that Alaska's climate is in fact warming rapidly, twice as fast as in the Lower 48 states. The average winter temperatures alone have increased by 6 degrees Fahrenheit (3 degrees Celsius; Joling 2014). According to the National Oceanic and Atmospheric Administration, the average temperature for the Lower 48 during January 2014, for example, was 30.3 degrees Fahrenheit (–1 Celsius), 0.1degree Fahrenheit (.05 degree Celsius) below the 20th century average. During that same month the Alaska statewide average temperature was 14.8 degrees Fahrenheit (8 degrees Celsius) above the 1971–2000 average, marking the third-warmest January in the 96-year period of record (NOAA 2014).Thawing permafrost, shrinking lakes, flooding, shifts in species migrations, and the like have already occurred, with more changes anticipated in the coming decades. The quantitative and qualitative data presented here suggests that, like the scientific evidence, changes in the state's and region's climate are ongoing, hard to pinpoint at any single moment, and, more relevantly, difficult to quickly anticipate and adapt to.

The Arctic Village community has proved to be highly resilient in the past, able to adjust over time. While a great deal may be learned from the discussion above, the takeaway message is that permanent changes are now occurring with ongoing regularity. However, another factor should clearly stand out: a decline in subsistence activity in Arctic Village today cannot be blamed on climate change alone (see also Dinero 2013: 131). Climate change may at times be a convenient scapegoat, but, as this and the previous chapter reveal, it does not completely explain the numerous social and economic changes now underway among the Nets'aii Gwich'in. A changing climate provides only one part—albeit a significant one—in influencing the community's future. For a more complete understanding of the larger, ever-evolving picture of Nets'aii Gwich'in development, I now turn to a final piece in the Arctic Village puzzle, namely the evolving role of the village youth. As will be seen in the chapter that follows, the values, attitudes, interests, and concerns of the coming generations dictate where the community is heading as the twenty-first century unfolds.

CHAPTER 7

The Youth Are the Future

Arctic Village is losing its young people. They have gone away to high schools and colleges in the outside world and rarely return now. The people want their children to come back, but a college education is of little value in the village. Almost all of the young people, therefore, have chosen to stay "outside," and without a new generation to hunt the caribou and fish the rivers, Arctic Village may die ...

— *Tundra Times*, 6 December 1968

The Youth in Historic Perspective

I begin with this quote if only to highlight the date when it was written. To suggest that concern for the state of the Native Alaska "youth" is a longstanding problem is to state the obvious. For some decades now, White outsiders and, indeed, Natives alike have feared for the youth, though not without reason. If one segment of the Alaska Native community can be said to still experience the greatest degree of change and its accompanying stress, turmoil, and overall angst during the late twentieth and into the early twenty-first century, that group easily would be identified as the youth, most especially those who live in bush villages. As such, the young people of Arctic Village well fit within this set of rapidly changing circumstances.

The youth—here defined as those under the age of 18, though this definition requires some flexible interpretation—are facing challenges from virtually every quarter including their parents and elders, their schools and teachers, and of course, one another. The strains are considerable. On the one hand, the youth are a resilient group, endowed with inherent elasticity and able to respond, adapt, and reconfigure themselves as the demands of a newly evolving society, economy, and culture require. On the other, however, the young generations are in some ways at a breaking point. If and how they are able to respond to the multitude of changes that now must be confronted will, in the final analysis, prove to be the determining factor in the strength and durability of Nets'aii Gwich'in society and culture going forward.

The Native youth now growing up in bush villages are, unsurprisingly, in many ways trapped in a state of anomie. These youth are coming of age during a time of major upheaval for the entire Alaska Native community (Condon 1990: 269). Over the past half-century, several developments have occurred that have affected age roles. Parental controls have lessened in the post-contact, post-settlement era. The youth are more involved with peers, that is, their key socializing group. In turn, the youth are making their own decisions more than in the past (271). Yet, such shifts come with a cost. As the importance of peers has risen, so too has peer pressure. This is particularly true in terms of substance use and abuse (Wexler 2009: 11). Lastly, as discussed at length in chapter 3, formal education has mostly replaced the informal.

Stacy Rasmus's study of Alaska Native youth is particularly illustrative. As she explains, the development of the "youth" is a relatively new construct shaped during the latter part of the twentieth century:

> In the Alaska Native villages the aboriginal mechanisms for managing emotions have changed, shifting the balance between internal state and external action. Athabascan socialization practices are no longer based on managing behaviors and emotions on the Land, through the human–animal relationships. Young people in the Village no longer grow-up learning how to manage their feelings through the indigenous emotional economy. People in the villages still exist on the very edge of survival, but the terms have changed such that they must now learn how to survive the hazards of the heart. (2008: 29).

This assertion requires some deconstruction. Before European contact, there was no time for "boredom" or hanging out. Young people were constantly moving, constantly working. There was no time to be "lonely" or "sad" (94). Rather, adolescence was a time when the intensification of relationships between the genders and between the human and animal worlds occurred (18). As the youth came of age, gender segregation, sexual awareness, and the opportunities and responsibilities associated with hunting, fishing, gathering, and, in effect, surviving on the land all came into play. As such the youth of the past were the most valued members of Alaska Native society. Though they were the in-between generation, no longer children but not yet adults, expectations placed on this group were considerable. These members of society were especially virile; they still needed to learn hunting and

Illustration 7.1 The joy of childhood (Arctic Village, August 2011).

gathering skills, not yet having mastered every aspect of maintaining a household, but at the same time, were energetic and capable, willing to explore and to push the limits of life experiences.

These years were a time of intense relationship building, as a love for the land was transmitted from the older generation to the younger, and from the younger into, on, and within the resources the land had to offer. Education was a process of socialization; social control was exercised by the elders, who maintained a significant relationship over the youth. The youth viewed their elders as storehouses of knowledge, as models in whose footsteps they would follow. Social sanctioning was strong; roles were strongly and tightly prescribed.

Given both the socio-sexual-psychological power of these dynamic relationships and the context of the state of subsistence and changing climate described in the previous two chapters, it is no wonder that today's Native youth appear to be under siege. As subsistence declines, human interactions are exaggerated, seemingly to the breaking point. Whereas in the past an interaction with the land served as the guidepost for cradle to grave social and psychological growth and development, this relationship is now in steady decline. "Over the last century the intensity of the human–animal relationship in Northern economies has diminished to the point where the Land no longer intervenes on behavior in the same way. Living year-round in the village limits the ability of individuals in these groups to become emotionally-distanced, and centers the intensification of relationships almost exclusively on human ones" (Rasmus 2008: 18).

New technologies, increased exposure to the outside world, formalized education—all this and more have affected the role of Alaska Native youth throughout bush communities. As the youth are increasingly separated from the land, those traits that were well suited to the past—risk taking, a willingness to explore (i.e., those helpful in the hunt)—only lead to risky or questionable behavior today. While the economic uncertainties of the past continue to be eliminated through the creation of new technologies, government assistance, and the like, such innovations, in turn, encourage "nonproductive behavior," idleness, or worse (Condon 1990: 272–73).

Indeed, the Western, neocolonial capitalist model has now become the norm throughout much if not all of Native Alaska. As such, wage labor is essential and highly valued, especially by the youth. New expectations, demands, and challenges pose greater difficulties for the present generation than, perhaps, any previous generation. In some ways, they are in a hopeless situation, considered "failures" before they

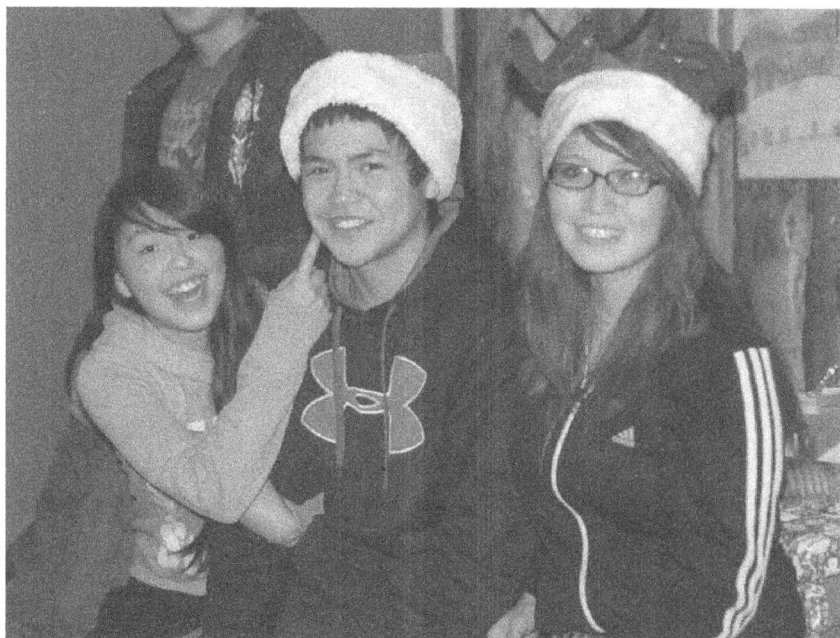

Illustration 7.2 The youth of Arctic Village (Christmas Eve 2011).

even begin their young lives (Wexler 2009: 17). Furthermore, there are very few employment opportunities available in the Native sector; as seen in chapter 3, education is increasingly emphasized but often there is a disconnect between school and the availability of local jobs (Condon 1990: 269). But more to the point, a separation from the land and, with it, a decline in subsistence activity comes at a very high cost. Often though certainly not always, today's village youth turn to dysfunctional behaviors, the result of a village life now turned upside down. As Lisa Wexler explains:

> As emerging adults, young people watch village grown-ups with critical eyes, and say that they will probably follow their lead and abuse alcohol, feel hopeless, and become "bums." These recriminations reflect the tensions of living between two worlds, blaming oneself and one's community for the struggle, and falling through the cracks in the meantime. Life starts out with such promise, but for many teenagers, their own failure is an almost foregone conclusion. (2009: 8)

Such critical assessments are harsh, unyielding and, to the degree that they are embraced, have taken a severe toll on Alaska Native youth in general and on Arctic Village youth specifically. They are sensitive issues, but to ignore or gloss over their existence is, in my view, a disservice at this critical juncture in the Alaska Native experience.

The Significance of Peers and the "Three S's"

The separation of Alaska Native youth from the land and its resources has occurred concomitant with a similar separation from elders and the knowledge, history, and heritage of their respective villages and communities. In turn, as the youth have moved away from the spheres of influence once afforded by parents, uncles, aunties, grandparents, and others, they have simultaneously fallen under the immediate influence of a new group, whose sway is now more significant than any other aforementioned group, namely peers. Peers have supplanted virtually all motivating forces among today's young Alaska Natives. This is particularly true when the "three S's" are considered—namely, substances, sex, and suicide. Together, these issues are a plague on the houses of the villages throughout the Alaska Native bush.

In seeking to address the issue of substance use and abuse, it has been suggested that repeated complaints of "boredom" among village young people, combined with the increased availability of substances in an age of improved modes of transportation, lend to these behaviors, as they create attractive distractions (Condon 1990: 269). To an extent, for adults and youth alike, substances serve as a form of self-medication. Substances of choice may be divided into a handful of problematic categories. These include tobacco-based products, various drugs, and of course, alcohol. To be sure, it is difficult to document let alone prove who is using and abusing which substances, not to mention to what degree. Self-reporting is perhaps the best approach, though the results are somewhat questionable if not altogether unreliable. That said, some statistics may help to provide a snapshot of the present situation of abuses among Alaska Native youth, particularly those residing in the bush village environment.

Among Alaska Native youth, there is a recognizable overrepresentation of tobacco use, which is more prevalent among the youth than any other substance. Alaska Native youth have higher smoking rates than other Native Americans (Hawkins et al. 2004: 308), and in one study, more than one in four youths were found to smoke or chew, compared to, for example, 16 percent of white youth (305). In another study, over half of Alaska Native adolescents reported some tobacco use (Thomas et al. 2010: 177). Tobacco use does not appear to correlate with gender, as studies among Alaska Native youth show that boys and girls use tobacco at similar rates (173).

Some research suggests that substance use is not an issue of age. Given their level of poverty, lack of jobs and so on, it is only "logical" that Native villagers—adults and youth alike—resort to selling and buying addictive substances (Fast 2002: 43). Yet, this contention is potentially prejudicial and incomplete. I agree that with settlement and the shift from a subsistence-based economy to a mixed economy that is dysfunctional at best, Alaska Natives have in effect become an impoverished underclass, displaying many if not all of the difficulties and social problems found across the globe in similar peripheral, subaltern communities. However, this does not fully answer why tobacco, for example, is so attractive. Put simply, the Alaska Native case is complex, drawing in a constellation of dysfunctional behaviors whose causes are difficult to assign to poverty alone.

One source notes a rate of tobacco use at 43 percent of Natives of all ages, almost double the rate of non-Natives (TCC 2015). Interestingly, studies on tobacco use have not found correlations between other social or economic criteria with one noted exception: whether one's mother used tobacco during pregnancy or thereafter (Angstman et al. 2007: 256–57). Needless to say, a dynamic relationship exists between parental and adult behaviors and those of the village youth that could be as much biological as it is behavioral. Substance-related behaviors and abuses may of course change as youths progress into adulthood, but usually with increased rather than declining frequency of use. Tobacco use, for example, tends to increase with age (Angstman et al. 2007: 256; Thomas et al. 2010: 173). Those who use tobacco in their young years will almost certainly continue use into adulthood.

Some Native adults are known to use and abuse a variety of illicit drugs, including marijuana. This is a wholly social activity and behavior less common among the young (Rasmus 2008: 186). Still, like tobacco, marijuana use is overrepresented among Native youth, with a third to about half having used it at one time or other by age 17 and 10 percent of high school seniors reporting daily use (Hawkins et al. 2004: 306–307). Drug use is more popular among Native youth and teens than the non-Native population of the same age. the public. That said, alcohol is the preferred drug of choice overall, desired by most youth—even more so than marijuana or prescription pills, which are favored by adults (Rasmus 2008: 186–87). Youth who use tobacco are also more likely to use alcohol and marijuana, to consider or attempt suicide, or to be involved in physical conflicts with peers—all additional signs of individual and communal distress (Thomas et al. 2010: 176).

Of course, the explanations for why alcohol is so popular among Native youth do vary. Quite clearly, alcohol is more readily available than any other substance, even in villages that are purportedly "dry." However, this merely explains the issue of supply, not demand and consumption. Native motivations to drink are both emotional and social (Rasmus 2008: 167), as drinking may allow for emotional release, freeing of pent-up feelings (170–71). In this regard at least, Natives are of course no different from any other social drinkers. Yet, given the social and economic changes described in the previous chapters, the virtual ecocide of Native America has created pressures that are hardly individual but rather have impacted entire tribes and peoples at a communal level. These tensions can potentially lead to explosive emotions (i.e., violence) and various risky behaviors, leading to both self-inflicted and internecine harm. At the same time, alcohol can also provide a "safe zone," or a soft, almost fantastical painless space that does not exist otherwise. Behaviors are "freed up," providing a psychosocial, emotional, "timeout" from what is otherwise a difficult time and place of uncertainty, lack of control over one's life-sustaining resources, transition, unpredictability, and constant change.

In short, the literature suggests that alcohol allows, albeit temporarily, for the freedom to step outside of oneself and to explore difference; it facilitates "craziness" and allows for "acting out." These are of course all of the indicators and watchwords that typify youth and adolescence. Furthermore, the perceived need to let go and at the same time find oneself also typifies increasingly what it means to be a Native in twenty-first century America. As the Tanana Chiefs Council, the agency most directly involved with offering counseling and other services to substance abuse patients in Arctic Village and throughout the Yukon Flats, concludes, "it is our belief that for Alaska Natives today, alcohol and drug use became a toxic way of coping with a loss of traditional Native values, cultural patterns, identities, relationships, and unresolved trauma" (TCC 2015). The Council of Athabascan Tribal Governments has a similar philosophy: alcohol addiction has been a problem among the Gwich'in for three generations, those who have this addiction must face this issue head on, and, above all, this issue affects the family as a whole, not just the individual (CATG 2015).

Native youth seek out and consume alcohol in a manner that is particular to their population, even as compared to adult Natives. As Elizabeth Hawkins et al. explain (2004: 307):

Research indicates that young people drink less frequently than adults but that they tend to consume larger amounts when they do drink … [However,] both American Indian youth and adults frequently consume large amounts of alcohol in a short period of time, a style often referred to as *binge drinking* (commonly defined as five or more drinks in a row for males and four or more drinks in a row for females).

Hawkins and her colleagues found that while levels of experimentation with alcohol by Native teens is comparable to the rates of non-Native youth, Native youth consumption is substantially higher when it comes to daily and excessive use—nearly double in the case of daily use, 6.1 percent versus 3.5 percent (306).

Discussion of the alcohol problem in Native America is very sensitive, though increasingly it has been discussed more publically, at least internally within villages and other communities. The goal here is not to overemphasize the issue, as this can lead to the furthering of stereotypes against Native peoples. On the other hand, a failure to discuss the issue would be unjustified. As Rasmus puts it bluntly, the existence of the drinking issue "is not good nor bad, it just *is* … The good or bad question about drinking is not the right question, because there is no real answer to it. The right questions have to do with drinking as a social fact of Native life" (2008: 161–62). This concisely summarizes the issue. Abuse of alcohol and other substances has become both a cause and an effect of other social difficulties across Native village life. It is rare for substance use not to lead to other dysfunctions; in turn, it is rare for other problematic issues not to ultimately lead youths

to substance abuse. As such, the entangled relationship among and
between substances and other social problems is legion. This constellation is most evident in the areas of sexual relationships (and abuse)
and suicide.

Alaska Native village youth spend a great deal of their time doing
very little—that is, "hanging out." Not a great deal is "happening" in the
village in the twenty-first century White definition of the term. To be
bored is to be alone; to have fun is to "hang out" with other youth who
also have little to occupy their time, particularly during the long sunlit
days of summer. While gender segregation is common, as girls spend
time chatting in pairs while boys drive about on four-wheel ATVs, the
youth generally have the run of the village and pairing off occurs easily
with little fear of detection. Parents or other adults will likely have no
knowledge of where the youth are at any given moment, let alone who
is doing what with whom. As such, the disciplinary structures of the
past are rapidly dissolving. Given that little happens without one "making it happen," relationships take on a crucial dynamic that cannot be
understated. As Rasmus notes, "fun-seeking behavior and avoidance
of boredom requires a level of sociality, cooperation, risk-taking and
hyper-arousal" (2008: 104).

While Rasmus contends that such qualities worked well in facilitating successful subsistence activity on the land—where alertness,
quick responses to environmental stimuli, and collaboration were
key—such traits in the twenty-first century village lead to other outcomes, such as casual, unprotected sexual encounters often accompanied by substance use. A resulting pattern of "babies having babies" is
not surprising. Yet, like other addictions noted in the literature (Fast
2002), mothering has now taken on a similar function. Fear, insecurity,
and an overwhelming need to be loved are apparently feeding into a
phenomenon in which increasingly younger Native girls are bearing
children, who are then adopted, formally or informally, by mothers,
grandmothers, aunties, cousins, or older sisters. In some instances,
these children are actually raised by their biological mothers, though
with help from other family members.

These young girls are displaying the attributes of what has recently
been termed the "bumpaholic." Like other addictions found in the
village setting, such behaviors are part of a complex constellation of
individual and communal interactions fostered by exogenous and en-
dogenous change:

Women who are obsessed with being pregnant are literally filling an
emptiness inside of them, just as alcoholics and drug addicts use sub-

stances to fill a psychological void … You want to have a purpose in this world. You want to feel less lonely. For some women, babies fill that gap perfectly. Infants are dependent creatures. They can give their mothers a clear identity; they can also become handy social buffers … a woman struggling with feelings of social anxiety or self-consciousness can hide behind the adorable infant in her arms. Any pressure to be cute or charming or funny disappears—your baby has that covered. Bumpaholics breed to blot out their feelings of insecurity. (Brockenbrough 2009)

The outcome of such a development is worrisome, for young Natives are increasingly bringing into the world children whose futures are unstable from the moment of conception.

Thus, Alaska Native youths' ability to successfully manage and maintain peer relationships within and across gender lines has taken on heightened levels of significance that revolve directly around matters of life and death. One's peers are literally and figuratively one's support system. Being separated or cut off from the community in the historic past was often a death sentence—survival depended on the succor and mutual support of all community members who worked together, carrying out physically arduous labor in order to facilitate the common good. In the twenty-first century, isolation can similarly lead to death, due not to starvation but to self-infliction brought on by a variety of stresses, alcohol-related accidents, or even suicide.

Alaska has the highest rate of suicide in the United States, averaging more than 20 deaths per 100,000 each year (the lowest being Washington, DC, with a rate of just over 6 per 100,000). The annual suicide rate among Alaska Natives is even higher, four times the national average, which hovers at about 13 deaths per 100,000. Less known is that 75 percent of these are young, unmarried males between the ages of 15 and 24. Native girls between the ages of 19 and 24 attempt suicide at even greater rates than males (Rasmus 2008: 20–22). Such behavior among the youth, male and female alike, provide further evidence of the self-loathing, hopeless or helpless, imploding nature of their condition today. The overall sense of futility among the youth is palpable: "In the contemporary context, suicide *is*, just like alcohol is, a part of life in the village. It is something that everyone has to deal with" (271).

While true on its face, such a contention is problematic. There is no doubt that suicide—as well as casual sex, pregnancy, and substance abuse—are givens among Alaska Native youth that are likely here to stay. The persistent, repetitive, dysfunctional cycle that has now developed across the state is indisputable. In other words, while recognizing such issues is essential as a first step to potential improvement, it can also lead to mere palliatives and passivity. It is not enough to accept that the three S's are now intrinsic aspects of Alaska Native village life. They must be recognized as the diseases that they are and thus exorcised. Lack of vigilance should not be an option.

Education as a Way In, or a Way Out?

If there is any "golden elixir" that, many believe, will help redress the developing culturally destructive phenomena noted above, it is formal education. As noted in chapter 3, education is now seen across Native Alaska as the gateway to success, but is it not also becoming a gateway out of the village and bush life altogether? It is increasingly common for youth to leave the village to attend boarding school at the secondary and sometimes even the primary level. High expectations are associated with a Western education; as noted in chapter 3, village schools remain of poor quality compared to schools outside of rural Alaska, which serve as magnets for the best and brightest of the youth. As a result, weaker students remain behind, providing further challenges for local schoolteachers.

Ironically, when boarding schools were first implemented in the latter part of the nineteenth and first half of the twentieth centuries, they were resisted, condemned, criticized, and, in general, despised. To this day, the scars of the boarding school experience remain for many who attended them (Dinero 2004: 408). Today, however, the boarding school option is increasingly attractive. It is viewed no longer as a place of deculturation but rather as a primary mechanism or transitory membrane through which one can easily and effectively leave the "boredom" and "monotony" of the Native village and pass into White America while simultaneously accessing a good, formal Western education. Boarding schools provide structure, discipline, and the economic scaffolding for success in an ever-globalizing world, all of which the village lacks (Rasmus 2008: 120–22).

Such schools—and indeed, formal education even inside the villages—are more likely to prepare Native youth for a life in White America than in the village (Seyfrit et al. 1998: 344). Today's youth are betwixt and between, being told one narrative at home and another seemingly contradictory narrative at school by authoritative outsiders armed with red pens (see chapter 3). Note Carole Seyfrit et al.: "In bush villages, traditional values and norms support subsistence hunting and fishing, community life, and the maintenance of family connections. College or migration require one to step away, at least partially, from these familiar activities, places and people" (1998: 346).

Formal education, especially acquired in a boarding school setting, seems to create and perpetuate the existence of almost as many problems as it resolves. Increasingly, more girls are sent out of the villages than boys (Rasmus 2008: 123; Seyfrit et al. 1998: 349). Seeking an education is gendered as a more female activity, while traditional hunting and fishing are still seen to be more male roles geographically fixed to the village environment (Seyfrit et al. 1998: 361). This has created major gender imbalances in numerous regions including Arctic Village, with ramifications for future social relationships including added sexual tensions among those who remain. Moreover, youth who leave the village to attend school are then likely to stay outside where they will seek jobs that can earn better salaries than are available in bush villages. Here too, wage labor positions are more available to women than to men, even women with less formal education (Condon 1990: 274–75).

In short, perhaps the most major challenge to Alaska Native youth today is that they are acquiring different values and lifestyles than

Illustration 7.3 Twenty-first century Nets'aii Gwich'in children (Arctic Village, Christmas Eve 2011).

their parents, grandparents, great-grandparents, or anyone in previous generations. These changes are due to exposure to national and global influences, especially those introduced through the imposing structures of formal education. Other challenges that today's youth face include increased exposure to White and Western society through television, social media, and relatively quick transportation from their village communities to larger urban centers. This rapid, unfiltered interaction with novelty, marketing campaigns, and excess has resulted in a virtual if not actual assault on traditional ideals, values, morals, communication networks, and so on. Elders often die without passing their knowledge on to the youth, since there are no youth who are willing or able to *listen* and thus to learn (UNEP 2007: 79).

I do not intend to paint a purposely grim picture of the future of the Native Alaska village youth. Quite the contrary, I seek here to recognize the numerous challenges that Alaska Native youth face—not to reinforce the myriad of stereotypes that White authors unfortunately tend to perpetuate but rather to merely acknowledge that several problems among the youth exist, just as they do among youth around the globe. Alaska Native youth are no better or worse than anyone else; they are just kids like any others, growing up in a world quite different from that of preceding generations. A close analysis of the Arctic Village youth will, I believe, help to put some of the difficulties the young people now face into sharper focus while offering hope for the future.

The Youth of Arctic Village: An Analysis

In the discussion above, some may view "the youth" of Native Alaska as a static group of dysfunctional people who are, as some of the literature suggests, "failures" in their ability to adapt to life in the "modern era." Such evaluations are harsh, prejudicial, and racist. Still, my observations in Arctic Village during the study period do suggest some similar areas of concern. As for this peer group being consistent in its difficulties and frozen in time, this of course is quite illogical; youth, like childhood and adulthood, is a stage of life, though relatively brief, through which everyone passes. Yesterday's youth are today's adults and tomorrow's elders. Thus, adolescents I may have encountered in Arctic Village at the beginning of this study (say, 16-year-olds) are now more than 30 years old. They surely have children of their own, who may now be moving ever so rapidly past childhood and into the stage of youth under discussion.

In looking at earlier generations, however, to be a "youth" in the past was clearly not the same as being a "youth" today. In the case of Arctic Village, developments in the late 1960s and early 1970s (see chapter 4) facilitated changes across the Nets'aii Gwich'in social spectrum. This alteration in family relationships, subsistence behaviors, technological advances, and more affected the youth, I suggest, more than any other sector of the community. Moreover, this sector continued to be impacted for generations—that is, those who were youth in the latter part of the twentieth century and those who are youth now, though entirely different people, are being adversely influenced by virtually the same social changes that began some forty-five years ago.

For example, analyzing an Arctic Village publication written largely by the local youth from the early 1970s (*Arctic Village Echoes,* 21 October 1969–17 December 1971) reveals the specific nature of those issues deemed relevant during that crucial time of change. By looking at the issues of the day, it is possible to get a sense of how the youth of the 1970s were experiencing social and economic change—change that continues to the present day. The *Echoes* repeatedly address issues related to hunting and fishing—who was hunting what, who was or was not succeeding in the hunt, and so on—and changes in the weather (it's warmer, cooler, or snowier than usual, etc.). Other concerns included activities in school, the arrival of the plane from Fairbanks, the arrival of visitors from outside of the community, and other new behaviors and activities.

The publication highlights some noteworthy events. There is mention, for example, of a "crisis" of sorts that occurred at the Midnight Sun (a local store) when it ran out of smokeless tobacco soon after the winter holidays (23 January 1970). A few weeks later on 16 February, Bingo was played as a communal activity for the very first time (20 February 1970), a highly popular activity in Arctic Village, although criticized by some. Soon thereafter, the village got its first pool table (3 April 1970), also popular with the local youth. Though a subsistence economy and culture still predominated, the transition to new, nontraditional foods was also manifest in Arctic Village during this time. Perhaps this shift was most obvious when, in lieu of drawings of caribou, moose, fish, cabins, and similar iconography representing the village environment usually found throughout the paper, the cover image of the *Echoes* depicted a Nets'aii Gwich'in youth eating a hot dog (see Illustration 7.4; 15 May 1970).

Indeed, by autumn of 1970, articles in the *Echoes* well reveal that change was under way in nearly every quarter of the Nets'aii Gwich'in community. A transition in thought and behaviors was rapidly taking

Illustration 7.4 Nets'aii Gwich'in boy eating hotdog on the cover of *Arctic Village Echoes* (1970).

place, and the youth of Arctic Village were in the crosshairs, caught between new ways of addressing these challenges and the tried and true values of the past:

> Two years ago much gasolinee [*sic*] was burned hunting but there were just not many animals in the country. Last year the animals were around but not in very large herds. It took both good luck and alot [*sic*] of driving

to get meat. So far this year hunting has been poor. The most animals taken are found only 20 air miles away but on snow-machines the distance covered was some where around 70 miles over rough ground.

A trip like that one took all day with stops to repair both machines in the middle of no where when one developed electrical trouble and the other messed its front drive pulley. The 6 animals which were brought in that day required a lot of work. So far there have been no herds anywhere near the village and there have been no reports of herds moving towards it. I sincerely hope that it will not be another hard year for meat. When everyone is used to having meat it comes as kind of a shock when you have to go several months without it. *Makes a person really appreciate the super market just down the street.* (6 November 1970, emphasis added)

To be sure, previous generations would not have expressed the values and attitudes here. Growing up at the time and in an age of exposure to new externally generated ideas, technologies, and opportunities, the youth could not help but be influenced by these changes, even in a village hundreds of miles from the nearest White settlement. An editorial in the *Echoes,* "Reflections on the Year So Far," furthers this contention, suggesting that the village at the time was filled with more advance technologies (a "superhighway" in the village teeming with snowgos), new infrastructure (the chapel, housing, improved roads), and greater connectivity with the outside (regular mail delivery and more CODs and food stamps than ever before). Yet the editorial concludes in a cynical, youthful tone—familiar to anyone who has ever raised a teenager—that it's been a poor year for the caribou and so asks, "How 'bout a MacDonald's [sic] franchise?" (25 November 1970).

In short, the views expressed in the *Arctic Village Echoes* well capture the era's sentiment that would provide the context for an analysis of youth behaviors, values, interests, and concerns decades later. In Native bush today, including Arctic Village, the younger generation of Alaska Natives is commonly referred to as "soft," no longer interested in hunting, fishing, or gathering as were previous generations. However, a transition has been under way for decades, and those who express these concerns were once accused of these very failings themselves. But to what extent are today's youth abandoning Nets'aii Gwich'in values and behaviors? Is subsistence in jeopardy? And are the youth more caught up in destructive behaviors, such as the three S's, than they are in their own culture and traditions?

In chapter 6, I addressed how a fluctuating climate and changes in subsistence behaviors now overall conflate, with ramifications for the community in general. Here, I add the ongoing dilemma of the particular role of the younger generations being played now and in the future.

In short, I seek to problematize the question of if and how much the community believes today's youth are not as active in Nets'aii Gwich'in values such as subsistence activities and behaviors as were their parents and grandparents. Afterward, I seek to determine what specific causes are at the root of these changes and how social, economic, and communal shifts contribute to the decline of subsistence among today's younger generation. Among these are, of course, shifts in priorities, values, and behaviors, including some of the abuses outlined in the previous section.

As seen in the previous chapter (Table 6.3), many in the Arctic Village community share the aforementioned concerns (i.e., the three S's). From the moment I stepped into the village in 1999, residents from every walk of life repeatedly told me that youth drinking was a problem and that the local council was struggling to intercede. In short, the consensus, which has changed little over the fifteen years since this study was conducted, is that drinking starts young and is often reinforced, albeit inadvertently, from within, as parents and others seek to protect their children from sanction. As passengers arrive at the airport from Fairbanks and the wet Gwich'in town of Fort Yukon, bags are repeatedly checked for contraband bottles, their contents poured out on the tarmac. Still, the issue has no doubt worsened since this research began and has resulted in several publically acknowledged accidents and even some deaths within the village.

To investigate issues of alcohol use, as well as drug use and sexual activity, among Nets'aii Gwich'in minors remains an ethically challenging task. I have certainly witnessed many problematic activities, heard a great deal from my children who accompanied me on several research trips, and learned much from adult interlocutors. Indeed, I also see much written on Facebook (see chapter 8) concerning a variety of social ills that are often discussed publicly, typically portrayed as problems by adults but sometimes celebrated as fun behaviors by the youth. To research and quantify such activities in a more formal fashion is risky business, given the small population in question and the uncertainties inherent in the sensitive nature of the issues (Stiffman et al. 2005).

Though such topics are sensitive, village elders and others have, at times, been willing to express their views about youth substance abuse and related concerns. Raymond Tritt, second chief and primary policing officer when I arrived in Arctic Village in 1999, told me in one of our first conversations that "the youth [here] get into trouble because they have nowhere to go. I wonder why they're drinking, or why they do drugs? Their mother isn't there, or she's on drugs or drinking. It

goes generation to generation. They see that their friends are doing it."
At the time, Tritt believed a youth center would make a huge difference
in discouraging negative behaviors, but even more needed was to "take
the teens into the woods"—that is, to encourage them to return to the
land and the subsistence activities that had long sustained the Nets'aii
Gwich'in body, mind, and soul. Still, though such a solution may be
seemingly self-evident, the many issues now facing the youth are considerable, the answers far from certain. Yet, this contention among
the Nets'aii Gwich'in persists. Many interviewed in the film *Gwich'in
Niintsyaa: The 1988 Arctic Village Gathering* (1988), for example, were
quick to suggest that the solution to substance abuse among Gwich'in
villagers young and old alike is "to get back to the land." In other words,
Gwich'in lifestyle, land, and tradition are the cures needed to fend off
the use and abuse of destructive and addictive substances.

Indeed, decades later, in the spring of 2014, the Tanana Chiefs Conference and the Alaska Department of Health and Social Services
jointly put out a public service announcement in an effort to address
the Nets'aii Gwich'in smoking issue (see Alaska DHSS 2014). The PSA
was notable on several levels. First, it used a formal classroom with
rather young children learning from a male and a female teacher about
the dangers of smoking. Second, the teachers are dressed in traditional
dress (beaded skin vests with fur trim) and everyone in the PSA speaks
the Gwich'in language, with English subtitles:

Female Teacher: Tobacco is not good for us. They cause over 600 deaths
each year.

Student: Why do they smoke if they know it will hurt them?

Male Teacher: Once we start smoking it is hard to quit. Drumming
our ancestors' songs strengthens our mind and body.
[Begins drumming on traditional drum.]

Narrator: Everyone has the right to breathe smoke-free air.

The message is clear: tobacco use can and must be fought. More to the
point, Gwich'in heritage—embodied by clothing that directly ties to a
proud, land-based tradition—will help the community to combat and
ultimately defeat such threats to the youth.

Once again, the idea is expressed that returning to traditional culture and values will deter substance use and abuse, but is such an argument truly valid? Are there correlations between declining subsistence
practices and communal social problems or dysfunction? Using data
collected in surveys in 2011, 2012, and 2013, I sought to determine
the degree to which, from the adults' perspective, the youth of Arctic

Village are in fact separating themselves from the land, ceasing subsistence behaviors, abusing substances, and more. At the same time, I
wished to acquire data from the youth themselves about how they see
their place in the village community and in the surrounding lands of
the Gwich'in Nation. In short, I sought information on how the youth
are perceived by adults and how they perceive themselves in the context of the ongoing development of the Nets'aii Gwich'in community.

As noted in chapter 5, the vast majority of adult villagers surveyed
in 2012 (81percent) agree that today's youth are not as interested or
engaged in subsistence activity as past generations were. Interestingly,
this contention is most pronounced among one group in particular:
duck hunters. Hunters from the older generation are especially critical
of the younger generation, as are Gwich'in speakers, who also tend to
be older. The belief in less subsistence activity among the youth directly and strongly correlates with believing that digital technologies—
including television, computers, cellphones, tablets, and video gaming
systems—are a problem. Alternatively, married respondents blame a
lack of parental guidance for the decline in youth hunting; single and
cohabitating respondents are less prone to do so, while divorced or
widowed respondents have mixed feelings on the matter.

Concern about the future of subsistence and the role of posterity
is central to virtually every conversation (see Table 7.1). The Nets'aii
Gwich'in of Arctic Village find it difficult if not impossible to separate
changes in the natural environment with changes now occurring in
Gwich'in culture and society at large. Many conversations may begin
with climate or subsistence but quickly devolve to the primary issues
of the day: the various social concerns and abuses that community
members feel keep the Nets'aii from developing and reaching their full
potential.

Other complaints about the youth may sound familiar to any culture today, insofar as they appear to be part of a growing narrative now
common among the baby boom generation. Many suggest, for example,
that the youth have no interest in attending church or in understanding Christianity. The village youth, like young populations globally,
are indeed expressing less affiliation with mainstream organized religion. Others speak of the present generation's lack of motivation,
noting how difficult things were before modern technologies. Others
even suggest laziness among today's youth, implying that the young
are spoiled and fail to appreciate what they have, especially compared
to the "old days." A generational difference of profound proportions is
unquestionably developing in Arctic Village. Even among adults, a split
in values and behaviors has occurred between the younger and the

Table 7.1 Arctic Village Adult Perspectives on the Youth

Villager 1: Now it's the end of spring hunting but the kids say it's boring. You have to stay out there where nothing is going on. It's not just camping, but the kids aren't interested any more. We wanted to do it [in the past]. The world was out there, but nowadays it's not like that. With TV and parents not going out there, it's not like that. Just the men and boys go. The costs are high so the whole family doesn't go. Sometimes we have to show them how to cut the caribou, they don't know how. We went out with dogs. Now they have 4-wheelers and snowgos and off you go, and then throw it all in the freezer. We had to dry the meat. Nowadays with the freezer it's all messed up.

The young ones get out of high school and then they are here and here and here. They have nothing. That worries me—how will they make a living? There aren't any jobs for them. There is hardly any tourism. Alcohol is a problem. We had a suicide and another froze to death from drinking. Another shot himself by accident. We have child abuse and endangerment. Someone was raped. And yes, I love to drink too! All the bootleggers are here too…

We have a lot of babies here and there isn't enough housing. They get out of high school and a year later they are pregnant and then they want welfare and a new house. Half the kids are like this and not qualified to work, and yet they are making babies. We have to get the logs to repair and replace the elders homes, and mean time the kids are complaining that they want a new house!

People are behaving themselves right now because they don't want to lose out on getting jobs for the summer. So there is less drinking right now. No one wants to get in trouble right now and move down on the job list.

--58, male

Villager 2: The problem is technology, the kids are into games. We didn't have video games. Now they have those things that stop them; they don't want to learn.

People are drinking a lot more. People are dying from it. My brother-in-law died. People are searching. Ninety percent smoke pot, 75% are doing some kind of pills—tronydol they're called. People are aging faster, they aren't as healthy as they were, they can't get up in the morning without it.

(continued)

Table 7.1 *continued*

The young kids are getting into nicotine products. By age 10 they're
chewing [tobacco]. Kids are selling things from their homes in order to
get money to smoke.

--27, male

Villager 3: The parents aren't doing stuff with the kids, taking them out
fishing. Do something to help their household, set traps, get wood! We
don't see that any more. We would like to see the parents more involved
with the kids, to show that they know something and don't expect others
to do it.

--33, male

Villager 4: There's technology, cable computers, games, all that. Our
traditional values aren't passed down. Our kids stay home rather than to
go out on the Land. The younger generation isn't growing up on
traditional foods. They are drinking pop, eating candy and microwavable
stuff. That's different from when I was a kid.

This past year I noticed some boys going out, around age 14, but in my
parents' generation, kids would go out who were younger than 10. That
traditional value is still there, it's just not being passed down as it used to
be. I make frybread, my daughter sees me beading. I cut up meat for dry
meat and she helps me. I grew up in the city, I wasn't raised that
traditionally either...

The main problem here is substance abuse. First it was alcohol, then
marijuana, now it's prescription pills. It's taking over people's judgment
of right and wrong. That's why I quit working at the Council. People's
reactions to their addictions—people aren't clear-headed.

--34, female

Villager 5: Games, IPods, these things get in the way. Why did they
invent that shit? They put on the Hunting Channel and that's hunting.
They just sit by the fire when we go out they just walk around.

--50, male

Villager 6: Parents don't hunt or do anything with the kids. They give them money to go to the store or the fair. I'm glad my father and husband do stuff with my kids. They don't do that with their kids. Experience it, see what it's like. But the parents and grandparents aren't doing it, they brush them off, say I'll tell you later. But I feel that they have to know these things.

--41, female

Villager 7: The kids live on junk food. They grew up on hamburgers and hotdogs and crap. There are a few who go hunting, you can't say all of them are like this. Maybe half. It's sad that not all of them are doing it. We don't teach them; they're too busy making money to teach their kids.

--65, female

Villager 8: I go out, but I don't see any kids out, and when they do go, they go maybe a half a mile [from the village]. Sometimes I wonder if they're scared of a bear or something. Maybe it's video games. We grew up the hard way. We knew this technology wasn't going to last. They [kids] prefer easy life. We grew up in the woods. We like it that way. They have Internet. Only thing we had was each other. Nowadays they have TV and all that. Things are more easy. They just jump on a four wheeler or boat or snow machine.

--54, male

older generations. In my 2011 survey (N = 46), for example, the key age appeared to be 40—that is, the answers provided by those born before 1971 differed significantly when compared to those provided by respondents born after 1971.

Anecdotal evidence suggests that the youth themselves also sense the losses and changes under way between generations. A feeling of ennui appears to have settled among young villagers, who try to explain their confusion in an age of ever-evolving expectations and roles. As one male villager in his early twenties told me:

I need to learn my traditional ways. I still don't know enough but I'd like to learn. Maybe I was raised to play video games; maybe I'm lazy … We're definitely losing our traditional ways of life. We don't want to say it aloud but it's true. I don't speak Gwich'in; I don't hunt. I have a lot to learn. I think what's holding us back is we have a lot of technologies—

what's holding us back is we have iPods, computers—I think that's what the problem is. I'm really worried. Unless they create some program, we're going to lose the Gwich'in language.

But yes, someday I'd like to get out of here, go to college. Right now I'm just having fun. No, we'll never be rich here, but we'll always have our animals. And we'll always have our caribou.

But how representative are such views? And to what extent are Arctic Village's young people engaging in new technologies in lieu of traditional subsistence activities?

Using chi-square analysis of data gathered in 2011, I determined that younger respondents, especially women, are more likely to use Facebook. Related to these findings, those on Facebook are less likely to speak Gwich'in or to receive federal or state assistance, and they tend to have more educated fathers. Younger-headed households are more likely to own a computer or gaming systems (e.g., Xbox). Predictably, younger respondents' parents are more likely to be high school graduates. Younger respondents were less likely to speak Gwich'in, a fact again confirmed in the 2012 household survey. Understandably, Gwich'in speaking correlates with the likelihood of one's children speaking Gwich'in.

My interest here, however, concerns not just young adults but young people as well, and not merely what is said *about* them (Table 7.1) but also their self-perceptions. In March 2013, I conducted a small pilot survey of the youth of Arctic Village (see "A Note on Methodology") between the ages of 8 and 17 (i.e., born between 1996 and 2005). Like all previous surveys, I paid the respondents ($10 in this case). Thirteen children qualified for inclusion, but two were absent from the village during the one-week period when I conducted the survey, and two refused to participate. Thus, the N for this survey amounts to only nine participants—still a rate of about 70 percent of possible participants. I expected a limited amount of statistical evidence to arise from such a small data set. Yet, all necessary provisos notwithstanding, the following findings offer some material worthy of discussion.

The first questions concern how the youth feel about their educations. While favorite subjects span from math to English to gym class (phys ed), some consistency is found among a handful of specific questions on student satisfaction—a question long asked of the children's parents in previous surveys. The results are as follows:

- The majority of respondents, 44 percent *like* their teachers. The same percentage *dislike* Arctic Village School;

- One-third say that they *dislike* their teachers. The same percentage, however, *like* the school.
- More than three-fourths, 78 percent, plan to attend college;
- One-third plan to stay in the village as adults; two-thirds plan to leave.

In order to gain a sense of how the village youth like to spend their time outside of school, I then posed a series of questions about what they would prefer to do (if they had total control of their schedules) daily, occasionally, or rarely. The results are in Table 7.2.

Given the number of young people residing in the village, the sample size could have been much larger had everyone been available, but the results nevertheless confirm that peer relationships, above all, are central to youth concerns today. The school experience itself is largely valued for its social component (Rasmus 2008: 123–24). Some basic statistical analyses found correlations between age, attitudes toward school, and peer relationships.

For example, the youth who responded that they "like to party" regularly (I did not specify what I meant by "party," allowing the youth to interpret the meaning for themselves) are less likely to enjoy math or science class than those who "don't party." As noted above, age makes a significant difference here; high school–aged respondents are more likely to admit an interest in occasional partying than are younger respondents, who said they "rarely" or "never" party. Respondents who favor math or science are more likely to want to attend college in the future than those with more interest in reading, English, or other subjects. Concerning new technologies, those who play video games more regularly are less happy in school, expressing particular criticism of their schoolteachers. These youth are less likely to have college-educated mothers and are more likely to spend their free time hanging out at the Youth Center.

This small sample clearly shows that the youth, both inside and outside of school, turn to one another for succor, though this has its ups and downs. As small environments with constrained exit strategies, villages can be like pressure cookers for young teens when relationships go sour. Like a small house with very few rooms, there is literally nowhere to go in the off-the-road bush village. On the one hand, spending time alone is not ideal, but on the other, to get away from someone undesirable is virtually impossible—whether one is a child *or* an adult. Native villagers do not like to be alone, but they also struggle with the day-to-day conflicts that inevitably arise out of living so close to relatives and peers. Perhaps it is no wonder that the respondents who

Table 7.2 Arctic Village Youth Preferred Activities

Activity	Percent stating agreement
Hang out with friends (daily if possible)	100
Watch movies on DVD (daily if possible)	78
Have a Facebook account at present Of these, those who would use daily if possible Do not have a Facebook account at present	78 44 22
Watch TV (daily if possible)	44
Play video games (daily if possible)	44
Do homework with friends (daily if possible)	44
Spend time with parents (daily if possible)	33
Spend time in town (daily if possible)	33
Spend time with Elders (daily if possible)	22
Spend time alone in room (daily if possible)	22
Spend time in Youth Center (occasionally if at all)	78

expressed the least desire to spend time alone (i.e., in their bedrooms) were most likely to want to spend time "in town" (i.e., Fairbanks).

Beyond these questions, I sought here to determine the merit of the ongoing contention often expressed by adults that Arctic Village's youth, distracted by new technologies, are not involved or interested in subsistence activity (see Tables 4.4 and 7.1). The short answer is that younger villagers do wish to be involved, but the longer answer, of course, is much more complex. One strong correlation seems to confirm these basic concerns: those youth who expressed greater interest in watching more hours of television are less likely to have gone fur trapping (a time- and labor-intensive activity) than those less interested in watching television. However, more regular Facebook users are also *more* likely to have cut firewood than less regular users, in part contradicting the assumption that the younger generation is not involved in both subsistence activities and computer technologies.

The survey makes apparent that overall, the youth are carrying out subsistence at lower levels than are their parents and elders (see Table 7.3). Nevertheless, the youth *are* undoubtedly active participants in subsistence activity, which is significant given that their primary commitment is to attend and perform well in school. Particularly noteworthy is that in the case of one activity, fishing, the youth are more active than are the older generations. This being said, some provisos are needed here that further confirm the gendered nature of subsistence going forward and the feminization of the boarding school option, which of course has major ramifications for the flight of girls out of bush villages. Those young people who hunt caribou and ducks and who cut firewood are predominantly male. Caribou hunting and wood-

Table 7.3 A Comparison of Adult and Youth Participation in Subsistence Activities (2012)

% Involved in Subsistence Activities (2012)	Adults	Youth
Hunt caribou	71	44
Hunt moose	15	0
Hunt sheep	8	0
Hunt ducks	60	33
Trap for furs	15	11
Fish (net/pole)	77	**89**
Gather berries	75	67
Cut wood	77	56

cutting are challenging activities, primarily limited to older children (that is, high school aged). Finally, the same youth are involved in several activities while others opt out altogether; those who hunt caribou, for example, are also more likely to hunt ducks and to cut firewood.

Concluding Thoughts

In every generation, in every society, parents and elders commonly look back on their own youth with some fondness, romanticism, and nostalgia. As fallible memories fade or even morph with the passage of time, perhaps it is only natural that they compare "today's youth" with those of the past. Rarely if ever can the youth of today "measure up" to the memories of yesterday.

In the case of the Nets'aii Gwich'in, of course, the past was a time of little exposure to the outside world, of a lifestyle based solely on total subsistence from the land, and when the youth were socialized from birth most directly by their parents and elders. The Nets'aii Gwich'in had once been isolated from the White world in virtually every way, but, as the previous chapters have shown, that all changed in the

Illustration 7.5 These children are the future (Arctic Village, July 2012).

mid-nineteenth century. The social and economic fabric of the village was undergoing total transformation during the late twentieth century, and by 1970, physical, social, economic, and political changes were underway that would affect all aspects of the Gwich'in culture. No one would be affected more than the youth.

It would be disingenuous to suggest that the youth's lives of the 2010s are similar to those of the 1910s—or the 1970s for that matter. My goal here is not to propose that life is now any better or worse than before. It is simply different. Still, one can only wonder what Chief Christian or, better yet, Rev. Albert E. Tritt might make of the present young generations growing up in Arctic Village—of the lifestyles, values, and priorities now developing in the village that they were so instrumental in creating. In the next and concluding chapter, I return to this very question: what can be made of the present social and economic situation among the Nets'aii Gwich'in of Arctic Village? And, more importantly, what might the future hold for this small Alaska Native community?

CHAPTER 8

We Don't Know
Where We Are Anymore

As the future approaches and passes away, the Indian will undoubtedly vanish with it. His race will be bred out, absorbed by the stronger breed of the Caucasian, but his blood will still flow in the veins of future northern whites. The Red Man's day is darkening into night, and his race is doomed to perish in exile from freedom.

On the farthest northern frontier, in the Land of the Takudh Kutchin, he is making his last stand and losing in the fight. But his blood will carry on through the ages, giving to the future white men something of the cheerful, care-free nature of those who are, in spite of all their misfortunes and adversities, in spite of the hard, hard life they lead, among the happiest and most contented of peoples.

— Michael H. Mason (1924)

Who Are We, and Where Do We Go from Here?

Since the first contact between White Europeans and the Alaska Natives, an ethnocentric if not racist belief has prevailed: in time, "modernity" will win the day, and the "primitive" faiths and practices of the Natives will fall by the wayside. This mentality, fed by a social Darwinist value orientation, exists to the present day, even if it is not voiced fully in our increasingly "politically correct, multicultural" society. It informed the introduction of Christianity to the territory. It supported and sustained formal education for youth. It was at the foundation of "modern" settlement and formalized government planning initiatives. It was—and is—at the center of an ideology that suggests monetization and with it the commoditization and sale of foodstuffs in stores must and will replace subsistence systems of hunting, fishing, and gathering.

In short, such biased attitudes were at the basis of past acts of wanton aggression and still inform every aspect of the ongoing contested relationship between Alaska Natives and White America today. Since contact, colonial and neocolonial ideals and values have perpetuated an onslaught on the social, economic, political, and geographic foundations of Native culture and society. In a take-no-prisoners barrage, White America has pursued a campaign of devastation and destruction. If there is any surprise here, it is only that the outcome of this carnage has not been even more severe.

As such, the previous chapters paint a picture of a community in what some might suggest to be a period of crisis. In just over a century, a once-proud, highly functional Alaska Native community has undergone change at such a rapid rate that it is difficult to document without a great deal of hesitation and numerous provisos. Even during the time this study was undertaken at the turn of the millennium, much has occurred in the community; to speak about what is happening in Arctic Village "today" is impossible, as "today" quickly becomes yesterday, seemingly in the blink of an eye. While some aptly argue that Alaska Native cultures are "resilient" and well able to adapt to an ever-changing social, economic, and physical climate (e.g., Carey 2009; Kofinas et al. 2010), coerced change is also rarely if ever accepted as positive, no matter how purportedly "good" that change might be.

Since I first began my research in Arctic Village in 1999, villagers commonly say to me, during our many formal and informal conversations, "We don't know *where* we are anymore." They did not say *who*; they always said *where*. At first, I did not understand this. I even thought there might be a linguistic issue that created confusion or a problem with translation. But, of course, I did not fully take into account initially that for the Gwich'in, a connection to place—that is, the land—and a sense of heritage, history, and, above all, identity, go hand in hand. Indeed, in what appears to be the first and only pre–World War II census in which the villagers participated, taken on 25 March 1929, Albert E Tritt and his followers all indicated that their places of birth, as well as that of their parents, was *athabasca takudh*—Gwich'in Athabascan (US Census Bureau 1930). In short, when asked *where* they and their families were from, they responded with *who* they were.

This sentiment well represents the Nets'aii Gwich'in worldview as it once was manifest. The people and the land were one. Though today's villagers live in the same geographic location as their ancestors did going back millennia, the earth seems to have shifted beneath their feet. As the previous chapters have shown, an earthquake of major proportions has taken place since the mid-nineteenth century, causing the

known, the certain, the expected, the recognizable, and the predictable
to have become virtually unfamiliar and unrecognizable, all in a matter of a few short decades. What the Nets'aii Gwich'in of Arctic Village
once *knew* is no more.

At one time—the local belief among elders contends—the Nets'aii
Gwich'in knew every mountain, every stream, every rock. They knew
every local animal, how it behaved, where it lived. They knew (and
still contend that they know) when the caribou would arrive each fall.
They knew when the first snowflake would fall and when the first crack
would appear in the spring ice. They knew how to navigate every river,
every creek, every trail. They knew where the biggest berries grew. They
knew where to hunt—and where *not* to fish. In short, as noted somewhat romantically in the 1988 documentary film against oil drilling
interests in the ANWR, they knew the land like a child knows a parent
(*Gwich'in Niintsyaa* 1988). But the colonial (and later neocolonial and
multicorporate) enterprise would shake the people from this foundation and, in the latter part of the twentieth century, further changes
only exacerbated the growing separation from the land and with it the
resulting social and economic disorientation.

Today, the world in which the Nets'aii Gwich'in live is in many ways
becoming a very foreign place. They do not know where they are anymore. In light of the transitions documented in the previous chapters,
it is only reasonable to ask, "What happens next? What will the future
bring to the Nets'aii Gwich'in, and to Arctic Village?"

Gary Moore, a planner and Athabascan Native familiar with Arctic
Village and its surrounding Gwich'in villages, suggested to me prior
to my first visit to the village in 1999 that the future viability of such
communities would depend largely on their ability and willingness to
become more attuned to how modern economic systems work. Little
physical infrastructure or commercial activity exists in bush villages
that can sustain or support strong, viable economies. In what amounts
to a catch-22, the ability for communities such as Arctic Village to at-
tract private business interests is limited at best (Moore 1999). As a result, the Gwich'in, who are hardly alone in this regard, expect state and
federal funding to compensate for a limited ability to internally gener-
ate needed private direct investment funding. In an age of tightening
budgets, such dependency is ill advised and ill fated. Native corporations are needed to invest in their own areas, yet they tend to invest in
the urban areas (Anchorage, Fairbanks) and not in the villages.

Moreover, in the case of Arctic Village, its choice of opting out of
the ANCSA means that it receives no support from Doyon. The Tanana
Chiefs Conference, Doyon's sister social services organization, does

work actively throughout the Yukon Flats, including Arctic Village, but again, the need here is for job creation, ideally in the private sector. As planner Moore noted at the time, villages expect government investment when they should be looking for job creation coming from private enterprise. Their economic bases are built on unsteady ground, with limited sustainability going forward. According to Moore: "Village corporation boards are little more than managers of portfolios. I don't see efforts to create jobs at the village level. [Instead] these boards are inclined to take low to medium risks in stocks, mutual funds, bonds. They don't really work on actual development" (1999).

Without these essential jobs, the youth will continue to leave communities like Arctic Village, never to return. Those who remain in the village will continue to rely on transfer payments (see Dinero 2003b), which, Moore has suggested, "can be viewed as a failure; this kills the incentive to be creative" (1999). Subsistence activities will also be jeopardized without adequate income to pay for equipment, tools, transportation, fuel, and so on. This dynamic creates a vicious cycle: without cash revenue, subsistence activities cannot be sustained, but without subsistence activities, the viability of the village and the ongoing desire to live in the bush are questionable. If one is no longer hunting, fishing, or gathering with any level of regularity, why live in a bush environ-

Illustration 8.1 The "new" Bishop Rowe Chapel built in the late 1960s (December 2011).

ment where dependable wage-labor jobs are scarce or nonexistent and conditions are difficult—other than for cultural or nostalgic reasons, which, in time, have less purchase relative to the realities of economic stress? For many, the urban option simply has greater allure.

Thus, before predicting what Arctic Village will look like decades from now, one might first ask whether the village will even exist. Planners like Moore are pessimistic, believing that "fewer than half" of all bush villages will survive in the coming decades (Moore 1999). But he does suggest that what is or is not done *today* in villages large and small will play a significant role in the future of the Alaskan Native bush communities—and in which communities have a fighting chance at survival.

"Plan Your Perfect Trip: Arctic Village"?

If there is one possible economic development strategy worthy of investigation, Moore has suggested, it is tourism. While he was quick to note during this early interview that no one solution exists for all villages and that if too many villages were to enter this field, there would be a glut as each competed with the other for limited tourist dollars, still, he suggests, this could be an option in some locales (Moore 1999).

As noted in chapter 4, the 1991 planning document calls for greater investment in a variety of economic development arenas, including tourism (Arctic Village Council 1991: 31). For years since the Moore interview, many of the Nets'aii Gwich'in of Arctic Village have asked for my help in pursuing such efforts. Microlevel tourism has long been viewed positively as an economic development opportunity that has not been fully exploited. In the 1999 household survey, 63 percent of respondents supported the idea of marketing the village more aggressively to tourists. In 2006, 62 percent supported the idea, and in 2011, 78 percent supported the idea of pursuing small-scale, environmentally sustainable tourism more aggressively.

Yet, the commoditization of the land, home, and livelihood is understandably controversial, like virtually all issues in the village today, and support is not universal. Women, for example, are significantly less enthusiastic about having tourists come to the village in larger numbers than are men. As one female elder told me back in 1999, "tourism is always as option, but we won't dance for the tourists!" In the same household surveys, I asked a theoretical question about creating increased access to the outside world, worded as follows: "If it were possible to build a road to connect Arctic Village to the South (i.e.,

Fairbanks), would you support this plan?" In 1999, only 9 percent said yes. In 2006, 23 percent supported the idea, and by 2011, 38 percent supported it. It is clear that some ambivalence toward outsiders remains, despite increasingly frequent contact with the outside, White world that was virtually unknown only a few short decades ago.

Still, tourism, especially ecotourism, may be one of the village's few realistic options given its small population and location. However, to date, tourism in the village has been irregularly planned and managed. In the late 1980s and 1990s, a director did try to organize tourism in the area but on a very small scale that brought in little money and was concentrated almost solely on the Japanese tourist market. But this activity, limited as it was, ended some years ago, and many economic development opportunities have been missed over the years since. For example, 1,200 to 1,500 tourists fly into the ANWR annually for hiking, rafting, and similar activities. All must pass through Arctic Village to change planes. The cost of these trips averages $4,000 to $4,500 per person, excluding airfare from one's point of origin (see Sierra Club 2016). Such ecotourists, who rarely stay in the village more than an hour or two, could offer cash inputs at a time when they are most needed.

Arctic Village's location, a bane when it comes to most aspects of private enterprise, may serve as its primary asset as a tourist desti-

Illustration 8.2 Snowgo at −35 degrees Fahrenheit (Airport Road, 21 December 2011).

nation. The village sits amid thousands of acres of beautiful wilderness teeming with charismatic fauna including caribou, moose, grizzly bears, wolves, and a variety of fowl and fish. The aurora borealis, also an attraction for many outsiders, is visible for several months each year. Lastly, the recently reconstructed Bishop Rowe Chapel (see chapter 2) is an attractive magnet for heritage tourists.

All of this being said, much work would be needed to transition the village into a twenty-first century tourist destination, assuming this is even a serious option worthy of consideration. The villagers would certainly want to control the flow of outsiders as much as possible. They would want to determine what kinds of activities outsiders are allowed to do, where they are allowed to go, and so on. For example, as hunting activity becomes more challenging due to climactic and other concerns, fear of competition with sports hunters and others has become increasingly acute. Such limitations may not be common in other types of touristic ventures, but the village is also a community, and even the few tourists who visit the village today are not always respectful of resident sensibilities. The challenge would be to pursue an economically viable enterprise in a culturally sensitive manner that includes villager buy-in and input while not suggesting in any way to the tourist that the village is some sort of Alaska Native theme park. In short, much additional groundwork and research are needed before such a cottage industry might be launched in Arctic Village.

What Is the Nets'aii Gwich'in's Status?

The use of tourism planning as an option for fostering economic development may help to bring badly needed revenue to the coffers of the Arctic Village Council, as well as to many of the Gwich'in residents in the form of labor wages. However, might this "solution" to a community in economic stress simply be pabulum, offering the Nets'aii Gwich'in too little, too late? Some statistics may be illustrative of this growing concern.

In 2000, Arctic Village reached its highest official population ever recorded, 152. The median age, according to the US Census, was 23.5, and 59 percent of all villagers were adults aged 18 and older. In 2010, the population remained unchanged at 152 villagers, but the median age was now 30, and 72 percent were adults. This is notable, as in 1990, the median age was 23, and 55 percent of the population was of adult age. And in 1980, the median age was 18.3, and 51 percent of all villagers were 18 or older (adapted from Alaska DCRA 2010). In other words, the population of Arctic Village is slowly but quite apparently aging. The "vill" may be a "fun" and free place for youth to grow up, play, and explore, but when it is time to pursue higher education or, more significantly, a wage labor position, the youth will and are urbanizing either to Fairbanks or, in fewer instances, Anchorage. And as they leave, one might contend, with them goes the future of "Gwich'inness."

But is this entirely true? Must this be the case? I would suggest that as the geographic Nets'aii Gwich'in space of Arctic Village contracts, an "imagined Nets'aii Gwich'in community" appears to be developing in concert with, if not in lieu of, the physical village. This community may be defined and qualified through an analysis of social media, particularly Facebook. Use of social media as a lens for studying present or future development trends is a newly evolving field, and not all would agree that what is seen on one's daily "timeline" is indicative of much of anything worthy of study or analysis. Social media use is now the norm for households worldwide; use varies by culture and region, and drawing conclusions based on limited data may be somewhat questionable. Analysis of textual and visual imagery of social media in diasporic communities is especially challenging (Ignacio 2012: 239–40). Despite the limitations (small sample size, lack of randomness, difficulty in assuming "representativeness" of data), such analyses do offer a window into communal and self-identity and meanings. Just as data from face-to-face interviews do not represent the views of all community members, data mined from social network sites like Facebook also must be seen as a snapshot, nonrepresentative of the whole while still providing significant insights (242).

The Nets'aii Gwich'in actively use Facebook in ways that, I argue, other casual users do not. As but one example, in November 2012 two women created "Athabascan Showcase," a closed Facebook group,[1] with the sole purpose of exchanging information about the design, marketing, and sale of Native crafts such as Nets'aii Gwich'in beadwork. With more than three thousand members as of early 2016, the site serves a multiplicity of purposes as members (mostly women) share ideas, materials, and experiences, and buy and sell products from one another. Such a group, carried on in the tradition established earlier in the decade with the website ArcticWays.com (see Dinero et al. 2006), is particularly notable and successful because it is developed and run by and for Alaska Native women.

Facebook is used in other significant ways as well. Communal celebrations such as Spring Carnival are now marketed actively through Facebook. Photos and videos of these events are then posted literally within moments of their occurrence, allowing others to virtually share in the celebration. Photos and other materials referencing Gwich'in history, culture, language, music, humor, and the like are also posted regularly. Often, conversations take place between sisters, cousins, and friends that extend over some days—all open to "friendly" comment by other users. What is interesting about these threads is that such communications often include, among others, Arctic Village residents living literally next door to one another, as well as thousands of miles apart. When tragedy strikes, such as the death of a young adult villager in the Chena River in Fairbanks in the summer of 2014, search and rescue team volunteers were sought and news was shared, all through this social medium.

In short, I contend that the introduction of Facebook into the Native community has allowed the Nets'aii Gwich'in to connect with one another in ways that are largely unprecedented since European contact. In order to prove this point and to better understand these connections, I carried out a structured analysis of Facebook statuses posted by Nets'aii Gwich'in users whose timelines I had access to during three randomly selected 48-hour periods in 2014: Monday, 4 August to Wednesday, 6 August; Friday, 5 September to Sunday, 7 September; and Wednesday, 8 October 8 to Friday, 10 October. In the August sample, there were 54 potential posters, and in the 48-hour period, 19 posted statuses. In the September sample, there were 61 potential posters and 29 posted statuses during the sample period. There were 57 potential posters in the October sample, and 23 posted in the 48-hour period.

As for the contributors, all were Nets'aii Gwich'in who still live in Arctic Village at present (approximately 80 percent of all possible posters, over 40 percent of the adult population of the village) or who were originally from Arctic Village but have since moved away. To be sure, there are fourteen other Gwich'in villages spanning the region into the Yukon Territory and the Northwest Territories (NWT) of Canada comprising perhaps three thousand villagers total, and some now live in one of these villages or beyond. These villages include Beaver, Birch Creek, Chalkyitsik, Circle, Fort Yukon, and Venetie (Alaska), as well as Old Crow (Yukon) and Aklavik, Fort McPherson, Inuvik, and Tsiigehtchic (NWT). Of these, however, only Venetie (2010 population 166) has a substantial Nets'aii community.

That said, issues of identity and the future of the Nets'aii discussed throughout this text (e.g., Gwich'in language retention) are worrisome across the whole of the Gwich'in Nation and not only among the Nets'aii. Those fluent in Gwich'in in both the United States and Canada *combined* now number fewer than 700 (Ethnologue 2014), just over

20 percent of all Gwich'in villagers. Given that Arctic Village is the case study here, some lessons may possibly be extrapolated from the data for other Gwich'in communities, but it must be recognized that this data are drawn from a limited sample.

All of those in the sampled Facebook statuses are Nets'aii and posted from their homes in Arctic Village, if not, Venetie, Fort Yukon, Fairbanks, North Pole, Anchorage, or Texas during the three selected study periods. Posters ranged in age from 19 to early 60s; the vast majority, however, were in their early 40s. In the first two samples, women were overrepresented by a two-to-one margin and in the October sample, by more than three-to-one. For the sake of confidentiality and to respect the Facebook users in question, I will not post any specific content of the posts here. While users of social media such as myself know that what we write is "public," few of us might imagine that this principle could extend beyond the Facebook "timeline." However, I have categorized the status content in general (Table 8.1). The values, ideas, behaviors, and attitudes listed provide an overview of those reflected in the Nets'aii Gwich'in use of Facebook.

Among the Nets'aii Gwich'in, the nature and content of the Facebook messages disseminated among tribal members are clear: in essence, this social media platform allows the diasporic community to reconstitute and reify Nets'aii Gwich'in identity across time and space. Posts on any given day well represent the values the Nets'aii Gwich'in pride themselves in and for which they are known, most especially: 1) embracing their children and posterity, 2) strong familial ties, 3) love for their neighbors and community, and 4) a good sense of humor during times of stress.

As the table shows, the statuses reflect several other issues but with far less frequency. One simple example is the role of the dog. Many of the villagers' comments in previous chapters indicate that once in the not-too-distant past, dogs played many central parts in Gwich'in culture: they pulled sleds, warded off predators, and attended the hunt. They were not, of course, pets; they were workers. But as Nets'aii behaviors, values, and technologies change, so too does the role of the dog. As Table 8.1 reveals, dogs are barely mentioned in any of the study's Facebook posts. Many villagers own dogs but often chain them to metal posts outside the house for several hours at a time; if the animals happen to get free, they are subject to other villagers' annoyance and occasional disposal via the .30-30 rifle. While some are fed dog food, many survive on fish or other remnants from the hunt. If food runs out, even an owner has been known to dispose of a few dogs in the same manner. In short, while owners may view dogs as pets or close family members, dogs in Arctic Village today have become not much more than nuisances for those who do not share these values.

Of far more significance to this study is what appears to be a declining interest in formalized religion, as discussed in detail in chapter 2. As seen in Table 8.1, the Gwich'in Facebook users barely post material about the Church, their beliefs, or the like in any of the three study periods; the most was 5 percent of users in the August sample. While this piece of data alone is inadequate for a proper assessment of the Episcopal Church's level of priority in Nets'aii society today, its combination with the data already noted reveals an increasingly apparent trend toward less involvement or interest in the Church, especially among the young. Several additional issues are mentioned but with inconsistent frequency. As but one example of a topic that did change, posts on health-related issues suddenly rose from August to September. One simple explanation could be the weather; during August, the daytime temperature in the Interior, where most of the posters live, was in the low 60s Fahrenheit (17 Celsius) while September temperatures reached no higher than the low 40s (with low 20s and blowing snow having fallen earlier in the week).

However, perhaps a more significant topic is hunting and subsistence. Little mention of hunting is made during any of the three sample periods, which is quite astounding given that the caribou began their annual migration across Dachan Lee during the interval between the first two sample periods. Some photos of the hunt were posted during this time, as was one set of photos of a grizzly bear as it approached too close to one of the hunting camps up mountain. Yet, the number of posts mentioning hunting or subsistence was lower in the second sample, and by a considerable margin. One might suggest there is a dichotomy here—that the use of social media and involvement in subsistence activity are somehow in contradiction—but this could not be further from the truth. As seen above, there is little correlation between the use of Facebook and involvement in subsistence activity or inactivity. Moreover, one need not actually carry out subsistence activity to elect to portray or discuss these topics on Facebook.

Similarly, one could argue that there is no need to show such images or to mention the hunt. A question appears to be implied throughout: "We know who we are, after all. Do we really need to talk about it or show it on a repeated basis?" But this contention also is not compelling in my view. All one must do is return to an earlier version of what could then be thought of as "social media," the VHS film *Gwich'in Niintsyaa: The 1988 Arctic Village Gathering* (1988), to recognize that historically, the desire to reify and concretize Nets'aii Gwich'in identity

Table 8.1 Breakdown of Topics Covered/Mentioned/Pictured in Nets'aii Gwich'in Facebook Statuses

Topic Discussed/Pictured	Percentage of statuses 7:00 a.m. ADT Aug. 4 - 7:00 a.m. ADT Aug. 6, N=223	Percentage of statuses 7:00 a.m. ADT Sept. 5 - 7:00 a.m. ADT Sept. 7, N=186	Percentage of statuses 7:00 a.m. ADT Oct. 8 - 7:00 a.m. ADT Oct. 10, N=152
Childhood/children/babies	15	18	16
Hope/faith/love/friendship	13	9	9
Home/family/community	10	19	13
Comedy/humor	10	12	10
Hunting/subsistence	7	1	1
Anger/violence/frustration	6	3	4
Prayer/God/religion	5	4	1
Popular culture	5	9	10
Food/meals	4	5	9
Alaska State Fair	4	0	0
Caribou	3	1	0
News/politics	2	2	8
School/education	2	2	2
Money/finances	2	2	1
Death/memorials	2	0	1
Weather	2	2	1
Work	1	1	3
Health	1	5	2
Dogs	1	1	2
Being Native	1	2	3
Gwich'in language	1	0	0
Tobacco/alcohol	1	0	1
Songs/music	1	1	0
Daily errands	0	1	0
Christmas	0	1	0
Halloween	0	0	2
Moose	0	0	1
The environment	0	0	1

was (and still is) constant, consistent, repetitive, and unshaking. As the film repeatedly notes, the Nets'aii Gwich'in *are* the Caribou People, full stop. No hesitation, no question, no discussion.

There is ample evidence found here that the most well represented issues (family, children, love, friendship, hope, humor) are increasingly nonspatial. As the Nets'aii Gwich'in diaspora grows and expands from the Yukon Flats to Fairbanks, from Fairbanks to Anchorage, and now from Alaska to the Lower 48, what ties the Nets'aii Gwich'in together— and what will likely tie them together well into the future—cannot and must not be limited to their connection to the land (i.e., subsistence, caribou). Simply put, in the past the "land" and the "Gwich'in Nation" were inseparable. Now, more Nets'aii Gwich'in are living outside of their historic homeland than within. While some may continue to hunt, fish, and gather, the majority will not.

Thus, like virtually every other indigenous, postcolonial community on the planet today, the Nets'aii Gwich'in are facing challenges that their ancestors could have never foreseen a hundred years ago, soon after European contact. Performing Gwich'inness has now taken on such a highly charged, politicized nature that a certain self-consciousness is found here. In other words, *being* Gwich'in versus *acting* Gwich'in appear to be increasingly at odds. When external perceptions of identity come up against the internal, such issues are difficult to reconcile.

Notwithstanding my efforts here, existential questions such as who the Nets'aii Gwich'in were, who they are, and who they are becoming are not to be answered by outsider academics. Rather, community members, such as those still residing at Arctic Village, now and in the coming years must make these determinations. As the preceding chapters have revealed, the Nets'aii Gwich'in have gone through two major periods of transformation: one externally generated, one more self-driven. In the first instance, European colonial contact influenced how the community taught its children and how culture in general was created and transferred. These were no small changes. But the community adapted in earnest, in the same manner through which they quickly acclimated to new forms of dwellings built with less permeable materials better suited to withstand the brutal cold of winters on the lower Brooks Range.

The second instance of change, however, was far less forgiving. The 1970s and onward saw the rapid introduction of new technologies (most significantly the four-wheeler, the snowgo, and the television) along with alternative attending values and attitudes that would impact the Nets'aii in permanent ways. Dependency on these technologies and the monetization of the local economy conflated, fostering other changes like a shift toward packaged (noncountry) foods, substance abuse, and a decline in the use of Native language. Recent global shifts toward a monolithic capitalist economy following the fall of the Soviet Union in the early 1990s and the concomitant rise of global temperatures as a result of climate change have all further worked against Nets'aii Gwich'in aspirations aimed at reclaiming their position as an independent and self-sufficient Alaska Native tribe. In short, "Gwich'inness" has become more of a liability, not an asset. It is associated with the markers of the underclass: dependency, poverty, unemployment, substance abuse, teen pregnancy, and various other social and economic struggles.

To be clear, this is not *my* definition of the Nets'aii Gwich'in in the early twenty-first century. But the village community itself is losing its historic connection to the land, as powerful external (pre-1970) and internal (post-1970) forces that the community neither asked for nor expected were imposed. As these processes have evolved, the Gwich'in are caught between an age-old culture and identity that prides itself on a longstanding commitment to communal hard work and self-sufficiency, independency, self-respect, and above all survival off the land but in reality is increasingly challenged by reliance government subsidies, internecine conflict, substance dependencies, and other social pathologies. There are times, such as Christmas, Spring Carnival, or the Fourth of July, when the village is a very happy and functional environment; at others, people struggle mightily, as financial woes, familial conflicts, and other challenges are rife.

I contend that several changes are possible going forward. First, a new definition of "Gwich'inness" may develop in the evolving global economy of the twenty-first century that does not merely give lip service to indigeneity but rather recognizes all Nets'aii Gwich'in, regardless of their exact "bloodline." Indeed, this portrait embraces Natives by virtue of their ongoing connection with the Gwich'in people, ancestry, heritage, language, and historical memory and legacy and, further, pushes back against dependency on the state by encouraging education, access to the formal workplace, and possibly even outmigration when appropriate. In such a scenario, one can be Nets'aii regardless of where or how one lives; valorizing and romanticizing the subsistence lifestyle does little to facilitate the betterment of struggling Native communities such as Arctic Village in an era when urbanity is, in truth, the preferred choice of so many, especially members of the younger generations. An alternative scenario is less tenable. If "Gwich'inness" is limited to a traditional definition of those who have two Nets'aii Gwich'in parents, speak the Gwich'in language, and live and carry out some form of subsistence in the Chandalar River valley—if these are the criteria for membership in the Nets'aii Gwich'in Nation, then indeed the community in trouble. In only a decade or two, no "Nets'aii Gwich'in" will fit this description.

An additional proviso may also be considered. As senses of "Gwich'-inness" are redefined by the changing, hybridized nature of the Nets'aii community today, so too is a further rethinking of the present direction of the village itself. Tables 4.4 and 7.1 and other qualitative material above suggest that the Nets'aii Gwich'in are rather divided given their small population. Once in the recent past, the entire Gwich'in tribe celebrated their connections as "one people," throughout the Yukon Flats and across the US–Canadian border (*Gwich'in Niintsyaa* 1988). But today, residents of Arctic Village are at a crossroads, struggling at times to see themselves as a unified community with a single mission, a single set of values, a single church to pray in each Sunday, a single land to love and protect, and a commitment to a single caribou herd from which they draw sustenance. To be sure, the villagers are well aware that until the divisiveness now extant along the Vashr'aii K'oo is contained and extinguished, little can be accomplished. This change is crucial to the future development of Arctic Village. Rev. Albert E. Tritt and Chief Christian found a way to bridge their differences and thus formed a village miles above the Arctic Circle on the East Fork of the Chandalar that thrived for generations. In their honor, it can—and should—be built again.

* * *

The Nets'aii Gwich'in have lived throughout the Yukon Flats for millennia. Their ancestors changed in several ways, yet the Natives still reside at Arctic Village today—still strong, still proud, still known for their sense of humor at times of stress and difficulty. If one thing can be said of the Nets'aii Gwich'in, it is that they are survivors, even if the lifestyles of many who reside in Arctic Village today do not exactly resemble those who founded the village just barely a century ago. But all peoples change, and the Nets'aii Gwich'in of northeast Alaska are certainly no exception.

And so, as I began, I end this narrative with a traditional story (Nickelson (1969b):

> It is told that one day it was quite cold even though the sun was shining. Chief Christian was out hunting. "I must find a moose or caribou. My family needs meat," he was thinking as he walked along.

> Chief Christian walked slowly looking for signs of moose. Suddenly he stopped. He looked carefully at a track in the snow. "That is fresh moose track. I will follow it and see if I can find the moose," he said as he thought how happy his family would be.

Very carefully Chief Christian followed the moose track. Ahead of him he saw something dark in the snow. As he got closer he saw that is was a dead moose. "I wonder what happened to that moose," Christian thought as he got closer. "It looks as though it had just been killed, but I know there is no one here but me," he thought as he carefully turned the moose over. "I think wolves killed it. I can see their tooth marks on the moose. I wonder where they are now. I can see their tracks all over the snow. Maybe I frightened them off. This moose has just been killed so I think I will skin it and take the meat," he was thinking as he started to skin the moose.

Chief Christian was working on skinning the moose. Suddenly he began to feel as if someone were watching him. He stopped skinning and looked up. What he saw made the hair on his neck stand up and he gasped in surprise. There were a lot of hungry wolves standing looking at him. He could see their sharp teeth and hear their snarls. "So you have come back," Christian shouted at the wolves. "I am going to take this moose meat home to my family. So it looks like we might have to fight over it," he said as he grabbed his rifle.

One wolf ran toward Chief Christian. Chief Christian shot the wolf before it could attack him. He began to scream and shout as he continued to shoot wolves. At last the rest of the wolves ran away.

Chief Christian got up and looked around. He saw eight dead wolves. "Well I have quite a load," he said, "one moose and eight wolves." Chief Christian finished skinning the moose. He skinned the wolves. He took the moose and the wolf skins back to his family. "We can eat moose meat and I will make a blanket of the wolf skins," said Christian's wife when she saw the skins and the meat.

"Yes, you make a blanket and I can take it to Fort Yukon to sell," said Chief Christian. "That way I can buy the things we need."

Chief Christian's family was happy. They had moose meat to eat. The wolf skins would buy many other things they needed.

Though a strong and resolute people, the Nets'aii Gwich'in of Arctic Village, Alaska, are now, like Chief Christian in this traditional story, in the midst of adversity. They are surrounded by threats from all sides— some social, some economic, some external but many originating from within. Now is a time of ongoing change and, for many, of uncertainty. The successes of the past are behind them, and they must now look ahead. The decisions made today and in the years to come are crucial to the future of this community. In an age of declining subsistence practices, a changing climate, ongoing oil drilling interests in the Arctic National Wildlife Refuge, and outmigration of the youth, there is much to contemplate and to concern any and all who call themselves Nets'aii Gwich'in, for indeed, theirs is a community now living on thin ice.

Note

1. Available at www.facebook.com/groups/139392279542401.

Postscript

It's 5 July 2012—John Fredson Day. The day feels suddenly hot. It hadn't been that warm till I got to this hill. I can barely see the four-wheeler at the top. Circle it, they told me, and then back down I go.

My breathing is heavy, my legs heavier. The mountain air is thin and dusty, the gravel beneath my feet angular and uneven. As I barely make it to the four-wheeler at the top and now turn back toward Arctic Village Center, I know at this point, at the head of the airport runway, I have about a mile or so yet to go.

My two young competitors—both easily half my age—are so far ahead of me that I no longer can see them. I cannot help but ask myself, "How did I, a 50-year-old university professor from Philadelphia, suddenly find myself running in Arctic Village's John Fredson Day Men's Long-Distance Run? What was I thinking? Am I crazy?"

* * *

This was not the first time that it occurred to me that my efforts in Arctic Village had faced a "few" obstacles. But then, I've never been one to surrender to barriers, though yes, sometimes the challenges there can be considerable. The obvious were of course logistical; Arctic Village is about as far from my home in Philadelphia as Dublin, Ireland, or Lisbon, Portugal. Going back and forth, sometimes more than once in a few short months, had proved challenging over the years.

Logistics aside, my residence on the East Coast also had raised questions among some skeptics that, as an "outsider," I could never really "get" Alaska. To a certain degree, they're right, especially when it comes to the contention among some that Alaskans are some sort of an ethnic group and that, as an "outsider," I just "wouldn't understand." There is no doubt in my mind that Alaskans—be they Natives or non-Natives—are a unique group of folks. That said, I never have accepted the idea that one has to live in the state to appreciate the issues that affect day-to-day life there.

Lastly, though one might guess that the greatest challenge to carrying out this research over the past decade and a half (or indeed, to writing a book about my findings) is the inability of a male, East Coast, White professor to be accepted, loved, and embraced by an Alaskan Native village Yet nothing could be further from the truth.

Historically, little good has ever come to an Alaskan Native village from outside without there being some sort of price to pay, so trust is certainly at a premium. However, generalizations are not helpful when it comes to working in the Native North. While many along the way "warned" me that I would never be accepted into the community, quite the opposite has proved to be true; I am privileged to say that over time, I became an honorary member of the Nets'aii Gwich'in community, and I do not take this honor for granted.

Thus, what I have written in the preceding pages reflects an honest assessment of time spent with a people that cautiously have grown to accept me, a people that know that I have done my best not to misuse or abuse their confidences. I have taken this responsibility seriously and as a spiritually blessed trust.

* * *

I look out ahead of me. Sweat is stinging my eyes. I can barely make out a few four-wheelers parked ahead at the finish line in front of Allo's house and the council building. And then I hear the growing chant: "Go, Steve, go! Go, Steve, go!"

I cross the finish line and am quickly handed a paper cup of cool water, from whom I do not know, as the sweat pours down, and an envelope with my prize for coming in third place (out of three runners). The crowd of Nets'aii Gwich'in Arctic Villagers claps and continues to cheer.

I sit down exhausted. Finally, the race is over. But for the Nets'aii Gwich'in, the contest continues.

Godspeed, *Shalak Nai*. *Mahsi' cho* to one and all.

Bibliography

Alaska Department of Education (DOE). 1995. "School Enrollment as of October 1, 1995." Office of Data Management. Retrieved 6 February 2014 from education.alaska.gov/Stats/SchoolEnrollment/1995SchoolEnrollment.pdf.

Alaska Department of Education and Early Development (DOEED). 2014 "Report Card to the Public" Accessed 6 January 2014. https://education.alaska.gov/reportcardtothepublic/Home/Index.

Alaska Department of Health and Social Services (DHSS). 2014. "Gwich'in Tobacco Free PSA." Video. Accessed 1 August 2014. www.facebook.com/permalink.php?id=165019316984839&story_fbid= 325902004229902.

Alaska Division of Community and Regional Affairs (DCRA), Municipal and Regional Affairs Division. 1991. "Yukon Flats Region Community Profiles: A Background for Planning." Juneau, AK: The Division.

———. 2010. Community Database Online. Accessed 5 August 2014. commerce.alaska.gov/dcra/DCRAExternal.

Alaska Natives Commission (ANC). 1994. "Alaska Native Education: Report of the Education Task Force." In *ANC Final Report*, vol. 2. Anchorage: Alaska Natives Commission.

Andrews, Elizabeth F. 1977. "Report on the Cultural Resources of the Doyon Region, Central Alaska, Vol. 1." Occasional Paper no. 5. Anthropology and Historic Preservation, Cooperative Park Studies Unit. Fairbanks: University of Alaska Fairbanks.

Angstman, Sarah, et al. 2007. "Tobacco and Other Substance Use among Alaska Native Youth in Western Alaska." *American Journal of Health Behavior* 31(3): 249–60.

Arctic Village Council. 1991. *"Nakai' t'iu'in* ('Do It Yourself!'): A Plan for Preserving the Cultural Identity of the Neets'aii Gwich'in Indians of Arctic Village." Community Development Plan (CDP).

———. 2002. "Bishop Rowe Chapel Reconstruction and Historic Preservation." Planning meeting notes, 19 July.

"Arctic Village: Crossroad in Time." 1968. *Tundra Times,* 6 December, 152.

Arctic Village Echoes. Village newspaper. 21 October 1969–17 December 1971.

Arnold, Robert D., et al. 1976. *Alaska Native Land Claims.* Anchorage: The Alaska Native Foundation.

Barnhardt, Carol. 1999. "Standing Their Ground: The Integration of Community and School in Quinhagak, Alaska." *Canadian Journal of Native Education* 23(1): 100–16.

———. 2001. "A History of Schooling for Alaska Native People." *Journal of American Indian Education* 40(1): 1–30.

Berardi, Gigi. 1999. "Schools, Settlement, and Sanitation in Alaska Native Villages." *Ethnohistory* 46(2): 329–59.

Berman, Matthew, et al. 2004. "Adaptation and Sustainability in a Small Arctic Community: Results of an Agent-Based Simulation Model." *Arctic* 57(4): 401–14.

"Bishop Rowe Chapel Restoration Project Budget, 2002–2005." Unpublished document. 20 January 2005.

Bockstoce, John R. 2009. *Furs and Frontiers in the Far North: The Contest among Native and Foreign Nations for the Bering Strait Fur Trade.* New Haven, CT: Yale University Press.

Boddy, Janice. 2007. *Civilizing Women: British Crusades in Colonial Sudan.* Princeton, NJ: Princeton University Press.

Brockenbrough, Martha. 2009. "Can You Be Addicted to Pregnancy?" *Women's Health,* 23 June. Accessed 8 July 2014. www.womenshealthmag.com/health/pregnancy-perks?page=3.

Callaway, Don. 1999. "Effects of Climate Change on Subsistence Communities in Alaska." In Gunter Weller and Patricia A. Anderson, eds., *Assessing the Consequences of Climate Change for Alaska and the Bering Sea Region: Proceedings of a Workshop at the University of Alaska Fairbanks, 29–30 October 1998.* Fairbanks: University of Alaska Fairbanks Center for Global Change and Arctic System Research, pp. 59–74.

Carey, Erin. 2009. "Building Resilience to Climate Change in Rural Alaska: Understanding Impacts, Adaptation and the Role of TEK." MS thesis. Ann Arbor: University of Michigan.

Carpenter, Murray. 2001. "The Gwich'in and ANWR: 'The Most Anglican Group of People in the World' Fight for the Right to Protect a War of Life." *The Witness,* January/February, 12–16.

Caulfield, Richard A. 1983. "Subsistence Land Use in Upper Yukon-Porcupine Communities, Alaska" (*Dinjii Nats'aa Nan KakAdagwaandail*). Technical Paper no. 16. Fairbanks: Alaska Department of Fish and Game, Division of Subsistence.

Chabot, Marcelle. 2003. "Economic Changes, Household Strategies, and Social Relations of Contemporary Nunavik Inuit." *Polar Record* 39(208): 19–34.

Chomicz, Dorothy. 2011. "Chandalar River Runs Red, Alarms Villagers." *Fairbanks Daily News-Miner,* 12 July. Retrieved 10 April 2014 from www.newsminer.com/chandalar-river-runs-red-alarms-villagers/article_49085080-8dee-5bec-a441-2cd086b721ee.html.

Condon, Richard G. 1990. "The Rise of Adolescence: Social Change and Life Stage Dilemmas in the Central Canadian Arctic." *Human Organization* 49(3): 266–79.

Cuomo, Chris, Wendy Eisner, and Kenneth Hinkel. 2008. "Environmental Change, Indigenous Knowledge, and Subsistence on Alaska's North Slope." *The Scholar and Feminist Online* 7(1).

Council of Athabascan Tribal Governments (CATG). 2015. "The CATG Story." Accessed 28 May 2015. www.catg.org/the-catg-story-3-of-5.

Dinero, Steven C. 1996. "Observation, Advocacy or Interference? Undertaking Research in a 'Fourth World' Community." *Humanity & Society*. 20(3): 111–32.

———. "'The Lord Will Provide': The History and Role of Episcopalian Christianity in Nets'aii Gwich'in Social Development—Arctic Village, Alaska." *Indigenous Nations Studies Journal* 4(1): 3–28.

———. 2003b. "Analysis of a 'Mixed Economy' in an Alaskan Native Settlement: The Case of Arctic Village." *Canadian Journal of Native Studies* 23(1): 135–64.

———. 2004. "The Politics of Education Provision in Rural Native Alaska: The Case of Yukon Village." *Race Ethnicity and Education* 7(4): 399–417.

———. 2005. "Globalization and Development in a Post-nomadic Hunter/ Gatherer Village: The Case of Arctic Village, Alaska." *The Northern Review* 25/26: 135–60.

———. 2007. "Globalisation and Development in a Post-nomadic Hunter/ Gatherer Alaskan Village: A Follow-up Assessment." *Polar Record* 43(226): 255–69.

———. 2013. "Indigenous Perspectives of Climate Change and Its Effects upon Subsistence Activities in the Arctic: The Case of the Nets'aii Gwich'in." *GeoJournal* 78: 117–37.

Dinero, Steven C., Parimal Bhagat, Timothy McGee, and Elizabeth Mariotz. 2006a. "Website Development and Alaska Native Identities: Hunting for Meaning in Cyberspace." *International Journal of Technology, Knowledge and Society* 2(1): 79–90.

———. 2006b. "Bridging the Technology Gap: A Culture-Based Model for Economic Development in Rural Alaska." National Science Foundation – Partnerships for Innovation, award no. EEC-0332608. Project report.

Doyle, Aaron, Judith Kleinfeld, and Maria Reyes. 2009. "The Educational Aspirations/Attainment Gap among Rural Alaska Native Students." *The Rural Educator* 30(3): 25–33.

Doyon Native Regional Corporation (Doyon). 2015. Accessed 16 September 2014. www.doyon.com.

Drane, F.B. 1921–22. Personal Journals. Episcopal Church of Alaska Records, Box 101b. Fairbanks: University of Alaska Fairbanks Rasmuson Library.

Ellis, Carolyn, Tony E. Adams, and Arthur P. Bochner. 2011. "Autoethnography: An Overview." *Forum Qualitative Sozialforschung / Forum: Qualitative Social Research* 12(1). Accessed 19 February 2015. nbn-resolving.de/ urn:nbn:de:0114-fqs1101108.

"Faith Endures in Arctic Village." 2004. *Fairbanks Daily News-Miner*, 15 August.

Fast, Phyllis A. 2002. *Northern Athabascan Survival: Women, Community and the Future*. Lincoln: University of Nebraska Press.

Ford, James D., et al. 2008. "Climate Change in the Arctic: Current and Future Vulnerability in Two Inuit Communities in Canada." *The Geographical Journal* 174(1): 45–62.

Fox, Shari. 2004. "When the Weather Is Uggianaqtuq: Inuit Observations of Environmental Change." PhD diss. Boulder: University of Colorado Boulder.

Frank, Kenneth. 2002. "Kenneth Frank Interviewed by Bill Schneider with Sidney Stephens in Fairbanks, Alaska on February 2, 2002." Tape no. H2001-113-05. Retrieved 24 April 2014 from jukebox.uaf.edu/ClimateChange/htm/kfrank.htm.

Fredson, John, and Edward Sapir Haa Googwandak. 1982. *Stories Told by John Fredson to Edward Sapir*. Fairbanks: Alaska Native Language Center.

Furgal, Christopher, and Jacinthe Seguin. 2006. "Climate Change, Health, and Vulnerability in Canadian Northern Aboriginal Communities." *Environmental Health Perspectives* 114(12): 1964–70.

Gagnon, Paul L. 1959. "Report on Village of Arctic Village." Juneau: Alaska Rural Development Board.

Gemmill, Danny. 2012. Arctic Village resident. Personal communication, 20 June.

Gilbert, Trimble. 1996. "Arctic Village History." Unpublished manuscript, 16 August.

Gitay, Habiba, et al., eds. 2002. "Climate Change and Biodiversity." Intergovernmental Panel on Climate Change Technical Paper V.

Gwich'in Niintsyaa: The 1988 Arctic Village Gathering. 1988. Dir. and prod. George Henry and Ruth Carroll. Yukon, AK: Gwich'in Steering Committee and Northern Native Broadcasting/CBC.

Hadleigh-West, Frederick. 1963. "The Netsi Kutchin: An Essay in Human Ecology." Unpublished PhD diss. Baton Rouge: Louisiana State University and Agricultural and Mechanical College.

Hamilton, Lawrence C., and Carole L. Seyfrit. 1994. "Female Flight? Gender Balance and Outmigration by Native Alaskan Villagers." *Arctic Medical Research* 53: 189–93.

Hannum, Rev. W.W. 1955. Priest-in-charge, St. Stephen's Mission, Fort Yukon. Correspondence, 26 July. National Archives, Pacific Alaska Region. Record Group No. 75 (Bureau of Indian Affairs), Box No. 253, 04/08/10(4). Education Program Decimal Files 1936–68. 806.1 (Individual State correspondence), A-Barrow, File: Arctic 1955–1960.

Harvey, David. 1996. *Justice, Nature and the Geography of Difference*. Malden, MA, and Oxford: Blackwell.

Hawkins, Elizabeth H., Lillian H. Cummins, and G. Alan Marlatt. 2004. "Preventing Substance Abuse in American Indian and Alaska Native Youth: Promising Strategies for Healthier Communities." *Psychological Bulletin* 130(2): 304–23.

Haycox, Stephen W. 2002. *Alaska: An American Colony*. Seattle: University of Washington Press.

Hirshberg, Diane, and Brit DelMoral. 2009. "An Exploration of Experiences and Outcomes of Alaska Native Graduates of Mt. Edgecumbe High School." Anchorage: University of Alaska Anchorage Institute of Social and Economic Research.

Hosley, Edward H. 1966. "Factionalism and Acculturation in an Alaskan Athapaskan Community." Unpublished PhD diss. Los Angeles: University of California, Los Angeles.

Ignacio, Emily N. 2012. "Online Methods and Analyzing Knowledge-Production: A Cautionary Tale." *Qualitative Inquiry* 18: 237.

James, Gideon. 2002. Arctic Village elder. Personal communication, 18 July.

James, Sarah. 1999. Arctic Village elder. Personal communication, 8 August.

Jester, Timothy E. 2002. "Healing the Unhealthy Native? Encounters with Standards-Based Education in Rural Alaska." *Journal of American Indian Education* 41(3): 1–21.

Jester, Timothy E., and Letitia H. Fickel. 2013. "Cross-Cultural Field Experiences in Alaska Native Villages: Implications for Culturally Responsive Teacher Education." *The Teacher Educator* 48: 185–200.

Joling, Dan. 2014. "Climate Assessment Warns of Dire Effects in Alaska." *Fairbanks Daily News-Miner*, 6 May.

Jones, Gary. 1999. Tanana Chiefs construction foreman. Personal communication, 5 August.

Jorgenson, Joseph G. 1990. *Oil Age Eskimos*. Berkeley: University of California Press.

Kleinfeld, Judith. 1992. *Alaska Native Education: Issues in the Nineties*. Retrieved 6 February 2014 from www.alaskool.org/native_ed/research_rep orts/nineties_issues/kleinfel.pdf.

Kofinas, Gary. 2002. "Community Contributions to Ecological Monitoring: Knowledge Co-production in the U.S.–Canada Arctic Borderlands." In Igor Krupnik and Dyanna Jolly, eds., *The Earth Is Faster Now: Indigenous Observations of Arctic Environmental Change*. Fairbanks, AK: Arctic Research Consortium of the United States, pp. 55–91.

Kofinas, Gary P., et al. 2010. "Resilience of Athabascan Subsistence Systems to Interior Alaska's Changing Climate." *Canadian Journal of Forest Research* 40: 1347–59.

Kollin, Susan. 2001. *Nature's State: Imagining Alaska as the Last Frontier*. Chapel Hill: University of North Carolina Press.

Kruse, John A. 1982. "Subsistence and the North Slope Inupiat: The Effects of Energy Development." Man in the Arctic Program Monograph no. 4. Anchorage: University of Alaska Institute for Social and Economic Research.

Langdon, Stephen J. 1991. "The Integration of Cash and Subsistence in Southwest Alaskan Yup'ik Eskimo Communities." In Nicholas Peterson and Toshio Matsuyama, eds., *Cash, Commoditisation and Changing Foragers*. Osaka, Japan: National Museum of Ethnology, pp. 269–91.

Local School Directory. 2014. "Arctic Village School." Accessed 6 February 2014. www.localschooldirectory.com/public-school/3000173/AK.

Lonner, Thomas D. 1986. "Subsistence as an Economic System in Alaska: Theoretical Observations and Management Implications." In Steve J. Langdon, ed., *Contemporary Alaskan Native Economies*. Lanham, MD: University Press of America, pp. 15–27.

Lonner, Thomas D., and Stuart Wilson Beard. 1982. "Part II: Arctic Village." *Sociocultural Assessment of Proposed Arctic National Wildlife Refuge Oil and Gas Exploration*. Anchorage, AK: US Department of the Interior by the Arctic Environmental Information and Data Center.

MacDonald, Mark. 2012. "Indigenous and Anglican: A Truly Native Church Emerges in the Anglican Church of Canada." In Ryan K.. Bolger, ed., *The Gospel after Christendom: New Voices, New Cultures, New Expressions*. Grand Rapids, MI: Baker Academic, pp. 315–26.

Mackenzie, Clara Childs. 1985. *Wolf Smeller (Zhoh Gwatsan): A Biography of John Fredson, Native Alaskan*. Anchorage: Alaska Pacific University Press.

Madsen, E. 1990. "The Symbolism Associated with Dominant Society Schools in Native American Communities." *Canadian Journal of Native Education* 17(2): 43–53.

Marker, M. 2000. "Economics and Local Self-Determination: Describing the Class Zone in First Nationals Education." *Canadian Journal of Native Education* 24(1): 30–44.

Martinez, Shawn. 1999. Arctic Village Council member. Personal communication, 4 August.

Mason, Michael H. 1924. *The Arctic Forests*. London: Hodder and Stoughton.

Mason, Arthur. 2002. "The Rise of an Alaskan Native Bourgeoisie." *Inuit Studies* 26(2): 5–22.

McBeath, Jerry, and Carl E. Shepro. 2007. "The Effects of Environmental Change on an Arctic Native Community: Evaluation Using Local Cultural Perceptions." *American Indian Quarterly* 31(1): 44–65.

McDonald, Rev. Robert. 1863. Journals, 6 March. Archives of the Ecclesiastical Province of Rupert's Land. ARCH M/F 98, Microfilm. Fairbanks: University of Alaska Fairbanks Rasmuson Library.

McDowell Group. 2001. *Alaska Native Education Study: A Statewide Study of Alaska Native Values and Opinions Regarding Education in Alaska*. Anchorage: First Alaskans Foundation.

McKennan, Robert. 1965. "The Chandalar Kutchin." Technical Paper no. 17. Calgary, Alberta: Arctic Institute of North America.

McNeeley, Shannon M. 2009. "Seasons Out of Balance: Climate Change Impacts, Vulnerability, and Sustainable Adaptation in Interior Alaska." PhD diss. Fairbanks: University of Alaska Fairbanks.

McPhee, John. 1977. *Coming into the Country*. New York: Farrar, Straus and Giroux.

Mishler, Craig. 1990. "Missionaries in Collision: Anglicans and Oblates among the Gwich'in, 1861–65." *Arctic* 43(2): 121–26.

———, ed. 1995. *Neerihiinjik: We Traveled from Place to Place: Johnny Sarah Haa Googwandak: The Gwich'in Stories of Johnny and Sarah Frank*. Fairbanks: Alaska Native Language Center.

Mishler, Craig, and William E. Simeone. 2006. *Tanana and Chandalar: The Alaska Field Journals of Robert A. McKennan*. Fairbanks: University of Alaska Press.

Moore, Gary. 1999. Former director of Planning Development, Tanana Chiefs Conference. Personal communication, 29 July.

National Oceanic and Atmospheric Administration. 2014. "National Centers for Environmental Information-National Overview January 2014." Accessed January 31, 2016. https://www.ncdc.noaa.gov/sotc/national/201401

Nelson, Richard K. 1986. *Hunters of the Northern Forest*. Chicago: University of Chicago Press.

Nickelson, Marian. 1968. "Primary Reading Program at Arctic Village Day School." Unpublished paper.

———. 1969a. "The Year Ahead: A Report on Educational Plans for the Arctic Village Day School for 1969–70." Unpublished paper.

———. 1969b. "Chief Christian Stories." Unpublished manuscript.

———. 2013. Arctic Village principal teacher, 1968–72. Personal communication, 12 June.

Norton, Ilena M., and Spero M. Manson. 1996. "Research in American Indian and Alaska Native Communities: Navigating the Cultural Universe of Values and Process." *Journal of Consulting and Clinical Psychology* 64(5): 856–60.

Nuttall, Mark, et al. 2004. "Hunting, Herding, Fishing and Gathering: Indigenous Peoples and Renewable Resource Use in the Arctic." Carolyn Symon, Lelani Arris, and Bill Heal, eds., *Arctic Climate Impact Assessment.* Cambridge: Cambridge University Press, pp. 649–90.

Okakok, Leona. 1989. "Serving the Purpose of Education." *Harvard Educational Review* 59(4): 405–22.

Osgood, Cornelius. 1936. *Contributions to the Ethnography of the Kutchin.* Yale University Publications in Anthropology, no. 14. New Haven, CT: Yale University Press.

Patty, Stanton H. 1969. "Deciding Arctic Village Schools Fate." *Fairbanks Daily News-Miner,* 7 April.

Peter, Katherine. 1992. *Neets'aii Gwiindaii: Living in the Chandalar Country.* Fairbanks: Alaska Native Language Center.

Peter, Kias, Jr. 1999. Arctic Village natural resource technician. Personal communication, 6 August.

Peter, Kias, Sr. 1966. "Arctic Village News." *Tundra Times,* 29 April, 18.

Pewewardy, Cornel. 2002. "Learning Styles of American Indian/Alaska Native Students: A Review of the Literature and Implications for Practice." *Journal of American Indian Education* 41(3): 22–56.

Poirier, Bernard W. 1975. "National Register of Historic Places Inventory—Nomination Form, AHRS Site No. ARC-056." Falls Church, VA: Iroquois Research Institute.

Poppel, Birger, ed. 2015. *SLiCA: Arctic Living Conditions: Living Conditions and Quality of Life among Inuit, Saami and Indigenous peoples of Chukotka and the Kola Peninsula.* Copenhagen: Nordic Council of Ministers.

Post, Eric. 2009. "Climate Change Taking a Toll on the Arctic." Interview with Ira Flatow on National Public Radio, 11 September.

Post, Eric, et al. 2009. "Ecological Dynamics Across the Arctic Associated with Recent Climate Change." *Science* 325: 1355–58.

Rasmus, Stacy M. 2008. "Indigenous Emotional Economies in Alaska: Surviving Youth in the Village." PhD diss. Fairbanks: University of Alaska Fairbanks.

Rattenbury, Kumi, et al. 2009. "A Reindeer Herder's Perspective on Caribou, Weather and Socio-economic Change on the Seward Peninsula, Alaska." *Polar Research* 28: 71–88.

Reed, Terry. 2013. Arctic Village School principal teacher. Personal communication, 11 March.

Sakakibara, Chie. 2010. "Kiavallakkikput Agviq (Into the Whaling Cycle): Cetaceousness and Climate Change among the Inupiat of Arctic Alaska." *Annals of the Association of American Geographers* 100(4): 1003–12.

Sam, Moses. 1987. "Moses Sam Is Interviewed by Rose Speranza on August 11, 1987 in Arctic Village, Alaska." *Arctic Village Elders.* Audiobook on cassette.

Seyfrit, Carole L. et al. 1998. "Ethnic Identity and Aspirations among Rural Alaska Youth." *Sociological Perspectives* 41(2): 342–65.

Sierra Club. 2016. "Outings." Accessed 25 June 2014. content.sierraclub.org/outings/national.

Slobodin, Richard. 1960. "Some Social Functions of Kutchin Anxiety." *American Anthropologist* 62(1): 122–33.

———. 1981. "Kutchin." In William C. Sturtevant, ed., *Handbook of North American Indians*, vol. 6. Washington, DC: Smithsonian Institution.

Snipp, C. Matthew, and Gene F. Summers. 1991. "American Indian Development Politics." In Cornelia B. Flora and James A Christenson, eds., *Rural Policies for the 1990s*. Boulder: Westview Press, pp. 166–80.

Stabler, Jack C. 1990. "Dualism and Development in the Northwest Territories." In James S. Frideres and Joseph E. DiSanto, eds., *Natural Resource Development and Social Impact in the North*. New York: Peter Lang, pp. 11–42.

Stathis, Tim. 2010. Speech at the Interior Education Summit on the YFSD Native Language and Culture Revitalization Initiative, 18 November. Fairbanks, Alaska.

———. 2011. Speech at the Interior Education Summit on the YFSD Native Language and Culture Revitalization Initiative, 16 November. Fairbanks, Alaska.

———. 2014. Director of Curriculum and Instruction, Yukon Flats School District (YFSD). Personal communication, 3 February.

Stern, Charlene. 2005. "Planning a Village in Social Transition: A Case Study of Arctic Village, Alaska." MA thesis. Albuquerque: University of New Mexico.

Stiffman, Arlene Rubin, et al. 2005. "Cultural and Ethical Issues Concerning Research on American Indian Youth." *Ethics and Behavior* 15(1): 1–14.

Stuck, Hudson. 1916. *Ten Thousand Miles With a Dog Sled: A Narrative of Winter in Interior Alaska*. New York: Charles Scribner's Sons.

———. 1920. *The Alaskan Missions of the Episcopal Church*. New York: Domestic and Foreign Missionary Society.

Tanana Chiefs Conference (TCC). 2015. "Alcohol & Drugs" and "Tobacco Prevention." Accessed 28 May 2015. www.tananachiefs.org/health.

Thomas, Janet L., et al. 2010. "Prevalence and Correlates of Tobacco Use among Middle and High School Students in Western Alaska." *International Journal of Circumpolar Health* 69(2): 168–80.

Thornton, Thomas F. 2001. "Subsistence in Northern Communities: Lessons from Alaska." *The Northern Review* 23: 82–102.

Tritt, Albert E. n.d. *Arctic Village Journals*. Box 1, Folder 8. Fairbanks: University of Alaska Fairbanks Rasmuson Library.

Tritt, Albert E. n.d. *Arctic Village Journals*. Box 2, Folder 17. Fairbanks: University of Alaska Fairbanks Rasmuson Library.

Tritt, Isaac, Sr. 1987a. "Isaac Tritt, Sr. Is Interviewed by Rose Speranza in Arctic Village, Alaska on August 6, 1987." *Arctic Village Elders*. Audiobook on cassette.

———. 1987b. "Isaac Tritt Is Interviewed by Rose Speranza on August 9, 1987 in Arctic Village, Alaska." *Arctic Village Elders*. Audiobook on cassette.

Tritt, Lincoln. 1999. "Ancestor's Journals Basis for Tritt's Perspective." *Alaskan Epiphany* 21(2): 8.

Tritt, Raymond. 1999. Second Chief. Personal communication, 6 August.

United Nations Environment Progamme (UNEP). Convention on Biological Diversity. 2007. *Revised Final Report: Composite Report on Status and Trends Regarding the Knowledge, Innovations and Practices of Indigenous and Local Communities, Region: Arctic*. Ad Hoc Open-Ended Inter-Sessional Working Group on Article 8J and Related Provisions of the Convention on Biological Diversity, UNEP/CBD/WG8J/5/INF/4.

US Census Bureau. 1930. Population of Arctic Village, Alaska, 25 March 1929. Retrieved 26 May 2015 from www.mocavo.com/1930-United-States-Census/126213/004955484/860.

US Department of the Interior (USDOI). 2012. "Proposal to Open Red Sheep Creek and Cane Creek Drainages to Non-federally Qualified Users." Document WP14-51. Retrieved 13 February 2014 from www.doi.gov/subsistence/councils/ns/upload/10-NS-WP14-51.pdf.

US Fish and Wildlife Service (USFWS). 2012. "Attention Sheep Hunters." Retrieved 12 February 2014 from http://www.fws.gov/uploadedFiles/Region_7/NWRS/Zone_1/Arctic/PDF/sheep25a.pdf.

VanStone, James W. 1974. *Athapaskan Adaptations: Hunters and Fisherman of the Subarctic Forests*. Chicago: Aldine Publishing.

"Village Focus: Vashr'aii K'oo—Arctic Village." 1991. In *The Council*. Arctic Village, AK. pp. 4–5.

VonThaer, Jack. 1999. Arctic Village schoolteacher. Personal communication, 3 August.

Wahrhaftig, Clyde. 1965. "Physiographic Divisions of Alaska." Geological Survey Professional Paper 482. Washington, DC: United States Government Printing Office.

Wexler, Lisa. 2009. "Identifying Colonial Discourses in Inupiat Young People's Narratives as a Way to Understand the No Future of Inupiat Youth Suicide." *American Indian and Alaska Native Mental Health Research: The Journal of the National Center*. 16(1): 1–24.

Wolfe, Robert J. 1991. "Trapping in Alaska Communities with Mixed, Subsistence-Cash Economies." Technical Paper no. 217. Juneau: Alaska Department of Fish and Game, Division of Subsistence.

Wolfe, Robert J., and Linda J. Ellanna. 1983. "Introduction to the Case Studies." In "Resource Use and Socioeconomic Systems: Case Studies of Fishing and Hunting in Alaskan Communities." Technical Paper no. 61. Juneau: Alaska Department of Fish and Game, Division of Subsistence, pp. 1–9.

Wolfe, Robert J., and Robert J. Walker. 1987. "Subsistence Economies in Alaska: Productivity, Geography, and Development Impacts." *Arctic Anthropology* 24(2): 56–81.

Wooten, D.T.F. 1967. "The Coming of Christianity to the Kutchin." Thesis. Canterbury: St. Augustine's College.

Yukon Flats School District (YFSD). "School Board Policies." Accessed 3 February 2014. www.yukonflats.net/board-policies.

Index